Rethinking Human Rights

Also by David Chandler

BOSNIA: Faking Democracy after Dayton

FROM KOSOVO TO KABUL: Human Rights and International Intervention

Rethinking Human Rights

Critical Approaches to International Politics

Edited by

David Chandler
Lecturer in International Relations
Brunel University

First published 2002 by
PALGRAVE MACMILLAN
Houndmills, Basingstoke, Hampshire RG21 6XS and
175 Fifth Avenue, New York, N.Y. 10010
Companies and representatives throughout the world

PALGRAVE MACMILLAN is the global academic imprint of the Palgrave
Macmillan division of St. Martin's Press, LLC and of Palgrave Macmillan Ltd.
Macmillan® is a registered trademark in the United States, United Kingdom
and other countries. Palgrave is a registered trademark in the European
Union and other countries.

ISBN 0–333–97716–5

This book is printed on paper suitable for recycling and made from fully
managed and sustained forest sources.

A catalogue record for this book is available from the British Library.

Library of Congress Cataloging-in-Publication Data
Rethinking human rights: critical approaches to international politics/edited
by David Chandler.
        p. cm.
    Includes bibliographical references and index.
    ISBN 0–333–97716–5
        1. Human rights. I. Chandler, David, 1962–
K3240.R48 2002
341.4981–dc21   2002074839

10   9   8   7   6   5   4   3   2
11   10   09   08   07   06   05   04   03

Printed and bound in Great Britain by
Antony Rowe Ltd, Chippenham and Eastbourne

For Harvey Tate

Contents

Part III   Human-Centred Rights?

Acknowledgements

This book would not have been possible without the funding and support provided by the Policy Research Institute, Leeds Metropolitan University, which kindly extended my Post-Doctoral Research Fellowship to enable me to complete the work of editing this collection. I would also like to acknowledge the support, ideas and suggestions from the contributing authors, who made the process of bringing this collective project together an insightful and stimulating one. In particular, I would like to thank Philip Hammond for his help and advice throughout.

Notes on the Contributors

David Chandler is a Lecturer in International Relations at Brunel University. He has written widely on international institutions, human rights and democracy, including *Bosnia: Faking Democracy After Dayton* (1999, Pluto Press) and *From Kosovo to Kabul: Human Rights and International Intervention* (2002, Pluto Press).

Barrie Collins is the author of *Obedience in Rwanda: a Critical Question* (1998, Sheffield Hallam University Press). He has taught the international politics of Africa at the School of Oriental and African Studies, London, and is currently researching African peace processes.

Fiona Fox is the former Head of Media Relations at CAFOD, the Catholic aid agency. She was commissioned by the Caritas Network to write a discussion paper on the Politicization of Humanitarian Aid in 1999, and has widely promoted debate on this theme within the UK aid movement. She has written articles for a variety of journals including *World Today*, *Tablet* and *Disasters*.

Chris Gilligan is a Lecturer in Sociology at the University of Ulster. He has written extensively on Northern Irish politics, culture and society and is co-editor, with Jon Tonge, of *Peace or War? Understanding the Peace Process in Northern Ireland* (1997, Ashgate).

Philip Hammond is Senior Lecturer in Media at South Bank University. He is co-editor, with Edward S. Herman, of *Degraded Capability: The Media and the Kosovo Crisis* (2000, Pluto Press).

Edward S. Herman is Professor Emeritus of Finance at the Wharton School, University of Pennsylvania, and has written extensively on political economy; among his books is *Manufacturing Consent: the Political Economy of the Mass Media*, co-authored with Noam Chomsky.

Jon Holbrook is a barrister and writer on legal and political issues. His articles have appeared in *The Times*, *The Independent*, and the *New Law Journal* on issues ranging from the International Criminal Court and

Pinochet to free speech and libel law. He has practised at the bar from Two Garden Court Chambers, London, since 1991.

John Laughland is a former lecturer at the Sorbonne and the Institute of Political Science in Paris. He is the author of *The Death of Politics: France Under Mitterrand* (1994, Michael Joseph) and *The Tainted Source: The Undemocratic Origins of the European Idea* (1997, Little, Brown; 1998, Warner). He also writes articles for various British national newspapers including *The Spectator, The Times, Mail on Sunday* and *Daily Express*. He is European Director of the European Foundation and a trustee of the British Helsinki Human Rights Group.

John Pender is an independent writer and researcher. His current interest is the shifting content of development policy for the world's poorest countries, focusing especially on the World Bank. His most recent published work, 'From "Structural Adjustment" to "Comprehensive Development Framework": Conditionality Transformed?' appears in *Third World Quarterly*, vol. 22(3), 2001.

David Peterson is an independent journalist and researcher based in the United States.

Vanessa Pupavac is a Lecturer in the School of Politics, University of Nottingham. She trained as a solicitor and has worked as a consultant for the UN, the ODI, the OSCE and other international organizations. She has published widely on children's rights, international conflict resolution and psychosocial work.

List of Abbreviations

BAE	British Aerospace
BBC	British Broadcasting Corporation
BHHRG	British Helsinki Human Rights Group
CDF	Comprehensive Development Framework
CNN	Cable News Network
DFID	Department for International Development
ECHO	European Community Humanitarian Aid Office
EU	European Union
FAR	Forces Armées Rwandaises (Armed Forces of Rwanda)
FBI	Federal Bureau of Investigation
GDP	gross domestic product
GOLI	Grand Orange Lodge of Ireland
GRRC	Garvaghy Road Residents Coalition
HRW	Human Rights Watch
ICRC	International Committee of the Red Cross
ICTR	International Criminal Tribunal for Rwanda
ICTY	International Criminal Tribunal for the former Yugoslavia
IMF	International Monetary Fund
IRA	Irish Republican Army
KFOR	Kosovo Force
KLA	Kosovo Liberation Army
KPC	Kosovo Protection Corps
MDR	Mouvement Démocratique Républican (Movement for a Democratic Republic)
MSF	Médecins sans Frontières (Doctors without Borders)
NATO	North Atlantic Treaty Organization
NGO	non-governmental organization
NIHRC	Northern Ireland Human Rights Commission
NRA	National Resistance Army
NSPCC	National Society for the Prevention of Cruelty to Children
OECD	Organization for Economic Co-operation and Development
OSCE	Organization for Security and Co-operation in Europe
PBS	Public Broadcasting Service
PPA	Participatory Poverty Assessment
PRSP	Poverty Reduction Strategy Paper
QC	Queen's Counsel

RPA	Rwandan Patriotic Army
RPF	Rwandan Patriotic Front
RUC	Royal Ulster Constabulary
SFOR	Stabilization Force
UK	United Kingdom
UN	United Nations
UNAMIR	United Nations Assistance Mission for Rwanda
UNDP	United Nations Development Programme
UNESCO	United Nations Educational, Scientific and Cultural Organization
UNHCHR	United Nations High Commissioner for Human Rights
UNHCR	United Nations High Commissioner for Refugees
UNICEF	United Nations Children's Fund
UNITAF	Unified Task Force
UNOSOM	United Nations Operation in Somalia
UNPROFOR	United Nations Protection Force
US	United States

Introduction: Rethinking Human Rights

David Chandler

Today, governments and international institutions claim human rights as one of the essential pillars of the international system, and they are proclaimed in the same breath as peace, democracy and the rule of law as a universal value of the highest order. The UN General Assembly President noted, in December 1998:

> The quest for the basis of human rights to which philosophers, jurists and politicians devoted their interest and concern in the past has ... lost its significance. We can affirm today that human rights, beyond the theoretical concepts that justify the sacred and inviolable character of human rights, must be recognized and protected simply because this is what all humankind believes and desires, and because this has been the express will of the international community as reflected in the Universal Declaration.
>
> (UN, 1998)

The concept of human rights is not merely accepted by policy-makers and governments, but also their critics in campaigning NGOs, the media and academia, because it is seen to provide a framework for a radical and transformative approach to international society. The discourse of human rights appears to go beyond the liberal democratic framework to aspire to a broader normative project of human progress, which celebrates the universal nature of humanity. This radical aspiration is reflected through the development of a human-centred approach to global questions, putting the value of human dignity above the search for economic gain or the narrow interests of particular national governments. This approach is seen as a progressive development from the divisions of the Cold War period, in which geopolitical competition

1

between the West and the Soviet Bloc led to the downplaying of questions of individual and group rights.

This book does not concern itself with the history of the human rights concept or with theoretical and philosophical questions raised by the term, but rather with the political implications of prioritizing human rights as a guide to policy-making in the international sphere. The following chapters seek to raise important questions which challenge the radical claims of the proponents of human rights approaches and suggest that rather than challenging political and economic inequalities in the international system, the human rights framework is facilitating new hierarchies of control and regulation. This introductory chapter seeks to establish the radical attraction and claims of the human rights approach and briefly considers their basis in the transformation of the international order, since 1990, as former mechanisms of international regulation have been recast reflecting the shift to a unipolar world. The consensus in favour of the process of prioritizing a human rights approach is highlighted as well as the limited nature of critical appraisals of this shift in international policy focus. Finally, the framework of the material to be considered in the following chapters is set out.

Ethical aspirations

The concept of human rights is seen by many commentators as establishing a radical framework for progressive change in international relations because it contains within it three powerful and interrelated ideas. Firstly, there is the idea of universality, on the basis that in an increasingly globalized world promoting human rights concerns is in the interests of us all. Secondly, there is the idea of empowerment, because unlike politics, which is often seen to legitimize the power of a government or elected elite, human rights are seen to redress the balance and provide support for the claims of individuals, oppressed minorities or socially excluded groups. Thirdly, there is the idea of a human-centred approach based on ethics and morality, rather than an adherence to grand political schemas connected to the politics of Left or Right.

Universal rights

The popular use of the concept of human rights has coincided with a growing belief that we are living in a global community, where our interests are closely connected to those of others who may not live in the same state or even on the same continent as us. As the British prime minister, Tony Blair, stated, after the terror attacks on the twin towers of the World Trade Center in New York:

> Round the world, September 11 is bringing governments and people to reflect, consider and change ... There is a coming together. The power of community is asserting itself. We are realising how fragile are our frontiers in the face of the world's new challenges. Today conflicts rarely stay within national boundaries. Today a tremor in one financial market is repeated in the markets of the world. Today confidence is global – either its confidence or its absence ... [T]his interdependence defines the new world we live in.
>
> (Blair, 2001)

International responses to the attacks have highlighted the developments analysed in the UN Report of the Commission on Global Governance, *Our Global Neighbourhood*, which suggested that international policy-making be increasingly posed in relation to global concerns of war, poverty, the rights of children, women and minorities and the environment (CGG, 1995). The concept of universality, inherent in the human rights approach, reflects the shift in political focus towards global concerns and away from the constrictions of the territorially bounded nation-state.

Human rights are considered to be universal in two respects. Firstly, and most importantly, because the subject of human rights is the universal citizen not the political citizen defined by the nation-state. The discourse of human rights 'inaugurates a new kind of citizenship, the citizenship of humanity' (Pieterse, 1997: 72). As Nicholas Wheeler writes: 'The notion of common humanity/human solidarity is diametrically opposed to the statist paradigm which is predicated on the contention that state leaders and citizens do not have moral responsibilities or obligations to aid those beyond their borders' (1997: 10). The prioritization of universal concerns over the national is sustained by the claim that the globalized nature of central issues, from international terrorism to ozone depletion and international drug trafficking to the spread of HIV/AIDS, means that we should be concerned with the needs of others no matter how far away they are or how different their lives.

Secondly, the idea of universality is a very powerful one because, in theory if not in practice, support for human rights is, in fact, universal. The Universal Declaration of Human Rights, adopted by the United Nations General Assembly in 1948, has been approved by virtually all governments representing all societies. As Louis Henkin states: 'Human rights are enshrined in the constitutions of virtually every one of today's 170 states – old states and new; religious, secular, and atheist; Western and Eastern; democratic, authoritarian, and totalitarian; market economy, socialist, and mixed; rich and poor, developed, developing, and less developed' (1990: ix). This international acceptance of human rights supports the position that they do, in fact, constitute a moral community of humankind, not confined to any political system, democratic or not. Therefore commentators argue that, because human rights cannot be bound territorially or to any social system, in any hierarchy of rights, human rights are at the top and in this sense 'trump' all other claims (Evans, 1997: 125).

Protections for the human rights of the 'global citizen' have been developed through the extension of 'universal justice'. The proposed establishment of an International Criminal Court, ad hoc tribunals for war crimes in former Yugoslavia and Rwanda, and UN and NATO actions in Somalia, Bosnia, Kosovo and East Timor in the 1990s, highlighted new developments in international law and new powers of intervention awarded to international institutions and states active in human rights promotion. The radical nature of this shift is demonstrated by the fact that the teachings of the US civil rights leader, Reverend Martin Luther King, are today held up by the US State Department as a guide to international action. His declaration that 'injustice anywhere is a threat to justice everywhere' is used to confirm the moral and political need for an activist foreign policy in the interests of all (Wagenseil, 1999: 13). The shift towards rights universality by the world's remaining superpower is highlighted in the US State Department's annual *Country Reports on Human Rights Practices*. The first report, in 1977, ran to 137 pages; the last report of the twentieth century, the largest ever, covered 194 countries, totalling 6000 pages (USDoS, 2000).

The prioritization of human rights issues has transformed the language and institutional practices of international relations. International bodies, from the UN and NATO to the IMF and World Bank, whose mandates may seem to be unrelated to human rights, have integrated these concerns and acted on them in ways unthinkable ten years ago (Bradlow and Grossman, 1995). Today the language of human rights infiltrates every discussion on international themes. For example, discussions about economic development, in United Nations committees, take the form of human rights debates over the priority of 'economic or developmental rights' in relation to civil and political rights. As one experienced commentator remarks: 'Today, practically no state can afford not to participate in some form of human rights diplomacy' (Müllerson, 1997: 5).

Even the states at the critical end of many human rights resolutions, such as Russia, China, Cuba, Syria and Libya, argue that they are upholding human rights principles and supportive of international action on the issue. They in turn raise human rights criticisms of the United States and other Western states regarding responses to poverty, institutionalized racism, prison conditions and aggressive militarism (see, for example: UN, 1996; UN, 1999).

In the field of international human rights interventionism, the shift in policy practices has been institutionalized in an ad hoc manner through the UN Security Council, which since 1990 has empowered itself to consider humanitarian emergencies as a threat to international peace and security (Weller, 1999a). In 1991, the Gulf War to 'liberate' Kuwait was followed by the international community's attempt to protect the human rights of the Kurds and Marsh Arabs through a 'safe haven' policy. With the UN Security Council's support, the US-led coalition established aerial exclusion zones in Northern and Southern Iraq, denying the government control over its own territory. Iraqi aircraft entering the zones, formally within Iraqi airspace, were considered hostile and shot down (Weller, 1999b: 94–5). Iraqi sovereignty was also undermined by UN provisions preventing Iraq from developing 'weapons of mass destruction' as well as from trading freely with other states. The international regulation of Iraq, in which sovereignty was subordinated to human rights concerns, was subsequently seen as a legal precedent for universal human rights-based intervention. This was acted upon the following year when the UN authorized unilateral United States intervention in Somalia to protect humanitarian food convoys. In Bosnia in 1993, the UN authorized a multilateral military intervention to protect humanitarian aid and, in 1995, a NATO force, in its first combat action since it was founded, was mandated to impose a peace settlement.

The international military action against Yugoslavia over the Kosovo crisis in 1999 was widely greeted as the first international military intervention against a sovereign state for purely human rights purposes (Klug, 2000: 2). As Tony Blair asserted, this was a war fought 'not for territory but for values' (1999a). The human rights discourse also provided a framework for the universal struggle of the 'war against terrorism' declared by Washington and London after the September 2001 destruction of the World Trade Center. Leading Western states claimed the right to take unilateral military action abroad, including the right to assassinate state leaders and depose hostile regimes, on the basis that they were acting for universal interests rather than their own. In President George W. Bush's words: 'This is the world's fight. This is civilization's fight.

This is the fight of all who believe in progress and pluralism, tolerance and freedom' (2001). Tony Blair assumed the mantle of 'the moral power of a world acting as a community' to argue that this moral mission would 'reorder the world around us' (2001).

Empowering rights

The idea of empowerment has also been a very forceful focus for the human rights concept. Human rights are seen as a protection against inequality and the domination of the powerful over the weak. David Forsythe asserts: 'It cannot be stressed too much that ... the idea of human rights is a defense against abuse of power everywhere' (2000: 219). Mary Kaldor argues 'many non-Western states are sources of stark oppression and denial of democracy' and that the non-state orientated approach of the human rights movement can 'facilitate the representation of the weak and powerless in the non-West' (1999b: 223). For Jack Donnelly: 'Human rights is the language of victims and the dispossessed' (1998: 20). Helena Kennedy QC argues that: 'The time has come to uncouple the law from the state and give people the sense that the law is theirs. Human rights are the privileged ground where we can bring the law back to the common conversation of humankind' (2000: xv).

The new focus on human rights has been held to have a radical and empowering impact. For many commentators, the shift in policy perspectives is seen to represent the influence of grassroots civil society movements on the international agenda. At the 1993 UN World Conference on Human Rights in Vienna, some three thousand representatives of over five hundred international NGOs attended, almost outnumbering the representatives of states (Boyle, 1995). At the UN World Conference on Women's Rights in Beijing, in 1995, there were around 35,000 participants mainly from NGOs (Korey, 1999: 166). Many human rights advocates have also suggested that the reason for this transition has been the influence of ordinary people, creating a 'people's politics' in which 'a campaigning mass movement is putting pressure on democratic governments to practise what they preach' (Robertson, 1999: 115).

It is often argued that one of the main achievements of the human rights movement has been the new legal protections put in place to protect minorities from persecution or oppression. International justice was once more on the agenda, and 'a start was at last made to capitalise on the Nuremberg legacy' through The Hague and Arusha tribunals for war crimes in the early 1990s (Robertson, 1999: xv). Many commentators highlighted that the tribunals marked an important change in international relations, as 'the seeds of a new resistance to evil have been planted' (Urquhart, 2000). In September 1998, the Rwandan tribunal sentenced Jean Kambanda, former prime minister and head of the Rwandan government, to life imprisonment for crimes against humanity. This precedent was in turn used by the UK House of Lords, which, in March 1999, ruled that General Augusto Pinochet had no sovereign immunity and could be extradited to be tried for crimes against humanity. This was the first time a former head of state faced criminal proceedings for breaches of international law while in office, in a foreign court (Bianchi, 1999: 255). Following this, a few months later, the indictment of a sitting head of state, Slobodan Milošević, for crimes against humanity was greeted as confirming that there had been 'a revolution in international law' (Moghalu, 1999).

Today it appears that both international and national courts can indict presidents and elected leaders if they are held to have abused their citizens' human rights. The empowerment of the vulnerable individual or group against government repression is seen as a major transformation in power relations. International institutions and new treaty bodies now have the power to prevent or punish abuses, which during the Cold War would have been protected by sovereign immunity. As Michael Ignatieff notes: 'Taken together, these changes amount to a revolution: they enfranchise the individual against the state for the first time in international law' (2000a: 201).

Human-centred rights

The idea of human-centred rights – putting people first, regardless of the sectional interests of big businesses or political parties – derives more from the spheres of morality and ethics than that of politics. For many commentators, the moral aspirations behind human rights claims gives them a legitimacy which cannot be gained merely through the institutional practices of state-based politics. In fact, some advocates would argue that campaigning on the basis of human rights is the opposite of a political approach, because it is about principles, not about making compromises, and about protecting minorities, as opposed to enforcing the power of majorities. Where politics is seen to be about the expression of self-interest and the competition of views, human rights is regarded as an expression of altruism and the collective values of a moral community, the articulation of 'an underlying moral consensus' (Kennedy, 2000: xiv). Putting people before profits and politics has been a powerful idea and is widely seen as a refreshingly positive view of human potential and human progress. In the view of Zbigniew Brzezinski, former US national security advisor, 'human rights is the single most magnetic political idea of the contemporary time' (cited in Forsythe, 2000: 33). For the *New York Times*, the 'great flowering of the idea of universal human rights ... is among the most important political legacies of [the last] century' (1999). Mary Robinson, the United Nations High Commissioner for Human Rights, speaks for many in her belief 'that the growth in the human rights movement is one of the most hopeful, optimistic developments of our time' (1999).

The human rights approach to international policy-making has struck a chord with many commentators, academics and activists because of its radical rejection of the ideology and politics of the Cold War era. The focus on protecting individuals, rather than operating on the basis of the needs of governments, challenges the international framework developed since 1945. At the 1993 UN international conference in Vienna the UN Charter was widely construed to mean that human rights should take precedence over sovereignty (Boyle, 1995: 85). By the end of the 1990s, with UN protectorates established in Kosovo and East Timor and the indictment of former Yugoslav President Slobodan Milošević for war crimes, international relations were no longer seen to be dominated by the need for inter-state consensus. Although human rights had been a concept of international agreements since the Second World War, before the 1990s the promise of concerted action on the issue had never been fulfilled. At its September 2000 Millennium Conference the UN confirmed the need for people-centred reforms of the institution and affirmed the rejection of its previous 'state-centred' framework (UN, 2000a). The change in approach on behalf of the international community has been greeted by human rights advocates as marking a new historical period for human rights: 'the age of enforcement' (Robertson, 1999: xvi).

As the role and remit of international institutions has been strengthened, international action under human rights mandates has been of a long-term nature as well as reactive. This was demonstrated with a number of international institutions acquiring powers of long-term administration over Bosnia in the Dayton peace settlement. These administrative powers were later extended on an indefinite basis and, in 1999, the UN acquired further powers of administrative regulation in Kosovo and East Timor. Through this process, the role of the UN Security Council has been fundamentally transformed from being a policeman of international security, concerned with the welfare of states, to a supranational 'government and administration body' supporting the human rights of citizens in situations of complex political emergencies (Thurer, 1999).

This new consensus behind international policy shifts in the 1990s suggests that international activism in support of human rights is likely to shape the international political framework of the new century. For many commentators this radical shift at the end of the 1990s meant that a century marked by world war and genocide ended on a positive and hopeful note. This optimism was founded on the belief that international policy based on human rights could make the twenty-first century safer and more just than the preceding one. As Bernard Kouchner (1999a) declared:

> Can we dream of a 21st Century where the horrors of the 20th will not be repeated? Where Auschwitz or the mass exterminations that took place in Cambodia under the Khmer Rouge, and later in Rwanda, and the killings in Kosovo, cannot happen again? The answer is a hopeful yes.

This optimism appeared to be fully justified in the international response to the World Trade Center attacks, where finally international society seemed willing to take on the 'moral responsibility' for tackling human rights abuses wherever they might occur (Blair, 2001; Woollacott, 2001). The US Defense Secretary, Donald Rumsfeld, argued that the military action in Afghanistan was in line with previous US-led interventions in Kuwait, Northern Iraq, Somalia, Bosnia and Kosovo 'for the purpose of denying hostile regimes the opportunity to oppress their own people and other people', adding that: 'We stand with those Afghans who are being repressed by a regime that abuses the very people it purports to lead' (2001). Far from stressing US national interests in responding to an attack on its major symbols of economic and military dominance, the US establishment and the coalition of supporting states stressed the ethical and humanitarian nature of the military response, which included the dropping of food and medical provisions. On the first night of the military campaign John Warner, a leading US senator, noted on *Larry King Live*:

> This is the first time in contemporary military history where a military operation is being conducted against the government of a country, and simultaneously, with the troops carrying out the mission, other troops are trying to take care of the innocent victims who all too often are caught in harm's way.
>
> (Solomon, 2001)

As Warner remarked, the dropping of humanitarian aid at the same time as Cruise missiles indeed marked a turning point in the presentation of international intervention. For many commentators, the Bush Republican administration's response to the twin towers attack symbolized the transformation of international politics since the Cold War, highlighting the consensus of support for a new ethical and morally committed world order, established on the basis of protecting and promoting human rights. This brave new world of human rights regulation has been hailed as an era of 'post-international politics' where states and fixed boundaries will no longer dictate whose rights will be protected and whose will not (James Rosenau, cited in Mills, 1997: 289).

Limited criticism

The application of human rights aspirations, in the policy practice of NGOs, the foreign policy of states and regional institutions, from the European Union to NATO, and in the activities of the United Nations, has not been without its detractors. Commentators across the board, from academics to journalists, state officials and NGO practitioners, have raised a large body of criticism.

This criticism has originated largely within the human rights discourse itself. The policy-makers and institutional actors have been criticized for failing to act on behalf of human rights in some areas of the world, or when they have acted, have been criticized for being too slow to respond or for merely taking half-measures. Much of this criticism has also been focused on the slow pace of institutional change at the international level, for example: the UN Security Council composition and power of veto; UN Charter restrictions on international intervention; the slow development of an International Criminal Court; the lack of institutional integration of NGOs in international decision-making; and the remaining outdated privileges of state sovereignty.

As Alex de Waal has noted, 'to date most sociological study of humanitarian action implicitly accepts the axioms of the humanitarian international'. Statements of human rights NGOs and states and international institutions acting in the name of human rights are often taken at face value, as if the nobility of aim conferred immunity from sociological analysis or political critique. He sums up the strength of consensus by analogy: 'It is as though the sociological study of the church were undertaken by committed Christians only: criticism would be solely within the context of advancing the faith itself' (1997a: 65).

Despite the rapid nature of the transformation of the language and powers of international institutions there has been little critical consideration of this change. The radical challenge of human rights to the postwar international framework has been accepted in essence, with discussion focusing on the nature of the required institutional changes and the speed with which they are possible.

It is becoming increasingly clear that the human rights discourse is rewriting the international law books and policy-making procedures from the starting point of ethics and universal values, and in so doing is challenging the previous frameworks of legal and political rights at both international and domestic levels. As Jack Donnelly notes, the discourse of human rights implicitly recognizes 'a new kind of accountability' (2000: 128). The shift away from forms of accountability linked to the nation-state opens up a series of theoretical and practical alternatives that did not appear possible during the Cold War period. Where the nation-state was previously seen to be solely responsible for the protection of the rights of its citizens, and state sovereignty upheld as the first principle of international society, today the global citizen is seen to require a more global or cosmopolitan political framework of rights protection. As the International War Crimes Tribunal at The Hague held in the *Tadić* case: '[it] would be a travesty of law and a betrayal of the universal need for justice, should the concept of State sovereignty be allowed to be raised successfully against human rights' (cited in Bianchi, 1999: 261).

There has been little discussion of the new forms of international law which would need to be developed and legitimized once the equality of sovereign states is replaced by a legal framework that prioritizes individual rights in the international arena. Another area which has received little discussion is the impact of these changes on the domestic political framework of states, particularly those subject to international regulation, once the political framework is determined by the universal ethics of human rights priorities. Just as the recasting of international law assumes a different starting point, so do domestic forms of human rights-based regulation: 'Democracy and human rights have very different, and often competing, theoretical and moral foundations' (Donnelly, 2000: 154). The challenge of the human rights discourse to the existing framework of international law and political decision-making is clearly a fundamental one, yet the broader consequences seem rarely to be considered. Most critical discussion is focused on particular crisis situations and the response made to them, and tends to assume that the broader long-term consequences of a shift to a human rights-orientated world must be entirely positive.

The lack of a critical consideration of the broader consequences of the prioritization of the human rights framework may be because the arguments have already been played out and the old political framework consciously rejected. It may be that this was justified because of its fail-ure to meet the new demands of universality, or inability to protect or empower minorities, or to provide a human-centred and progressive framework of social relations. Yet a study of the academic literature on human rights seems to bear little evidence of such a conscious level of consideration. For many commentators, the human rights framework appears to be justified as a *fait accompli* because governments and inter-national institutions have already accepted it. Richard Rorty, for exam-ple, argues human rights are so well established that 'the question whether human beings really have the rights enumerated in the [1975 OSCE] Helsinki Declaration is not worth raising' because 'human rights culture' is now 'a fact of the world' (1993: 115–34). Jerome Shestack puts the issue more forcefully, arguing that theoretical debate is now redun-dant because the arguments have 'been overtaken by the fact that human rights have become hegemonic and therefore essentially global by fiat' (1997: 568). For other commentators, critical discussion of the human rights framework is simply held to be unproductive and danger-ous. Louis Henkin asserts that seeking theoretical or philosophical justi-fications for human rights claims would be 'disruptive and unhelpful' (cited in Mutua, 1996: 629). Mary Midgley acknowledges that for aca-demics there may be uncertainties about the central justification for human rights, but warns that academics should not take an approach that is 'predeterminedly destructive'. Instead they should be positive about the 'mysterious' power of the human rights concept which has emerged as a result of the 'immense enlargement of our moral scene' (1999: 160–1).

Rethinking human rights

The rationale for this edited collection is the authors' shared concern to raise some questions over the assumptions often made on behalf of the human rights approach in the international sphere. The authors have different theoretical and professional backgrounds in the law, academia, media and the aid industry and bring with them a variety of concerns with the human rights approach in these areas. Whether the focus is humanitarian aid, economic development, international law, civil soci-ety and democracy, war and genocide, peace processes, children's rights, the media or military intervention each chapter raises serious concerns which go to the heart of the assumptions behind the consensus on human rights. The book is divided into three parts, each addressing one of the three ethical claims of the human rights approach.

Part I, 'Universal Rights?', consists of three chapters which question the assumption that a human rights policy-orientation necessarily represents a universal approach. The universality of human rights reflects the decline of Cold War barriers to international regulation and interference in areas which were previously seen to be the preserve of the sovereign state. Although the sphere of rights which can be claimed is enlarged, the capacity to act to enforce these rights has become the preserve of the major powers. While the United States and its allies acquire new rights to judge which regimes deserve to remain in power and which should be deposed, states which lack major military and economic resources become sidelined in international affairs and the object of new mechanisms of international regulation. The contributing authors suggest that the claims of the human rights discourse need to be measured against the policy practice of international institutions and governments which seem to indicate that the universalization of human rights concerns reflects the institutionalization of new mechanisms of great power regulation.

The central focus of Chapter 1 by Fiona Fox is the adoption of new human rights approaches to the provision of humanitarian aid. She suggests that rather than univerzalising the right to aid in situations of humanitarian need, the human rights framework reflects the increasing politicization of aid by Western governments and the creation of new regimes of control through aid conditionality. John Laughland, in Chapter 2, highlights how the development of international law to give greater emphasis to protecting universal human rights has undermined the previous legal equality of nation-states. The new framework of law-making has politicized the law under the guidance of leading Western states, with the power to establish new crimes and new courts for the prosecution of the governments of weaker states, while the international laws which restrained the predatory instincts of major powers, such as the UN Charter's indiction against 'waging aggressive war' are quietly dropped. In Chapter 3, Vanessa Pupavac draws attention to the new hierarchies of international regulation established under the human rights framework of the UN Convention on the Rights of the Child. She suggests that the universal claims of promoting the rights of all children legitimizes international policy practices establishing mechanisms of therapeutic governance which challenge the rights of both governments and parents in non-Western states.

Part II, 'Rights of Empowerment?', questions the view that the human rights framework can be assumed to empower people held to be excluded or marginalized from the political process. Rather than granting new rights, the authors suggest that the rights of advocacy claimed by international bodies provide little accountability for those they claim to act on behalf of, while potentially undermining existing rights of democracy and self-government. Each of the four chapters in this section considers that the human rights framework, in fact, empowers international institutions or governing bodies charged with defining and adjudicating on human rights questions or claiming to represent or articulate the 'voices' of those excluded from government. The problems at the level of accountability are seen to undermine human rights advocates' claims of facilitating broader participation in decision-making and to create barriers to the process of political consensus-building.

In Chapter 4, Chris Gilligan considers the human rights protections built into the Good Friday peace agreement in Northern Ireland and charts how the redefinition of rights away from the political sphere of democracy and self-government has allowed the British state to regulate the province by disempowering political representatives on both sides of the religious divide. He suggests that the removal of political accountability in the mechanisms of conflict resolution established by the peace process may result in institutionalizing divisions in Northern Irish society rather than ameliorating them. John Pender, in Chapter 5, analyses the World Bank's revision of its development policies to prioritize human rights under the Comprehensive Development Framework, designed to give voice to and empower the poor. He concludes that the 'Voices of the Poor' approach can be easily manipulated to suit the World Bank's own agenda, and questions whether the focus on poverty reduction can meet the needs of the poorest and most vulnerable in poor societies. David Chandler, in Chapter 6, assesses the claims of cosmopolitan democracy and asks whether the global citizen is empowered in the proposed frameworks held to expand democracy at the international level. He highlights that the mechanisms of regulation based on conceptions of international civil society, cosmopolitan governance and cosmopolitan citizenship involve no relationships of political accountability and reflect the new freedoms of action claimed by leading world powers. Chapter 7, by Jon Holbrook, considers whether the proclaimed right of humanitarian intervention effectively empowers people in the societies concerned and questions whether human rights advocates are right to assert that sovereignty is a barrier to the protection and promotion of human rights. He argues that international interventions, which externally impose political settlements, will fail to provide sustainable solutions to humanitarian crises.

The third, concluding part deals with human-centred rights and suggests that while human rights advocates may argue that they are putting humanity at the centre of policy-making concerns, their conception of humanity is a deeply problematic one. Far from seeing human potential for problem-solving and conflict resolution, the human rights framework often appears to assume that human beings cannot be trusted to act in a rational and responsible manner. Understanding conflict within the framework of human rights abuser and victim has resulted in the development of a moralized 'black and white' or 'good and evil' view of participants which rarely considers the underlying causes of conflict and portrays both sides as lacking the capacity for rational decision-making. The moralized approach to conflict portrays one side as morally incapable of choosing right from wrong and the other as damaged and needy victims incapable of recovering without international sponsorship and support.

In Chapter 8, Barrie Collins suggests that analysis of the Rwandan genocide within the human rights approach of abuser and victim has neglected the broader political and social context in which mass killing occurred, dehumanizing Rwandan society rather than analysing conflict in rational terms. He concludes that this approach has ignored the role of international interference in destabilizing Rwandan society and has been used to legitimize military repression and the denial of democracy in present-day Rwanda. Chapter 9, by Philip Hammond, assesses the claims of human rights journalism. Examining examples from the coverage of Bosnia and Rwanda, he argues that public understanding of these conflicts has been distorted by advocacy journalists calling for military intervention against demonized human rights abusers. Chapter 10, by Edward S. Herman and David Peterson systematically challenges the claims made by leading advocates of international military intervention over Kosovo and illustrates how human rights intervention can easily become a dehumanizing project of bombing and sanctions in the cause of great power interests.

Part I
Universal Rights?

1
Conditioning the Right to Humanitarian Aid? Human Rights and the 'New Humanitarianism'

Fiona Fox

Introduction[1]

Over the past decade, a new 'human rights-based' approach to aid provision has achieved prominence. This approach, often termed a 'new humanitarianism', is geared to strengthening those forces in society that can bring peace and stability to crisis situations in the developing world. It offers humanitarian relief agencies a new 'moral banner' under which to work, helping agencies to cope with the new international situation and the new and complex emergencies that have emerged since the Cold War. Most importantly, the 'new humanitarianism' clearly presents itself as a break from the past. It sees traditional humanitarian aid provision, which was avowedly apolitical and politically neutral, as a naive illusion. New humanitarian aid provision is overtly political, embracing a politically conscious aid strategy which, it is argued, can positively impact on the politics of a conflict or post-conflict situation.

This chapter urges aid agencies to practise caution in their embrace of this new approach. It seeks to spell out the potential dangers of many of the new trends in emergency relief. It questions whether some aspects of the new, human rights-based humanitarianism may conflict with the core values of many humanitarian aid agencies, in particular the respect for every human life. It is suggested that new humanitarianism, with its attempt to place humanitarian aid as part of a broader strategy to promote human rights and resolve conflict, may weaken the humanitarian imperative to assist all those in need regardless of where and who they are. The following sections explain where new humanitarianism has come from and how its practical application will impact on people caught up in conflicts in the Third World. They outline the changing role of international humanitarian NGOs, the changing nature of humanitarian principles within the human rights framework, and some of the potential dangers of this new approach.

The changing role of humanitarian NGOs

The end of the Cold War has seen a dramatic shift in the relationship between humanitarian and political action. During the Cold War there was little attempt to hide the fact that development aid was delivered on the basis of the strategic interests of the donor governments. Pragmatism triumphed over principle as donor nations openly sided with their Cold War allies. As President Franklin D. Roosevelt famously said of the Nicaraguan dictator General Anastasio Somoza: 'He may be a son of a bitch, but he's our son of a bitch.' Many aid agencies were also happy to be seen working in solidarity with those fighting for justice and identi-fied themselves with national liberation struggles such as those in Latin America and South Africa. However, governments and aid agencies drew a clear line between development aid and humanitarian relief. The latter, it was assumed, would be free of political conditions and delivered purely on the basis of need. While it may not always have happened, there was an expectation that humanitarian aid would be separated from foreign and defence policy.

The end of the Cold War marked an important change in the way NGOs operate in humanitarian emergencies. During the Cold War, strong authoritarian states exerted strict controls over NGOs, dictating the limits of international humanitarianism. The collapse and weaken-ing of many national governments, particularly those in the South and those formerly within the Soviet Bloc, has given NGOs unprecedented freedom to operate within these nation-states. One particular conse-quence of the weakening of the nation-state in the Third World is that, increasingly, donor governments are deliberately circumventing local governments and channelling any money for emergency relief through their own NGOs. This is a major change. In the past, the role of interna-tional NGOs was to fill the gaps in the official relief programmes run by the national government of the affected country. Since the 1980s, how-ever, NGOs are expected to be the primary response mechanism in any disaster. Within hours of the news of any major disaster, the media will announce the arrival of agencies like Oxfam and Médecins sans Frontières (MSF). During Hurricane Mitch in 1998, the media criticized international NGOs for not being operational on the ground quickly enough. The question of the Nicaraguan and Honduran governments running the relief operation was not even considered.

All these factors have contributed to the massive growth in the power of international humanitarian organizations. From the mid-1980s, relief and humanitarian expenditure witnessed an unprecedented sixfold increase. Agencies like the International Committee of the Red Cross (ICRC), UNICEF and UNHCR are billion dollar global operations, commanding significantly more power and resources than the poor countries in which they operate. Many aid agencies acknowledge that NGOs are filling the political vacuum in many of these nations. Mark Duffield makes the point that the growth of humanitarian NGOs is itself part of broader socio-political developments in the post-Cold War world: 'The enhanced ability of agencies to respond to need is, itself, part of a wider and complex process of globalisation and demise of political alternatives' (Duffield, 1998).

On the political level too, there have been developments that add to the relative power of international relief agencies. Human rights groups and aid agencies welcome the willingness of Western powers to reject national sovereignty as an obstacle to humanitarian interventions. The language of human rights and poverty, once the preserve of aid agencies and radical campaigners, now trips off the tongues of the leaders of the most powerful nations of the world. Tony Blair regularly described the NATO war against Serbia as a 'humanitarian war' with a 'moral purpose', the triumph of good over evil. No more, it seems, are wars fought for national interest or to exert power, but for a new set of universal values that have emerged in the post-Cold War world. Michael Ignatieff comments on the triumph of these new values: 'Instead of there being two competing human rights cultures in the world – one socialist, one capitalist – there is now one set of minimum norms to which every regime in the world formally subscribes' (1998a: 89).

This new human rights culture has challenged the notion of sovereignty as a barrier to international intervention. Although, so far at least, the implications of this shift have only been felt in the Third World or in marginalized East European countries, the forcible intervention into a state's territory in pursuit of humanitarian aims is now common and acceptable. If anything, the powerful nations are criticized for not doing it enough. The arrest of General Augusto Pinochet, the international war crimes tribunals for Rwanda and Bosnia, and the NATO bombing of Serbia are all examples of how sovereignty is no longer a block on intervention. For many, these are positive developments.

Bernard Kouchner, founder of MSF and former minister in the French government has welcomed the fact that 'the age of strict national sovereignty is over and a new era of intervention has begun' (Kouchner, 1999b). In November 1999, when MSF won the Nobel Peace Prize, several commentators remarked that the agency was ahead of its time in terms of condemning human rights abuses and challenging national sovereignty. In an editorial, the *Guardian* praised the agency for giving a lead to the Western governments: 'MSF's assertion of the right to enter sovereign states – in order to alleviate human suffering – was a bold precursor of an argument which is now embraced, however spasmodically, by governments' (*Guardian*, 1999).

These social and political changes have thrust humanitarian agencies into a new role. Very often aid workers are key actors in politically sensitive areas in which nation states and civil society have all but collapsed. Far from just delivering aid, they have become major players in their own right, wielding significant political influence and commanding massive resources. As the first people on the spot, they also play a major role in internationalizing conflicts and emergencies. The role of aid agency press officers is to draw media attention to humanitarian crises in remote areas of the world and use that spotlight to galvanize the international community into action. The humanitarian agencies' perception, rather than that of the local government or warring faction, is likely to be the one listened to by the world's political leaders. According to Peter Hawkins, Head of Operations at Save the Children: 'We have become hugely powerful, filling the political vacuum and influencing international opinion. Very often what we say goes.' Some critics of humanitarianism have pointed to the way in which the internationalizing of relief aid has reinforced the weakness of Third World governments and has undermined the whole concept of local solutions. Alex de Waal makes this point clearly: 'This process of internationalisation is the key to the appropriation of power by international institutions and the retreat from domestic accountability in famine vulnerable countries' (Waal, 1997a).

However, far from revelling in this newly acquired power and influence, humanitarian agencies are undergoing a profound identity crisis. Under attack from many quarters, humanitarians find it impossible to mount a robust defence of their new role because they are still grappling with the enormity of the changes. Many seasoned emergencies personnel feel increasingly uneasy with their new role. In many ways, humanitarians are the victims of global forces way beyond their control and some would happily return to the days when they filled the gap in official relief under clear and tight controls from the affected government. However, those days are hardly likely to return and humanitarian agencies need to gain a new confidence if they are to maintain public support.

Aid agencies have come under fire from many quarters over the past ten years. It is now commonplace to hear humanitarian aid accused of prolonging wars, feeding killers, legitimizing corrupt regimes, strengthening perpetrators of genocide and creating new war economies. In short, for many, humanitarians have gone from being angels of mercy who can do no wrong to being part of the problem. Unfortunately for NGOs, the media have played a major role in popularizing these criticisms (see Hammond, this volume, Chapter 9). During high-profile emergencies like those in Zaire (1994 onwards) and Sudan (1998), the role of humanitarian agencies came under massive scrutiny. Critics like de Waal were given copious amounts of airtime to accuse aid agencies of feeding killers and prolonging conflicts. The UK's Secretary of State for International Development, Clare Short, has said that she is 'haunted by the risk of relief maintaining conflict' (cited in IDC, 1999). During the 1998 famine in Sudan, Short very publicly suggested that delivering relief rather than pushing for a political solution could only prolong the war.

The level of criticism has persuaded many humanitarian agencies that there is an urgent need for change. The European Community Humanitarian Aid Office (ECHO) openly admits that the move towards a new human rights-based approach to humanitarian action has been driven by external criticism: 'Business as usual for the Commission as humanitarian aid donor would mean courting the risk of growing criticism and isolation in the donor community, and a loss of credibility generally' (ECHO, 1999). However, the crisis in humanitarianism is not just a result of sustained criticism. It also reflects the enormity of the changes engulfing the humanitarian system. It is worth noting that the humanitarian aid system evolved largely in relation to natural disasters. Agencies are still struggling to understand the complex emergencies in which they find themselves operating. In the past, humanitarian relief was considered a short-term stopgap, in situations where long-term development had to be put on hold. More recent emergencies, like those in Sudan and the Great Lakes, are seen as requiring long-term relief, which creates a whole new set of issues.

All these changes have produced a sustained debate about humanitarianism within agencies themselves and in academic circles. Most commentators agree that humanitarianism is in deep crisis and in need of reform. Indeed, reading the literature around this subject, it becomes clear that few can even clearly explain what the term means today.

There is certainly no common understanding of what good humanitarianism should look like. Despite frequent initiatives to improve standards and develop guidelines for humanitarian work, for example, the new Code of Conduct, the Sphere Project, and the concept of 'Do No Harm', there is still no clear framework for a new humanitarian system. NGO analysts, such as Hugo Slim, are critical of the 'semantic manoeuvring' in the debate around humanitarian principles, which masks chronic confusion amongst the main actors: 'The variety of these redefinitions creates something of a cacophony and has not yet given the humanitarian community a decisive moral banner under which to go about its business' (Slim and McConnan, 1998).

For many commentators and some aid agencies, the traditional ICRC view of humanitarian relief, based on the principles of humanity, impartiality and neutrality, is in need of updating in line with the changing international framework. The following section considers the important differences between the old ICRC principles and those of the 'new humanitarianism'.

From universal need to the conditionality of human rights

When Jean Henri Dunant happened upon the slaughter on the battlefields of Solferino in 1859, he was shocked to see thousands of soldiers from both sides lying side by side dying in agony with absolutely no help. There and then the wealthy Genevan sent for medical supplies, enlisted local women and set about tending to the wounded. The concept of humanitarian relief during war was born. A few years later, Dunant and his colleagues institutionalized the concept in the form of the ICRC. From the beginning, neutrality and universal assistance were at the heart of the ICRC's mandate. The agency makes no distinction between good wars and bad, between just and unjust causes, or even between aggressors and innocents. The ICRC's principles of neutrality and impartiality in the provision of aid, enshrined in the Geneva Conventions of 1864, were adopted by the plethora of humanitarian agencies that emerged throughout the last century. But over the past ten years, these principles have been seriously questioned.

In the new moral, human rights culture of international politics, the notion of universal and impartial aid provision has become increasingly controversial. The ICRC's refusal to speak out against human rights abuses and to remain neutral in every conflict has earned it criticism from newer agencies. There is growing international backing for the approach of 'human rights' humanitarians, like MSF, who argue that humanitarian intervention cannot be neutral between Serb militiamen and Albanian civilians or between Hutu genocidaires and their Tutsi victims. The ICRC has been criticized by journalists for refusing to give evidence to the international war crimes tribunals for Rwanda and Bosnia, and revelations about the agency's silence during the Holocaust have been presented as evidence that the universal approach, based on neutrality, can be morally repugnant. Journalist Ed Vulliamy used a conference of aid agencies and the media to air his strong views on the principle of neutrality:

> To be neutral is to be on the side of the criminal. There are moments in history when crimes are being committed, when neutrality is not neutral at all, but complicity in the crime ... I think the time has come for aid workers to challenge the commandment of neutrality – to draw a line, stand up and be counted.
>
> (Vulliamy, 1999c)

Vulliamy need not fear. As Hugo Slim and Isobel McConnan noted, after consulting all the UK's main humanitarian relief agencies about these principles, 'neutrality has become a dirty word' (1998). Today, neutrality is seen as undesirable, either because it is considered amoral, remaining silent in the face of human rights abuses, or simply because the central role of NGOs in highly political emergencies makes it impossible to achieve. As more and more agencies abandon the principle of universal assistance, a new humanitarianism based on the concept of human rights has emerged.

The ICRC's view that war is a political matter, to be dealt with by governments, is rejected by the new human rights tradition, which sees war as a moral violation. For these agencies, part of the goal of humanitarian action is to act within the political sphere in order to diminish the incidence of war and conflict. These humanitarians feel that it is wrong to remain neutral between the war-maker and his victim and argue that the role of humanitarians is to speak out against human rights abuses wherever they see them.

While agencies like Oxfam, Save the Children and UNICEF have all adopted a human rights approach in recent years, the leading advocate of the new human rights humanitarianism is MSF. The agency was set up in 1971 by doctors who were disgusted at the studied neutrality of the Red Cross during the horrors of the Biafran war. Now, thirty years on and with a budget of $250 million, their brand of political humanitarianism is in the ascendant, with aid agencies and governments alike. The 1999 award of the Nobel Peace Prize to MSF was a highly significant statement of support for the politicization of humanitarian aid, as acknowledged by the agency's founder, Bernard Kouchner: 'MSF's work was political from the start. I hope the prize marks the recognition of a type of humanitarian work which fights injustice and persecution, in contrast to traditional organisations' (cited in Sanction, 1999).

In a barbed reference to the ICRC's refusal to compromise its neutrality by condemning human rights abuses, Phillipe Biberson, MSF's President, said: 'If we are not sure that words can save, we do know that silence kills' (cited in Daley, 1999). However, despite this pressure, the ICRC continues to insist that speaking out against human rights abuses would undermine its humanitarian principles and threaten its ability to help those in need on all sides in a conflict. For example, in 1997 when aid agencies called on the Red Cross to cease humanitarian aid in Afghanistan because of the Taliban's position on women, the agency refused and promptly adapted their programmes to comply with the Taliban's instruction to segregate men and women. Meanwhile, those agencies with a human rights-based approach, including Oxfam, suspended their programmes in Taliban-controlled areas (Ignatieff, 1998a: 140–8).

Speaking at a public meeting to commemorate the 50th anniversary of the Geneva Conventions, Cornelio Sommaruga, President of the International Committee of the Red Cross, defended his agency's refusal to enter into the new rights-based humanitarianism (1999). He explained how the ICRC's refusal to publicly condemn Serb atrocities in Kosovo allowed him to personally visit President Milošević to negotiate access to Serbia. As a result the Red Cross became the only international agency able to deliver humanitarian relief to the victims of the NATO bombing and to the subsequent flow of Serb refugees from Kosovo.

The human rights-based approach to aid, being adopted by more and more aid agencies and donor governments, demands that all aid be judged on how it contributes to the goal of promoting and protecting human rights. This has led some agencies to reject the universal approach of traditional humanitarianism in favour of a new one, which moves beyond basic needs towards delivering justice and a political framework which can ensure that human rights are safeguarded: 'When considered through the justice lens, the mere provision of foodstuffs or medical support is an insufficient response to a humanitarian crisis' (CRS, 1999). It is important to note that human rights-based humanitarianism will mean withholding aid in some instances, as was the case in Afghanistan in the late 1990s.

A recent ECHO discussion paper, which presents a strong case for mainstreaming human rights into ECHO's humanitarian activities, clearly acknowledges that access to those in need would no longer be the overriding objective: 'From a rights perspective, access to victims of humanitarian aid is not an end in itself and will not, therefore, be pursued at any cost ... Access will be sought if it is the most effective way to contribute to the human rights situation' (ECHO, 1999). The ECHO paper looks at the case of the Ethiopian famine at the end of the 1980s, as an example of the modern dilemma facing human rights humanitarians. In that case, speaking out against human rights abuses meant risking losing access to those in need. MSF did speak out and the agency was expelled from Ethiopia. ECHO believes that history has judged MSF right: 'It is worth noting the criticism to which the international response to famine in Ethiopia has been subjected subsequently – above all for its "political blindness". This assessment appears to endorse MSF's strategy' (ECHO, 1999).

Closely linked to the new rights-based humanitarianism are the concepts of 'developmental relief' and 'goal-orientated humanitarianism'. During the Cold War, relief and development were considered to be distinct and discrete. However, the protracted and complex nature of many of today's wars has forced humanitarians to rethink the link between the two. Like the new human rights-based humanitarianism, goal-orientated humanitarianism is an attempt to move away from the strict ICRC tradition of delivering aid to all, based on immediate human need rather than the long-term political consequences. Increasingly, the old values of humanitarianism – impartiality and neutrality – are regarded as hampering the pursuit of peace and justice. From the late 1980s onwards, many agencies began to think beyond straightforward relief and to think of their interventions on the basis of how they could contribute to longer-term, sustainable development as well as enhancing the prospects for peace and justice.

Using aid to strengthen the prospects for a peaceful resolution of conflicts has now become the subject of a major case study commissioned by the OECD's Development Assistance Committee. Peter Uvin, author of the synthesis report, is clear that this approach is now a significant trend in conflict situations: 'There clearly is a broad trend towards an increased use of humanitarian assistance as part of a more comprehensive strategy to transform conflicts and decrease the violence' (Uvin, 1999). This trend is partly a response to the accusation that relief aid can prolong war and exacerbate conflict. In the late 1980s the buzz phrase became 'do no harm' (Anderson, 1996), a plea to humanitarians to ensure that, at the very minimum, aid does not make things worse.

Stung by criticisms of humanitarian interventions, agencies began to question whether there were ways in which humanitarian relief could be managed so that it could strengthen positive processes in conflict situations rather than inadvertently fuelling conflict.

Goal-orientated humanitarianism marks a fundamental shift from traditional humanitarian principles. Unlike the many goals implicit in long-term development, humanitarian relief was notable for its minimalist aim of saving life. Returning to the image of Dunant and his helpers, patching up soldiers on the fields of Solferino, it was irrelevant to Dunant whether these soldiers survived only to don their uniforms and fight again. The new goal-orientated relief, however, does question the long-term consequences of intervening 'merely' to save lives. Hugo Slim sums up the new goal-orientated humanitarianism like this: 'Rather than having the saving of life as its overriding and prophetic concern, a new humanitarianism has emerged that bases actions (or inaction) on the assumed good or bad consequences of a given intervention in relation to wider developmental aims' (Slim, 1997).

This new trend was highlighted during the controversy over the delivery of aid to over a million Rwandan refugees in the camps in Zaire in 1996. From the very beginning, agencies were condemned by human rights groups for saving the lives of 'genocidaires' who would survive only to reorganize and re-invade Rwanda to 'finish off' the genocide. In an unprecedented move, humanitarian agencies, including MSF, withdrew humanitarian aid from these camps on the basis that there was a risk that relief would be used to strengthen armed forces, thus prolonging the conflict. Pursuing the strategy of developmental relief or goal-orientated relief allows agencies to reassure the public that they are not politically naive and will withdraw humanitarian aid if it could have negative effects. Tess Kingham MP, a member of the British government House of Commons International Development Committee, put the case for this new approach very convincingly: 'Surely taking a view of the wider good – for the long term interests of people – to actually achieve real stability and development ... it may be better to withdraw aid now – to ensure that in the long term, it is in the best interests of the people' (IDC, 1999).

Short's criticism of voluntary agencies' fund-raising for humanitarian relief in Sudan in 1998, when what was really needed was a political resolution of the war, also illustrated this approach. In Sierra Leone too, the UK government called on humanitarian agencies to suspend all relief because it would serve to legitimize the 1997 military coup and therefore could postpone the return of democracy. While this approach seems to be common sense, it also projects humanitarian agencies into a much more explicitly political role. There is a danger of the unelected, often unaccountable and usually foreign, aid worker becoming judge, juror and politician in Third World conflicts. He/she is asked to reach a verdict on a highly complex political crisis, to decide which strategy would best deliver peace and stability and to predict the impact of humanitarian aid on the future development of a given conflict. For the first time, this approach introduces conditions into the delivery of humanitarian aid. As the UK-based Disasters Emergency Committee has noted: 'Agencies and donors alike have downgraded the humanitarian imperative in favour of conditional assistance linked to peace-building processes' (DEC, 1998).

While most Western governments continue to take a formal position that humanitarian aid is unconditional and should only be based on need, it is becoming increasingly clear that this principle has been seriously undermined. As Mark Duffield points out: 'While the formal position remains unchanged, the blurring effect of developmental relief has contributed to humanitarian assistance becoming a more indistinct, equivocal and contested activity' (1998). The new trend towards conditionality in humanitarian aid, delivering aid on the condition that it 'does no harm' and does not impede long-term peace and justice, directly challenges the fundamental principle associated with humanitarian aid, that of universality. Increasingly, the universal right of every man, woman and child to relief at times of disaster, which is enshrined in international law, is being undermined, as relief becomes dependent on peace-building and the promotion of security and stability.

Goal-orientated relief also pushes the humanitarian aid community to attempt to predict the long-term impact and outcome of the delivery of relief in each crisis. Yet, in the complex emergencies of the past decade, where outside aid is just one of many internal and external factors, this is not easily achieved. Nick Stockton, former Head of Emergencies at Oxfam, emphatically rejects the notion that aid agencies can predict the long-term impact of humanitarian interventions: 'No matter how much we want to act in a way beneficial in the long term, it's pretty much an exercise in ideological vanity – polishing one's own political correctness in public.' Stockton refers to Oxfam's experience in the Biafran war where, he argues, the agency took sides and predicted a humanitarian disaster which never unfolded: 'The truth is we're very good at retrospective analysis but very bad at getting it right at the time or at predicting the future consequences of our actions.'[2]

The other trend, visible in goal-orientated relief, is the attachment of conditions. If relief aid is to be used to tackle the underlying causes of the conflict and contribute to its peaceful resolution, then it may well be necessary to use it in a carrot-and-stick way to change the course of events. While withholding development aid until certain conditions are met is common practice, to apply this principle to humanitarian aid is a dramatic departure from traditional policy. After hearing all sides in the debate on humanitarian principles, the International Development Committee delivered its verdict that there was a case for withdrawing humanitarian aid in some instances: 'There are occasions where that moral imperative cannot be obeyed, where relief must be suspended or delayed until certain conditions are met' (IDC, 1999).

Michael Barfod, a senior officer at ECHO, neatly summarized these changes in the fundamental understanding of 'good humanitarianism' in his comments to the International Development Committee. Barfod began by stating that he believed that humanitarianism had moved away from the traditional model based on the universal principles of impartiality, neutrality and independence. He then contrasted the old and the new model in a way which left little doubt as to his preference for the new approach. Describing (some would say caricaturing) the old Red Cross model, he stated:

> You don't get mixed up with development and you don't get mixed up with human rights, that is none of your business. You certainly do not speak out because that is dangerous. The whole thing is action-orientated and it's morally self-justifying because when you provide humanitarian aid you are doing something good.
>
> (IDC, 1999)

Barfod is much kinder about the new model and quite explicit in claiming that the new human rights humanitarianism, and the concept of using humanitarian action to promote peace and justice, amounts to the politicization of humanitarian aid:

> Here you would actually say, there is no way we can handle a situation without linking up with human rights issues, without linking up with development, to understand the real impact. We have to be part of the political process leading to peace, that is what we are really there for.
>
> (IDC, 1999)

The dangers of politicizing humanitarian aid

The desire to link humanitarian aid with human rights, peace and development goals begs the question as to whether humanitarian aid agencies are in a legitimate position to pass judgement on complex political prob-lems. The move towards attempting to evaluate the impact of humani-tarian aid on any given conflict situation has forced agencies to grapple with new moral dilemmas. One obvious dilemma is 'Who are we giving aid to? Are they killers? Could our aid be used to help them kill again?' In the past, aid agencies did not generally ask these questions before deliv-ering relief. Giving aid in conflict or post-conflict situations has often brought agencies into contact with elements of a defeated army or mili-tia, or the communities that had sided with them. However, when human need was the primary concern, aid was delivered. Once this assumption is no longer made then aid agencies are thrown into a com-plex process of judgements on who is 'deserving' and who is not.

De Waal has criticized humanitarians for not openly taking the side of the local forces that put an end to the Rwandan genocide (i.e. the Rwandan Patriotic Front). Michael Ignatieff has also said that the logic of the new humanitarianism is that we should choose the right side and support it: 'We may have to intervene on the side that appears to be most in the right and assist it to consolidate power' (1998a: 160). The power of NGOs in debilitated Third World societies, and their influence with Western governments, means that agencies are often called on by donor countries to provide an analysis of the political situation and to put forward particular solutions. But there is concern among some that Western agencies are not qualified to rule on complex political crises like those in Sudan and the Great Lakes region. Many operational agencies have only been present in the region since the beginning of the crisis and their judgements are necessarily superficial.

Many commentators have suggested that the way to avoid making the wrong decisions or taking sides on a simplistic or emotional basis is to ensure that agencies hone their analytical skills. The demand to 'scale up' on political analysis has been taken seriously by many agencies working in complex emergencies. The Department for International Development (DFID) and other government development departments are currently in the process of jointly developing a standard practice for 'Peace and Conflict Impact Assessment'. This is designed to help humanitarians to assess the potential impact of their project on the political landscape. There is clearly a potential tension here between resisting the pressure to become more political while developing ever more sophisticated levels of political analysis. 'Scaling up' may well exacerbate the trend towards the politicization of aid.

There has been much discussion amongst the UK's aid agencies about whether the British government is politicizing humanitarian aid.

The feeling of many people in NGOs is that DFID has taken the positive thinking about a rights-based humanitarianism from the aid agencies, and then adapted it to fit into the government's foreign policy objectives. The formal position of the Department is that humanitarian relief remains immune to political conditionality and is based only on need: 'We will seek to promote a more universal approach in addressing humanitarian needs. People in need – wherever they are – should have equal status and rights to assistance' (DFID, 1999). However, a quick glance at the government's practice suggests another story. There is now some evidence that the British government may be prepared to withhold humanitarian aid where it believes that this is justified by the wider goals of human rights promotion in a specific political context. A closer look at where the government stands, in relation to the debate on humanitarian action and humanitarian principles, reveals that the government subscribes to the 'new humanitarianism' that sees human rights and goal-orientated humanitarianism as the way forward.

Short makes no secret of the fact that her Department and the Labour government now speak a new language when it comes to international affairs. In an important speech on humanitarian aid, Short emphasized that human rights have now become the central tenet of the government's policies on international development: 'This means refocusing all aspects of our work – including our approach to humanitarian issues' (Short, 1998). As if to emphasize the extent of this refocusing, Short never once used the word 'humanitarian' in the speech without some prefix. We were encouraged to support the government's espousal of 'ethical humanitarianism' or its 'rights-based humanitarianism', these two phrases being subsumed under the 'new humanitarianism' rubric. She was at pains to stress that this new humanitarianism did indeed represent a break with the past: 'This new rights-based humanitarianism goes well beyond private charity or governmental largesse' (Short, 1998).

It is clear that Short and the UK government have bought into the new human rights-based humanitarianism and the developmental relief or goal-orientated model. In a memo to the International Development Committee, DFID emphasized that human rights were at the centre of the government's humanitarian work: 'Protecting and promoting human rights in conflict, particularly those of women and children, is central to our crisis response strategies' (IDC, 1999). In her speech on the 'Principles for a New Humanitarianism', Short clearly came out in favour of using humanitarian aid to achieve particular goals:

> Many want to go beyond charity which simply alleviates the worst symptoms of crisis to search for and support a just regulation of the

conflict. The end of the Cold War provides the prospect of people being able to push their government and NGOs to act to remove the causes of conflict in a way which was impossible in the Cold War years.
(Short, 1998)

Today, the traditional aim of humanitarian relief – 'simply alleviating the worst symptoms of the crisis' – is no longer considered acceptable. Short has acknowledged that using humanitarian relief to tackle the causes of conflicts and promote a just resolution is an innately political activity: 'I think that the duty is whenever you are doing it [delivering humanitarian relief] to always be looking for the political consequences – who is getting it? Are we strengthening any negative forces?' (Short, 1998).

At a meeting of aid agency programme officers in 1998 senior officials from DFID emphasized that the Department's project was necessarily a political one. Correspondence to the directors of several UK NGOs indicated that agencies should expect the Department's decisions on funding humanitarian relief to reflect political outcomes to a much greater degree than in the past. The UK government argues that one of the key reasons for promoting a new kind of humanitarian action is the strong evidence that traditional humanitarian action has done harm. Short believes that relief has been used to prolong wars and legitimize corrupt regimes. This fear of the misuse of relief aid by warring factions has been used to justify unprecedented decisions made by this government to withhold humanitarian aid from people in need. In defending the UK government's refusal to fund humanitarian assistance for the victims of the coup in Sierra Leone, Short said: 'We made those decisions on humanitarian grounds and on the principle of not allowing humanitarian assistance to be misused by fighters and thus prolonging wars' (IDC, 1999).

Perhaps the most obvious risk of a new, more political, humanitarian action is that warring sides will no longer accept the neutrality of aid workers in crisis. The increased use of 'humanitarian protection' in war-torn societies has seen the institutionalization of military support for humanitarian relief efforts. We now regularly hear about the military creating humanitarian corridors or providing armed protection for relief workers and their logistics networks. While humanitarian workers may have little choice but to avail themselves of this protection, it does compromise the neutrality of NGOs. The Red Cross has rejected the protection of national armies, preferring to pay for reputable private security firms to protect its independence. The increasing use of the military in the delivery of humanitarian aid also compromises the independence of NGOs. For British aid workers during the Kosovo crisis, being managed by soldiers in NATO-run camps at the same time that NATO forces were bombing civilian targets inside Serbia did little to enhance their image of independence.

Moving towards a more political humanitarianism would undoubtedly lead to an increase in the targeting of aid workers. Indeed, this trend is already evident. There are also several unpleasant examples of warring sides targeting people from certain nations who are regarded as having taken sides in Third World conflicts. For example, the Hutu militia who kidnapped tourists in Uganda in March 1999 separated out the English and Americans, killing them while sparing the lives of other nationalities. The new human rights-based humanitarians have accepted that speaking out carries a risk of losing access to those in need. Again, there is nothing new about individuals being thrown out of countries for opposing government policies: it has been happening in countries like Kenya for many years. What is different is the more frequent decisions of agencies to speak out in the midst of a humanitarian crisis. Slim and McConnan note this trend in their review of humanitarian principles and point to the dangers: 'Agencies cannot expect immunity or "humanitarian space" if they are leaning towards solidarity' (1998).

The politicization of aid by donor governments therefore also carries the risk of undermining the ability of humanitarian agencies to do their work. The British government's attempts to deter UK NGOs from working in places like Afghanistan and Serbia, for example, carries a serious risk of undermining the capacity of humanitarian agencies to reach all those in need. It is crucial to the ability of humanitarian agencies that they are not seen as tools of government policy. As Joanna Macrae, from the Overseas Development Institute, states: 'It is vital that aid workers can convincingly state that they are not an instrument of British foreign policy.' Action Aid openly accused the DFID of restricting humanitarian aid to Sierra Leone after the 1997 coup as a deliberate component of the UK government's policy of reinstating the Kabbah government (IDC, 1999). Action Aid saw this as part of a broader trend:

> There have ... been signs that donors might be increasingly inclined to use the granting or suspension of emergency aid as a lever to pursue particular political or military responses to conflicts. This in turn endangers the impartiality of humanitarian aid.
>
> (IDC, 1999)

Short insists that, while the human rights-based approach may leave suffering people without relief, achieving the right outcome makes this 'principled humanitarianism': 'I have to say, NGOs often talk as though giving them money to provide humanitarian support is the principled thing to do and it is not always the principled thing to do' (IDC, 1999). The reason the government believes that withholding humanitarian relief can be principled is that it subscribes to the concept of developmental relief or goal-orientated relief. It is therefore argued that unless aid agencies can show that humanitarian relief can help contribute to resolving a conflict, or promote justice and human rights, it may be better in the long term to withhold that aid. This argument was used in making the case against delivering humanitarian aid in Sudan, Sierra Leone and Afghanistan. While there was some disagreement on the levels of need in all these crises, the government was still prepared to stand back from meeting human needs in the interests of a long-term solution.

At the very minimum the new rights-based, conditional humanitarianism preferred by the government does raise issues about which rights are pre-eminent. Even if one accepts the DFID position that withholding aid to Sierra Leone was nothing to do with British foreign policy, it is still worth questioning the government's judgement that basic rights to relief are secondary to the right to democratic government and peace. Even humanitarians who enthusiastically embrace the human rights approach are troubled by this tension. For example, Emma Bonino, the then EU Commissioner for Humanitarian Aid, expressed this dilemma in a 1998 meeting on the human rights approach to aid to Afghanistan when she questioned whether she could justify a policy that effectively saw young boys suffering because agencies were withdrawing aid in order to stand up for the rights of young girls.

Introducing a new conditionality into what was once considered a universal, unconditional right to relief in times of crisis has caused considerable concern to many in humanitarian circles. While increasing numbers of agencies accept that humanitarian aid can 'do harm', moving towards a situation where people are left in dire need, as in Sierra Leone, for example, in the interests of a long-term political solution, is anathema to many humanitarians. A number of agencies have raised their concerns with the British government, pointing to a number of instances where DFID policy appears to have been prepared to see short-term needs as less important than longer-term political objectives, as, for instance, in Action Aid's public criticism of the government's position on Sierra Leone. Some leading aid workers have expressed concern about the way in which new humanitarianism forces agencies to replace the doctrine of universal need with a hierarchy of victims. Oxfam's Nick Stockton has spoken passionately about the new vogue for 'deserving and undeserving victims' in relation to Rwandan Hutu refugees. He highlights the point that there is a danger in the new goal-orientated humanitarianism of abandoning the principle of a universal right to relief:

> The concept of the undeserving victim is therefore morally and ethically untenable, and practically counter-productive. It represents an outright rejection of the principles of humanity, impartiality and universalism, fundamental tenets of human rights and humanitarian principles.
>
> (Stockton, 1998: 355)

As the universal right to relief is superseded by the human rights approach, there is a risk that more groups of people will fall into the 'undeserving victim' category. The concept of an undeserving victim is a major challenge to the humanitarian system. In his comments on the criminalization of Hutu refugees, Stockton concluded:

> Withholding humanitarian assistance on the grounds that those in need may be criminals ... is the arbitrary application of punishment before trial and it constitutes cruel, inhumane and degrading treatment on a massive scale, such treatment is arguably a crime against humanity.
>
> (1998: 354–5)

Conclusion

To a large extent the discussion of the human rights approach to humanitarian aid provision has downplayed the real dangers involved in rejecting the universal right to assistance and in politicizing humanitarian action. Action Aid and other agencies have called on the government to separate the activities of DFID and the Foreign Office. But accusing the government of subordinating humanitarian aid to the dictates of foreign policy is not the grave insult it would have been during the Cold War. Short is proud of the convergence of all wings of the government's international policy and reminds us that foreign policy, defence policy and international development are now all run according to a new set of moral values with human rights at the core. A new 'ethical' foreign policy is deemed to have replaced the bad old days when foreign policy was based on the strategic interests of the Empire. When NATO powers go to war for 'humanitarian values' it is clear that the old distinction between a national foreign policy and neutral humanitarian aid has disappeared.

On an international level also, the accusation that humanitarian aid is just another arm of national foreign policy now sounds rather dated. In his study of aid in conflict, Peter Uvin notes that the current thinking of NGOs and donor governments is that all elements of intervention should be coordinated to create a positive impact. The move towards goal-orientated relief means that separating the delivery of relief aid from the overall military and political strategies of international governments will fail to promote the peace and stability required. Instead an integrated approach in which aid is just one aspect is now accepted as preferable. Uvin notes 'the close co-operation of all policy instruments (diplomacy, military, trade and development co-operation) based on their respective comparative advantages is required' (1999). Humanitarian aid has now become a 'policy instrument'. Unquestionably, this gives humanitarian aid a more political role than in the past.

It is no coincidence that MSF was the humanitarian agency selected over and above all the others to win the Nobel Peace Prize on the eve of the twenty-first century. To many they signify all that is positive in the move away from traditional humanitarian action:

> MSF's two major contributions to the continuing debate on humanitarian matters are, first, the right and duty to speak out on controversial subjects (in contrast to the Red Cross), denouncing corruption and injustice wherever they exist: secondly, the right and duty to intervene in the affairs of sovereign states where human rights are violated.
>
> (Woodrow, 1999)

MSF seems to have succeeded where other agencies have failed in finding what Slim calls 'a moral banner under which they go about their business'. The international recognition for this agency's political approach to humanitarian action seems to prove what many argue – that the universal principles at the core of the Red Cross model are a thing of the past. It is clear that the UK's Department for International Development, the European Community's Humanitarian Office and some agencies have openly embraced the need for a new politicized form of humanitarian action. But this debate is by no means over.

Notes

1. This chapter is an amended version of 'The Politicisation of Humanitarian Aid', a discussion paper written for Caritas Europa in June 2000.
2. In discussion with the author in response to an earlier draft of this paper.

2
Human Rights and the Rule of Law: Achieving Universal Justice?

John Laughland

> *Of course* we're non-political. The real power always is.
> C. S. Lewis, *That Hideous Strength*

Introduction

The advocates of the extension of international legal norms and the establishment of new international tribunals argue that these measures are necessary to prevent political and military leaders escaping accountability for human rights abuses. They assert that the doctrines of sovereign immunity and long-standing international bars on external interference in domestic legal jurisdictions seek to defend the indefensible. They embellish their arguments with appeals to the natural and deep sense of outrage people feel when atrocities are committed, and by insisting that what they are trying to do is to bring law and justice into a legal and moral vacuum. Many leading lawyers and theoreticians call for the return to moral principles and an 'international social idealism', establishing universal norms of human rights legislation which can be ruled on by an international judiciary (for example, Allott, 1999; Booth et al., 2000).

This chapter claims that these arguments are mistaken. The development of international legal tribunals will not necessarily lead to a more just world, because the premise that states cannot themselves render justice is false. It is also false to assume that international bodies are necessarily objective and non-political. On the contrary, human rights activists are in danger of aggravating the very thing they say they want to eliminate, namely the wielding of power without responsibility, because international bodies are, by definition, beyond the reach of democratic accountability.

The reason why this danger is real is that the central claim of the proponents of the new supranationalism is flawed. That claim, that state sovereignty means that there is no law higher than the state, betrays a deep ignorance of the history of political philosophy. On the contrary, the paradox that the prince is both author and subject of the law is one of the oldest topics of political thought. Aristotle is one of the most famous proponents of the natural law tradition; the principle that the prince or the state is subject to natural law continued to influence political thought for over a thousand years up to Aquinas and beyond. In the pre-Reformation Western Christian tradition, it was always quite explicitly recognized that princes govern subject to God's law. Even monarchs whose names are associated with the doctrine known as absolutism never claimed that they were absolved of their duties towards God and the principles of eternal justice. All that the doctrine of state sovereignty affirms is the circular argument that there is no civil law higher than the state, for the simple reason that if a state is subject to a higher body then that higher body becomes sovereign.

It is only in the modern secular period that states have regarded themselves as literally absolute. Hobbesian positivism and Rousseau's 'general will' do indeed seem to suggest that the highest law is the state's arbitrary will. In our own century, the theories of Hans Kelsen have also added grist to the absolutist mill by attempting to define value-free state structures. As we shall see, it is no coincidence that people from such positivist traditions, especially Kelsen, are precisely those who advocate world government. Because they do literally believe that government is simply a structure of essentially arbitrary commands, they see no problem is subjecting the whole planet to one single system of 'governance'. This chapter will seek to show, by contrast, that sovereign states, i.e. independent self-governing political entities, are the ones most likely to govern in accordance with natural justice.

The claims of moral universalism

The last three years of the twentieth century saw a sudden institutionalization of the view that 'morality' should now be introduced into the allegedly nihilistic world of state sovereignty. Key events succeeded each other very rapidly. The treaty bringing the International Criminal Court into being was signed in July 1998. The former Chilean president, Augusto Pinochet, was arrested in London in October of that year on a Spanish extradition warrant; he was held in Britain for over a year on charges relating to crimes allegedly committed against Chileans by the

Chilean police in Chile. NATO launched its high-altitude bombing campaign against Yugoslavia in March 1999, ostensibly because the need to protect universal human rights demanded it. The following month, NATO formalized this 'new strategic concept' and claimed the moral right to intervene unilaterally against sovereign states because of their domestic policies, something specifically ruled out by the United Nations Charter. In turn, in May 1999, the International Criminal Tribunal for the former Yugoslavia indicted six serving members of the Yugoslav and Serb governments, including the serving head of state, Slobodan Milošević, for crimes against humanity – an event which seemed to give a legal basis to NATO's military intervention. In February 2000, 14 EU states introduced diplomatic sanctions against Austria because the Freedom Party was included in the federal government coalition: the domestic politics of Austria were said to be a matter of common concern.

In June 2000, the International Criminal Tribunal at The Hague effectively endorsed the legality of NATO's new strategic concept and *ipso facto* of the bombing of Yugoslavia when it washed its hands of claims that NATO had itself committed war crimes. It reported that it had no competence to adjudicate over crimes against peace, thereby rescinding perhaps the single greatest advance in international law made at Nuremberg when, using perfect sovereignist logic, the International Military Tribunal ruled that all war crimes derive from war and that therefore the primordial war crime is the 'crime against peace', i.e. military aggression against another sovereign state (Rabkin, 1999). In October 2000, the United Kingdom, the one country in the industrialized world which had maintained a legal *ancien régime* without a written charter of rights, integrated into its domestic law the European Convention on Human Rights. All British parliamentary legislation was thereby subjected to the jurisdiction of judges and ultimately UK law was subjected to the views of the unelected judiciary sitting in the European Court of Human Rights in Strasbourg. In December 2000, the European Union adopted a Charter of Fundamental Rights at Nice; another article in the same treaty allowed EU member states to suspend the voting rights of a member state if it felt human rights were threatened by that state.

In December 2000, the outgoing Clinton administration signed the Rome treaty on the International Criminal Court. In May 2001, Belgium announced that its jurisdiction extended to the whole world where human rights were concerned and so it put two Rwandan nuns on trial for complicity in genocide. In June 2001, Slobodan Milošević was abducted from Belgrade and delivered to The Hague, in direct contempt of a ruling by the Yugoslav constitutional court. This act was welcomed by human rights activists in the same way as they had welcomed the arrest of General Pinochet in London: they said it was both ground-breaking and also well-grounded in existing law.[1] In July 2001, a group of Danes applied for the arrest of the Israeli ambassador to Denmark because of his stated support for the use of torture against Palestinians, while Belgium also announced that it was preparing an indictment of the serving Israeli prime minister, Ariel Sharon, for his role in the Sabra and Chatila massacres of 1982 – events which had already been the subject of a judicial inquiry in Israel itself. All these events testify to the increasing consensus that the doctrine of universal human rights should override the traditional privileges of states and their parliaments.

It is important to understand the philosophy which animated these seminal developments. Human rights advocates assert that the purpose of human rights law is to subject supposedly lawless sovereign states to the rule of law. The new international law should therefore be understood as a body of law directed specifically against the state, its officials or any other body claiming political power. As British human rights lawyer, Geoffrey Robertson QC, clarifies:

> What sets a crime against humanity apart both in wickedness and in the need for special measures of deterrence is the simple fact that it is an act of real brutality ordained by government – or at least by an organisation exercising or asserting political power. It is not the mind of the torturer but the fact that this individual is part of the apparatus of a state which makes the crime so horrific.
>
> (2000: 338)

In other words, if the police in the United Kingdom discover – as they often do – that a drug dealer employs torture on rival dealers or clients who will not pay, the torture committed there would not be prosecuted under the Human Rights Act but instead under the normal criminal law. By contrast, if the police themselves were accused of using undue force or of practising torture, then the alleged crime would be regarded as an attack on human rights. Similarly, rape has now been included as a war crime in the jurisprudence of the International Criminal Tribunal but only when committed in war and in spite of the fact that it is already a crime in the normal criminal code of most states. The same is obviously true of murder which has also made its way into human rights law under the awkward term 'violation of the right to life'.

Because they are directed specifically at actions taken by states and their officials, or by people claiming political power, international legal measures concerning human rights are obviously of very great constitutional importance. The claim is repeatedly made by supporters of human rights law that it removes the alleged 'immunity' (often deliberately confused with 'impunity') of state officials. If the declared purpose of human rights law is to usher in a new world order in which states are no longer sovereign,[2] then questions about the constitutional implications of these new arrangements must be posed. If heads of state and state officials may now be prosecuted by bodies other than those of the states (including their own) on whose territory they allegedly committed their crimes, then it is imperative to examine whether the new powers which will accrue to human rights tribunals, especially international ones, carry political responsibilities with them or are subject to any control. In particular, the danger must be addressed that officials of these bodies might begin to believe that they are somehow above the normal human realm of politics.[3]

Morality and law

The claims made for the legitimacy of the new international law and its institutions rest on moral universalism. It is very common to hear the advocates of international humanitarian law justifying the jurisdiction of their new international tribunals by saying that the crimes judged there are so heinous as to be 'beyond human forgiveness' (Robertson, 2000: 374). The idea is that if an act is criminal in all places and at all times then it should be subject to the jurisdiction of an international tribunal.

This reasoning is doubly false. First, even if one accepts that a certain act is always and everywhere criminal, it does not follow that a body with universal jurisdiction must be created to judge it. On the contrary, when the Convention on the Prevention and Punishment of Genocide was signed in 1948, it enjoined the signatory states to prosecute those accused of genocide in their own courts. It is noteworthy that the International Criminal Tribunal for the former Yugoslavia has unilaterally rescinded a key provision of this treaty, duly ratified by the parliaments of the states which signed it, when it declared that it, not national courts, alone had jurisdiction over persons accused of genocide in the former Yugoslavia.

Second, however, the claims made for moral universalism are highly problematic in the terms in which they are presented. To put it bluntly, there is precious little evidence of universality in the way human rights activists operate. As many opponents of NATO's war against Yugoslavia in 1999 argued, that war, waged in the name of universal standards, was in fact a perfect example of double standards. Why bomb Yugoslavia in the name of human rights but tolerate the Russian attacks on rebels in Chechnya? Why indict the Yugoslav leaders and exculpate NATO or the Albanian rebels from any war crimes?

Indeed, in the view of this author, the attacks on Yugoslavia were merely the high point of a decade of terrible double standards practised by the human rights industry and its Western governmental support-ers.[4] Pronouncements on human rights matters, especially in the former Soviet bloc, have owed far more to Western policy goals than to any objective truth. One stark example of such double standards is the con-trast between the way in which Russia and Belarus have been treated in the 1990s. When President Yeltsin of Russia faced opposition from the State Duma in 1993, he sent in the tanks to shell the parliament build-ing and succeeded in changing the constitution to reduce the power of the State Duma, turning Russia into a presidential dictatorship (Williamson, 2000 and forthcoming). But when President Alexander Lukashenko of Belarus found his government systematically stymied by parliamentary opposition in 1996 and called a referendum to introduce a semi-presidential system, he was branded a dictator.[5]

By the same token, the long-serving prime minister of Slovakia, Vladimir Mečiar, was constantly branded 'authoritarian' during his period in office and accused of harassing the media. In fact, only the main state television channel was supportive of the government: all the press and much of the electronic media was in the hands of the opposi-tion. When the new government took power, by contrast, it took over the state TV as well and therefore all media, press and electronic media included, were pro-government. The opposition under Mečiar then had no media outlets at all. Moreover, the new government proceeded to conduct a war of attrition against its political opponents and the coun-try's judicial authorities, yet these attacks were met with deafening silence by human rights campaigners in the West (BHHRG, 2001).

No doubt such claims of double standards are open to debate. But it is precisely debate which the discourse of moral universalism stifles. Acts of politicians such as those mentioned above can only be evaluated properly within an open democratic state system; they should not be subject to the say so of unaccountable NGOs who have no stake in the societies they so mercilessly attack.

How human rights law changes over time

Even leaving aside the objection about double standards, it is surely quite impossible to continue to sustain the view that international humanitarian law has the right to trump national law because the former is universal when, in fact, international humanitarian law changes over time. But how can an act which is supposedly at all times and in all places a crime disappear from the canon of international humanitarian law? History shows that this is exactly what happens.

One of the clearest illustrations of the flexible and politicized nature of these so-called universal moral norms is the shifting approach taken to the fundamental question of war crimes. The first international attempt at setting down laws against war crimes was the International Peace Conference held at The Hague in 1899. Its final Act made three Declarations, one of which forbids belligerents from dropping bombs from the air (Declaration 3: 'To prohibit the launching of projectiles and explosives from balloons or by other similar new methods'). Although passed before the aeroplane had been invented, this article was formulated explicitly in the light of the great speculation that a flying machine would soon come into being. According to the International Committee of the Red Cross:

> The attempts (at the Second Peace Conference at The Hague) in 1907, to adopt a permanent prohibition of the discharge of projectiles from the air led to the insertion in Article 25 of the Hague Regulations on land warfare, which prohibits the attack or bombardment of undefended towns, villages, etc., of the words 'by whatever means' in order to cover attack or bombardment from the air.
>
> (ICRC, 1907)

Article 25 of the Regulations contained in that 1907 Convention indeed states: 'The attack or bombardment, by whatever means, of towns, villages, dwellings, or buildings which are undefended is prohibited.' There was also a specific 'Declaration on the Launching of Projectiles from the Air', dated 18 October 1907. It is worth noting, in passing, that this prohibition on aerial bombardment had no effect whatsoever on the way in which wars were waged in any subsequent conflict, particularly not in the Second World War.

Contemporaneously with this interdiction on aerial bombardment, a provision was drawn up at the first Hague conference specifically outlawing dum-dum bullets. Named after the suburb of Calcutta where these bullets were first made, they were referred to in a rather cumbersome way as 'bullets which expand or flatten easily in the human body, such as bullets with a hard envelope which does not entirely cover the core or is pierced with incisions'. This exact same phrase about bullets which flatten, etc., has somehow made its way down the century unchanged and is reproduced, verbatim, in the section of the Rome Statute on the International Criminal Court of July 1998 which defines war crimes (Article 8, 2 (b) (xix)). This is in spite of the fact that it is over one hundred years since dum-dum bullets first excited passions. As with aerial bombardment, it is doubtful whether this interdiction has actually had any effect: the Palestinians have accused the Israelis of using dum-dum bullets to suppress the Al Aqsa Intifada. But, in striking contrast to the provision on bullets which flatten, etc., the legal interdiction against aerial bombardment has been quietly dropped from the texts on international humanitarian law. It does not feature, for instance, in the 1998 Rome treaty.

It is obvious why this is so. The Second World War, the Vietnam War, the Gulf War and the NATO war against Yugoslavia were all fought with the massive use by the great powers of aerial bombardment. With the wars against Yugoslavia and the daily reconnaissance flights and regular bombings over Iraq, aerial bombardment has indeed effectively become an integral part of American foreign policy (Burnham, 2001). Its frequent use is not even merely a matter of military technique: aerial bombardment is also highly symbolic of the almost millenarian moralism in which American diplomacy and the supporters of international 'humanitarian' intervention cloak themselves.[6] Bombing has thus acquired an almost mystical importance which was made quite explicit during the attacks on Yugoslavia when the Supreme Allied Commander of NATO, General Wesley Clark, said that for Mr Milošević, the vast air power being used against him 'must be like fighting God' (SHAPE, 1999). In the same vein, a noted British defence commentator wrote, in an article on the military use of air power, that: 'Technology and international morality now march in step' (Keegan, 2001).

In other words, in one hundred years, aerial bombardment has gone from being a crime of unsurpassable evil to an instrument of the highest morality, or even of God. Yet if the values embodied in human rights documents are supposed to be objective and universal – a crime against humanity is 'a crime so black that it does not admit of human forgiveness', according to Robertson (2000: 374) – it is extremely difficult to see how they could evolve over time. It might be possible for new crimes to be added as time goes on: one could argue that the moralists had 'discovered' new evils and tried to codify interdictions against them into law. But it is impossible, in the philosophical framework proposed by human rights activists, for aerial bombardment to be considered so wrong in 1899 that it merited a special international conference and yet not even deserve a mention a century later.

The same must be said of the notion of 'crimes against peace'. It was one of the main advances in international humanitarian law at Nuremberg to define the violation of state sovereignty by force as a criminal act. Crimes against peace were the first category of crimes established at Nuremberg: the Nazi leaders were all indicted under the charge of planning and executing an aggressive war. Supreme Court Justice Robert Jackson was convinced that aggressive war was the *fons et origo* of all war crimes. His view, codified at Nuremberg, was immediately adopted in the Charter of the United Nations and, in both cases, reflected a very old traditional principle of international law that states are not allowed to attack other states.

Indeed, it is important to understand that the primacy given to national sovereignty by Nuremberg and in the UN Charter had a key anti-fascist political purpose. That purpose was to institutionalize an antithesis to the Nazi theory of international relations. State sovereignty was considered, after the Second World War, to be the answer to the fascist view that international relations should be based on the concept of *Großraum* or 'great space' (Bennhold, 1999). According to that theory, the international system was (or should be) divided up between centres of power. Some states had the right to dominate others or to bring them into their sphere of influence within the *Großraum*. The Nazi philosopher of law, Carl Schmitt, expressed this theory in his book, *Völkerrechtliche Großraumordnung mit Interventionsverbot für raumfremde Mächte* (A Constitutional Order based on the Concept of Great-Space, with a Rule against Intervention by Powers outside the Great-Space) published in 1941. As the title suggests, the theory of the unequal sovereignty of states accorded the right of the hegemonic power to wage war against other states within its sphere, while naturally denying the right of other states in other *Großräume* the right to wage war against them. Each great power had to deal with its own back yard. Indeed, many Nazi theoreticians – like Marxists – believed that state sovereignty was an artificial construct which should be discarded (see, further, Laughland, 1997).

It was this theory which the postwar institutions were intended to bury. Put in legal terms, what the postwar order denied was the *ius ad bellum*, the right to wage war. State sovereignty was naturally used as the best legal instrument to express this absolute interdiction against war, except in self-defence, an interdiction which the fascist theory of international relations specifically denied. Consequently, the right to wage war was specifically and repeatedly denied as a basis of the international order in all international postwar documents. All wars of aggression were forbidden and the principle of the friendly coexistence between states emphasized as the driving thought behind the new international order. Indeed, not only is the use of force illegal in postwar international law; even the threat of the use of force is illegal according to Article 2(4) of the UN Charter. Meanwhile, any treaty obtained through the use of force or the threat of the use of force is null and void, according to Article 52 of the 1969 Vienna Convention. So radical, indeed, is the interdiction against war in international law that the International Pact on Citizens' and Political Rights of 1966, which otherwise guarantees freedom of expression, even makes war propaganda illegal.[7]

One would have thought, then, that the 'crime against peace' would continue to enjoy overriding importance as human rights law 'advances'. In reality, the opposite has happened. The 1998 Rome treaty on the International Criminal Court mentions crimes against peace but does so in such a way that they cannot be adjudicated: it has left to a panel of experts a later decision on how this matter should be formulated.[8] In other words, it will be killed off in committee. Meanwhile, the statute which established the International Criminal Tribunal for the former Yugoslavia (ICTY) does not even mention 'crimes of aggression' or 'crimes against peace'. When it was asked to adjudicate on whether NATO had committed a war crime by attacking Yugoslavia, the Tribunal's Prosecutor commissioned a report which concluded that:

> The *jus ad bellum* regulates when states may use force and is, for the most part, enshrined in the UN Charter. In general, states may use force in self defence (individual or collective) and for very few other purposes. In particular, the legitimacy of the presumed basis for the NATO bombing campaign, humanitarian intervention without prior Security Council authorization, is hotly debated. That being said, as noted in paragraph 4 above, the crime related to an unlawful decision to use force is the crime against peace or aggression. While a person convicted of a crime against peace may, potentially, be held criminally responsible for all of the activities causing death, injury or destruction during a conflict, *the ICTY does not have jurisdiction over crimes against peace* [emphasis added].
>
> (ICTY, 2000)

The spirit of Pontius Pilate therefore is alive and well and resides in The Hague. The fact that the primary international organ responsible for Yugoslavia chooses to wash its hands of the suggestion that NATO's aggression might have been illegal – especially in the context of very detailed speeches by world leaders arguing for a new *ius ad bellum* to overturn the old UN prohibition against war (Blair, 1999b)[9] – means that, to all intents and purposes, the notion of crimes against peace has been more or less dropped from the canon of international humanitarian law. But if the most fundamental principle of international humanitarian law can be quietly dropped, then the claim to universality looks pretty threadbare.

The philosophy of human rights

These problems associated with the claims to moral universalism are not coincidental. The theory itself is flawed. To be sure, it is noteworthy that, as traditional morality collapses at home, a highly moralistic attitude in international affairs moves in as if to compensate. Just as it might be argued that the drive towards European integration is a kind of substitute for the reality of the disintegration of the traditional state and the family, so the increasing moral nihilism of Western societies in traditional areas is now being compensated for by a vehemently moralistic attitude in new ones. The black and white terms in which much foreign policy and international humanitarian discourse is posed may give a comfortable sense of moral superiority to the speaker and, of course, humanitarian intervention is invariably perpetrated by strong states against weak ones. But is it true that objective truth exists only in the abstract or universal realm, as our humanitarian activists claim, or might it be the case that it inheres instead in the real and the particular?

An article of this length cannot, of course, resolve an issue which has bedevilled Western philosophy for millennia. Suffice it to say that the international humanitarian operates within a Kantian framework (and not only Kantian) whose key concept is that of universality. Kant held that moral truths (and indeed all ultimate truths) are to be found only in the realm of abstract universals and not in the realm of the real or the particular. The moral agent becomes moral only to the extent that his motives are detached from all contingency. The 'categorical imperative' – the cornerstone of Kantian moral and legal philosophy – must, for Kant, be formulated in such a way as to enjoin universal rules. It is categorical if and only if it is universalizable.

The Aristotelian and Thomist view, by contrast, is that objective truth is to be found in the real world, not only in some unknowable abstract realm. Whereas, for Kant, the faculty of judgement consists in deciding how to operate according to universal and abstract rules, the Aristotelian tradition regards the real world – and especially the polis – as the appropriate framework within which to judge the value of acts. This faculty of judgement is essentially comparative: the value of an act is ascertained by comparing it with other acts in the public sphere. Philosophers in this realist tradition believe, unlike idealists, that reality is itself intelligible, that the created world is fundamentally ordered and meaningful, and that truth can be found in it.

In the Aristotelian and Thomist tradition a right is a right to a thing and law is the right proportion in the distribution of things. Justice is real, not ideal, although it is of course based on a transcendent notion of equity. It is precisely because civil law is about discerning how individual cases exhibit general principles that it is legal nonsense to talk about universal human rights. Since a right is a claim to a thing, it is obvious that human rights conflict with one another. The whole point of having a judicial system is to adjudicate between these competing claims and to judge each individual case on its merits. What this means in practice is that it is unnecessary and largely nonsensical to try to define universal crimes or universal rights. No one doubts that genocide or rape is always evil. The question is whether certain individual acts fall into certain categories and if they do what to do about it. Because both these questions are questions of practical reason, law is always political in the sense that it is always about the right regulation of the polis. It is a matter of weighing up competing claims between citizens with a view to preserving the social order within specific political and territorial boundaries.

Consequently, any judicial system – even if it is based on so-called moral universalism – operates politically. This much is obvious from the behaviour of the International Criminal Tribunal for the former Yugoslavia, which allows lenient treatment of indictees if they agree to testify against other indictees. According to this logic, the former Bosnian Serb president, Biljana Plavšić, indicted for genocide, the ICTY's most serious charge, was allowed in 2001 to return to Belgrade to live quietly there because she has agreed to testify against Slobodan Milošević. Not only does this decision by the ICTY shock the moral senses; it also reflects the Tribunal's own institutional-political imperatives. It is far more important for the ICTY's overall mission as the embryo of a future International Criminal Court to indict and convict a real head of state like Milošević: therefore it can afford to plea-bargain with a woman who is constitutionally less important even though, at the time of her release, she was accused of worse crimes than he.

This example and the preceding considerations should show that the right legal response to atrocities is not purely moral outrage. The right response is, instead, to consider what legal and political structures are best suited to safeguarding rights and liberties. Above all, it is essential to question the philosophical basis for the claims to legitimacy made for international human rights tribunals and to ask what mechanisms there are for submitting such tribunals to political accountability. It is clearly problematic for human rights activists and Western governments to claim that they are 'ending the culture of impunity' if, in the process, they set up institutions with dubious claims to legitimacy which are themselves apparently above the law. Human rights activists cannot claim that states are necessarily worse at rendering justice than international organizations unless they prove it empirically and constitutionally.

Human rights and political accountability

It is unfortunate that many advocates of human rights do not appear to recognize that the new powers claimed for human rights institutions themselves beg new questions. The *non sequitur* which claims legitimacy for international bodies in the name of objectivity or universalism appears to assume that international bodies somehow rise, by a mysterious process of political levitation, above the normal realm of human affairs and take on especial wisdom and neutrality simply by virtue of being 'international'. But why should individuals be regarded as having special virtues simply because they sit on a committee with individuals from other nations? It seems rather that the opposite assumption should hold. International organizations – the United Nations, the European Union, or for that matter the High Representative in Bosnia and Hercegovina – have agendas of their own which should be regarded as political in the same way as any national government or governmental body is political. Human rights activists seem not to understand that the power wielded by, say, the International Criminal Tribunal for the former Yugoslavia in The Hague is itself political and that it must, as such, be subjected to the usual checks and balances which we generally associate with the liberal order.

The view that mechanisms of accountability are not required flows ultimately from the Gnostic assumptions which underlie the human rights framework. Instead of asking, 'Who guards the guardians themselves?' human rights activists seem to argue that they have a right to judge others because of their supposedly superior knowledge of universal truths. The ordinary person – on whose behalf human rights activists claim to be acting – is, it seems, too preoccupied by the imperatives of day-to-day life to think about universal truths. He or she therefore needs to be guided by self-appointed elites. One egregious example of this attitude is the statement by Aaron Rhodes, the Executive Director of the International Helsinki Federation:

> The 'Western' public seems incapable of identifying moral and political principles by which to interpret very complex conflicts and, through that exercise, to come together on a course of action. *Indeed, it is romantic to think that the 'public' should be responsible for identifying those principles. That is the job of those more concerned with principles than with the here and now,* more concerned with things that are true regardless of historical contexts and routine life. *In other words, it is the responsibility of intellectuals* [emphasis added].
>
> (Rhodes, 1999: 193)

Not since Plato's parable of the cave in Book VII of *The Republic*[10] has there been a more brazen claim for the rights of 'philosopher-kings' over the pettifogging self-interest of ordinary people. Such statements only make explicit what is in fact the basis for all human rights ideology, namely the view that the 'non-political' judgements, which are said to flow from human rights norms, depend for their validity on the claims to a 'higher truth' accessible to self-selecting elites but apparently beyond the political sphere of democratic decision-making. The claim to be above the 'petty interests' of the political sphere is thus the cornerstone of the alleged legitimacy of human rights ideology. Human rights activists use it to argue that international human rights legislation, which they falsely equate with objective and universal justice, overrides domestic legislation and domestic constitutional law.

In reality, this claim of superiority over the state misrepresents the doctrine of state sovereignty in order deliberately to delegitimize existing states and so that international or supranational institutions can step in to take their place. But it is false to allege that the doctrine of state sovereignty necessarily affords legal immunity to state officials. This mistaken view is clearly stated by Geoffrey Robertson (1998):

> It has taken half a century [i.e. since the proclamation of the Universal Declaration of Human Rights in 1948] but we seem at last to be working out a way to bring tyrants to justice. Why did it take so long? The problem is that the world has always been organized on the principle of 'sovereignty' of the state ... There must be no intervention in their internal affairs.

However, the doctrine of state sovereignty never holds that the state can do what it likes without fear of recourse. Instead, the doctrine simply means that political power always obeys a certain constitutional logic. That ineluctable logic applies as much to international tribunals or political systems as to national ones. Put simply, the doctrine of state sovereignty means that, while state power is of course subject to higher moral laws, those laws cannot be implemented over and above the state without it disappearing as a state and transferring its quality of sovereign statehood to the higher power which does the implementing. That higher power must, in turn, be based on some kind of legitimacy. It is this simple but unavoidable constitutional fact which the discourse of moral universalism seeks to avoid.

Sovereignty, in other words, simply describes the structures within which political authority is exercised. Without the conceptual framework to delineate lines of responsibility and to show where the buck stops, accountability can never be ensured. Because the concept of state sovereignty makes explicit what the ultimate source of authority is and what powers flow from that, it is the pivotal point on which all other political and legal norms rest: without knowing which body of rules are operative in a state, you cannot know who is responsible for what. If sovereignty is discarded as a concept, as human rights ideologues demand it should be, then power will be wielded without responsibility. In sum, without the concept of sovereignty you cannot make sense of that body of rules which we associate with the term 'the rule of law' (see Laughland, 1997: ch. 4).

Far from introducing lawless absolutism, in other words, the doctrine of sovereignty is the only legal bulwark against it. This is true as much of domestic (municipal) law as it is true of international law. For just as state sovereignty describes the boundaries of political authority within a state, so it provides a legal focal point for that state's interaction with other states in international relations. Sovereignty in international law is thus the exact equivalent of personhood in civil law: it is the legal concept which we use to enable states (or persons) to undertake obligations and enter into contractual agreements with others.

There is absolutely no contradiction between the sovereignty of a state and the subjugation of its political or military leaders to the rule of law. On the contrary, state sovereignty is the prerequisite for such subjugation. The body of rules governing the exercise of political authority within a legal order will include things which the prince is allowed to do or forbidden from doing. No doubt in many states the rules are too generous for heads of state. But any body which seeks to change them – an international tribunal, for instance – is itself wielding political power and must therefore have legitimacy and be accountable.

Human rights ideologues are quite right when they draw a distinction between customary international law, based on contractual agreements between states, and the new international law they seek to introduce, which will have a constraining power over states.[11] However, the key problem is that, by supplanting the sovereignty of states, the new bodies with the power to wield this constraint will themselves assume sovereign powers. There is no evidence that the supporters of such moves have thought about the constitutional implications of this.

Because they are based on a contempt for the very principles of constitutionality itself, the international tribunals which currently exist behave in a highly questionable manner. Consequently, the dangers for the rule of law are already apparent. In its zeal to punish alleged criminals, the International Criminal Tribunal for the former Yugoslavia has broken almost every rule in the book. Instead, it makes up new rules as it goes along, as Louise Arbour stated: 'The law, to me, should be creative and used to make things right' (Laughland, 1999a). The procedural shortcomings of the ICTY are becoming a byword for unfairness, as the Tribunal picks and chooses from legal systems around the world to find excuses for its actions. In one case, the Prosecutor defended the Prosecutor's office against charges that it had illegally seized documents from the Bosnian government by saying that the seizure had been compatible with the law in Paraguay. Even The Hague's formal legitimacy itself is open to question, since it was not established by law but instead by a fiat of the UN Security Council. Its existence has not been ratified by the statute of any law-making body. Instead, the ICTY was created by and is funded by Western governments or private organizations with very close links to those governments. This may be why the ICTY has refused to undertake investigations into NATO's war crimes, as the NATO spokesman, Jamie Shea, said on 17 May 1999, when he was asked whether the ICTY might investigate NATO for war crimes:

> As you know ... without NATO countries there would be no International Court of Justice nor would there be any International Criminal Tribunal for the former Yugoslavia because NATO countries are in the forefront of those who have established these tribunals, who fund these tribunals and who support on a daily basis their activities.
>
> (Shea, 1999)

Ultimately, therefore, the approach of human rights lobbyists is hostile to the political and legal mechanisms of liberal democracy. It is based on the view that rights can be enjoyed outside of the political framework, as well as on the implicit assumption that statehood is always at least incipiently if not actually an instrument of repression. It is not unrelated, therefore, to the doctrine of the withering away of the state, a central plank of Marxism. Lenin understood perfectly well that statehood and democracy were antithetical to Communism and that Communism would supersede them. In his essay, 'A United States of the World', Lenin wrote that 'the complete victory of communism (would) bring about the total disappearance of the state, including the democratic state' (1965: 270).

Ultimately, of course, state structures will not disappear under universal human rights any more than they did under Communism. On the contrary, it is precisely one of the most sinister aspects of the anti-sovereignty argument that it will break down precisely those barriers which do protect individuals from oppression. In fact, a seminal work on human rights makes warm references both to the apparent fact that 'the whole notion of autonomous self-hood has been called into question' (Eagleton, 1999: v) and to a totalitarian-sounding future in which freedom will not be freedom 'from the state' but through it (Savić, 1999: 5). NATO's attacks on Yugoslavia showed how dangerous any potential New World Order will be and seemed to confirm Alexandre Kojève's prediction that the universal order would be a universal tyranny:

> Even though the end-state embodies the deepest hopes and dreams of mankind, Kojève did not assume that everyone would be wise enough to submit willingly to the principles of the universal and homogenous state. He assumed that there were bound to be people who were recalcitrant, obstinate and irrational enough to pit themselves against the universal order. The universal tyrant is therefore necessary to coerce or imprison those who constitute *inconveniences* to the rational order of the end-state. Nevertheless, it is important to keep in mind that this is no ordinary tyranny. The universal tyrant is but a 'cog in the machine,' an incarnation of the rationality of the final order of things ... Kojève's depiction of the tyranny of reason is daunting. The end of history is the apotheosis of the Gulag parading as the victory of reason.
>
> (Drury, 1994: 45)

Conclusion

This chapter has argued that the attempt to universalize human rights protections is political and legal nonsense. The attempt to separate statehood from law is based on a misrepresentation of the true relationship between law and the state. The nation-state, essential to the derivation and application of the law at both domestic and international levels, is misrepresented as a barrier to the rule of law, while the law itself is idealized and held to be generated independently of the political process and capable of application without a constitutional framework of legal equality. As the above section considering the changing nature of the definition of war crimes demonstrates, it is necessary to be aware of the political way in which allegedly universal norms are applied. Without any mechanisms of accountability, these attempts to replace domestic with international jurisdictions can only lead to greater arbitrary rule and to the further erosion of the rule of law.

Notes

1. See the contradictory statements by Human Rights Watch: 'Milošević Arrest Breaks Ground on International Justice' (28 June 2001) and 'Transfer of Milošević Founded in International Law' (2 July 2001). On the latter occasion, Richard Dicker, the Director of HRW's International Justice Progamme, tried to square the circle by saying incoherently that the transfer of Milošević was 'a historic precedent with a sound basis in international law.' See <http://www.hrw.org/press/2001/07/hague0702.htm>.
2. Many commentators argue that the end of state sovereignty is an inevitable historical development, the result of anonymous and unstoppable historical forces. See, for example, Cooper (2000).
3. An amusing example of this came on 26 July 2001 when Florence Hartmann, the spokesperson for the International Criminal Tribunal for the former Yugoslavia (and a former correspondent for *Le Monde*) attacked a statement made on 24 July by the Bishops' Conference in Croatia as 'political' (*Agence France Presse*, 2001). Like the Office of the High Representative in Bosnia and Hercegovina, whose spokesperson has similarly attacked the Bishop of Mostar for 'being more of a politician than a priest', it seems never to have occurred to the people who work for the ICTY that their own activities might also be vulnerable to the same charge.
4. It is commonly supposed that the 'non-governmental organizations' which proselytize human rights are in fact non-governmental. However, this is not so. There is often a very deep intertwining between the personnel of the large so-called NGOs and governments. Governments also very often fund these organizations. Often these associations – especially the funding – are openly admitted on NGOs' web pages. On other occasions, the association is more covert. An intriguing account of the way NGOs are funded by the US government to promote American foreign policy objectives abroad is given by Thomas Carothers, an official at the Carnegie Endowment for International Peace (2001).
5. See the reports on Belarus by the British Helsinki Human Rights Group, of which this author is a trustee: <http://www.bhhrg.org>. See especially the 1997 report published after the much-criticized 1996 referendum. The anathemas heaped on this constitution, and on the referendum which ratified it, were based largely on a report by the EU's Venice Commission about an early draft of the constitution which was not, in the end, adopted.

6. For the history of American millenarianism, see Tuveson (1968). For a good example of the structural faults of such thinking, see John Rawls (1993). Rawls divides the world into 'ordered' and 'disordered' societies and allows the former to intervene against the latter in the name of the law of peoples. His article is an early articulation of the concept, which was later popularized with the term 'rogue states'. The division between ordered and disordered societies – it is never suggested that the same society might be both, or that it might evolve from ordered into disordered – recalls the Manichean division of mankind into 'the elect' and 'the damned'.

7. Like many articles of international law, this one has proved futile. The Kosovo war was notable for very brazen war propaganda, especially on the atrocities allegedly committed against Albanian civilians. See my own articles on this (Laughland, 1999b and 1999c); Phillip Knightley's classic, *The First Casualty: the War Correspondent as Hero and Myth-maker from the Crimea to Kosovo* (2000), and also Philip Hammond and Edward S. Herman (eds), *Degraded Capability: the Media and the Kosovo Crisis* (2000).

8. Article 5 stipulates that the crime of aggression does come under the Court's jurisdiction but adds: 'The Court shall exercise jurisdiction over the crime of aggression once a provision is adopted in accordance with Articles 121 and 123 defining the crime and setting out the conditions under which the Court shall exercise jurisdiction with respect to this crime. Such a provision shall be consistent with the relevant provisions of the Charter of the United Nations.' Unlike all other war crimes, 'aggression' is then not mentioned anywhere else in the treaty.

9. Blair's speech was a straightforward attempt to rewrite existing international law. He said, 'We are all internationalists now … We cannot refuse to participate in global markets if we want to prosper. We cannot ignore new political ideas in other countries if we want to innovate. We cannot turn our backs on conflicts and the violations of human rights within other countries if we want still to be secure. On the eve of the Millennium we are now in a new world. We need new rules for international co-operation and new ways of organising our international institutions.'

10. In Book VII, 'On Shadows and Realities in Education', Socrates says: 'You must not wonder that those who attain to this beatific vision are unwilling to descend to human affairs; for their souls are ever hastening into the upper world where they desire to dwell; which desire of theirs is very natural, if our allegory may be trusted. Yes, very natural. And is there anything surprising in one who passes from divine contemplations to the evil state of man, misbehaving himself in a ridiculous manner; if, while his eyes are blinking and before he has become accustomed to the surrounding darkness, he is compelled to fight in courts of law, or in other places, about the images or the shadows of images of justice, and is endeavouring to meet the conceptions of those who have never yet seen absolute justice?'

11. The difference was once powerfully expressed by the Chief Prosecutor of the International Criminal Tribunal for the former Yugoslavia, Louise Arbour, who declared: 'We have passed from the era of co-operation between states to an era in which states can be constrained' (*Le Monde*, 6 August 1999).

3
The International Children's Rights Regime

Vanessa Pupavac

Introduction[1]

The virtually universal ratification of the 1989 UN Convention on the Rights of the Child has been hailed as inaugurating a new era of international human rights. Mobilization around children's rights through international initiatives such as the Global Movement for Children is viewed as significant not only for child welfare but for promoting universal human rights values. The cause of children is regarded as capable of transcending national, political and social divisions and enlisting people globally to counter social problems and militate against disorder and conflict. Echoing the UN Charter's opening declaration 'We the Peoples', the Secretary General's end-of-decade review entitled *We the Children* encapsulates how the UN Convention on the Rights of the Child is increasingly being invoked as a core international document to develop human rights protections in the new millennium (UN, 2001). The cause of children has indeed come of age. No longer confined to the agenda of international welfare organizations or human rights advocates, children have received unprecedented interest in the last decade. In all areas of international policy-making, from development strategy to security matters, the rights of children are being taken up. Even the Security Council has begun to highlight children's issues in its deliberations, reflected in various resolutions on their behalf.[2]

This normative turn in international relations has generally been welcomed as a progressive move away from realpolitik (see Chandler, this volume, Chapter 6). The institutionalization of children's rights in international law is viewed as advancing more equitable international politics. Most analysis focuses on the gap between children's rights provisions and their realization in practice. The normative framework created by the international children's rights regime has been subject to relatively little interrogation save from cultural relativist perspectives. The virtues of children's rights are treated as self-evident. Indeed to challenge the children's rights paradigm risks being branded a heretic outside the contemporary legal, moral and scientific order (King, 1997: 173). However, examining the underlying precepts of the international children's rights regime brings to light disturbing anti-humanist and authoritarian trends.

This chapter questions whether the new normative approach represents a shift towards a more universal and empowering framework of domestic and international relations. The chapter first provides a brief outline of the international children's rights regime. Following this, there is an analysis of the assumptions underlying the concept of children's rights and the elevation of childhood. Finally the chapter discusses the implications of the children's rights paradigm for the well-being and freedoms of both children and adults. Rather than providing a framework for more humane relations, improving the lot of children globally, the chapter concludes that the international children's rights regime is legitimizing a new era of authoritarianism and inequality. One that is antithetical to the universal of a more humane childhood, the world that proponents of children's rights seek to secure.

The international children's rights regime

The scope of the international children's rights framework is considerable. The framework does not merely consist of the text of the UN Convention, but may be characterized as a regime. The concept of regime has been defined as a set of 'principles, norms, rules and decision-making procedures around which actors' expectations converge in a given area' (Krasner, 1983: 2). The international children's rights regime is part of an evolving system of global governance characterized by privatization of previous state functions, informal networks of norm entrepreneurs and norm-setting processes. The academic Mark Duffield neatly captures the essence of contemporary global governance which eschews formal institutional accountability: 'While disciplinary regimes attempted to alter the conduct of individuals within the confines of institutions, regulatory regimes attempt to alter the wider social systems, the web of interactions, exchanges and identities in which individuals behave' (2001). The informal, fluid and dispersed nature of these networks means that their significance as constituting new regulatory regimes is often underestimated. Furthermore, their authoritarian character is elided. This is because the new regulatory regimes take the form of 'therapeutic governance' appealing to self-realization (Pupavac, 2001a). As Duffield outlines, within regulatory systems, individuals 'are aggregates of different potentialities that are to be realised through processes of life-long learning, continual self-improvement, perpetual assessment and the never ending management of risk' (2001).

The core document of the international children's rights regime is the UN Convention on the Rights of the Child (1989). The Convention has received virtually universal ratification. The only countries not to have ratified are Somalia and the United States, the former due to its lack of goverment, the latter due to political reasons. However, although the United States has not ratified, it should not be assumed that the United States is absent from the international children's rights regime. The therapeutic norms underlying its approach originate in US culture and reflect Anglo-American social policy (Boyden, 1990; Lasch, 1977 and 1978; Nolan, 1998). US experts and NGOs have been very important in setting the norms of the children's rights regime and their dissemination. Even US organizations opposed to ratifying the Convention have supported its application in other countries. Here the implications of the children's rights normative framework are nevertheless explored in relation to predominantly British examples, because of the United Kingdom's ratification of the Convention as well as its comprehensive assimilation of therapeutic norms in relation to children.

The Convention is formally monitored by the UN Committee on the Rights of the Child which consists of ten international child experts who meet to consider the reports of state parties which have to be submitted within two years of ratification and every five years thereafter (Article 44). The formal monitoring mechanisms under the Convention do not properly indicate the international weight of the Convention today. More significant is how the Convention informs the work of the UN specialized agencies, notably UNICEF, whose role in promoting children's rights is specified under the Convention (Article 45), and non-governmental organizations (NGOs). The latter, predominantly Northern-based NGOs, such as Amnesty International the Defence for Children International and Save the Children played a crucial role in the drafting of the Convention and appeared to have more influence on the final text than official delegates from developing countries (Detrick, 1992).

The relative authority of international agencies and NGOs as compared to Southern states in the international children's rights regime is important to stress. Not only has the role of Northern NGOs been important in the drafting process, but they are key in the dissemination of the human rights-based approach under the Convention. Irrespective of the high-profile disputes over human rights versus Asian values, what is striking is the pace of the convergence of child policies globally which are based on contemporary Northern norms and policy perspectives. This convergence of policies is facilitated by the 'thickening of international aid networks' (Duffield, 2001). Just one example of expanding norm entrepreneurship is the British-based National Society for the Prevention of Cruelty against Children (NSPCC). While the NSPCC has acquired a central role in British child policy, it has not traditionally been involved in international work. Nevertheless, in the last decade NSPCC staff have been seconded to public institutions in Russia and Eastern Europe to work on their policy reform. In this way, the programmes of UNICEF and other international agencies are echoed by numerous much smaller projects and initiatives, highlighting the creation of new networks of influence. Meanwhile there is a growing body of supplementary international or regional norm-setting documents, for example the International Labour Organization's Convention Concerning the Prohibition and Immediate Action for the Elimination of the Worst Forms of Child Labor (ILO Convention 182, June 1999), the Organization of African Unity's Charter on the Rights and Welfare of the African Child (OAU Doc. CAB/LEG/ 24.9/49, 1990), and the National Plans of Action arising from the 1990 World Summit for Children. UNICEF's annual publications, *State of the World's Children* and *Progress of Nations*, are also increasingly important in setting the international policy agenda.

The remarkable global convergence of policy formation demonstrates the growing reach of the international children's rights regime. For proponents, this convergence indicates the universality of the norms under the Convention, which is regarded as embodying universal humanist principles and as representing the culmination of the struggle for recognition of universal human rights. Children's rights are treated as having the force of international law by international policy-makers who are now prepared to override long-standing principles, of national sovereignty and non-interference in internal affairs, in their name. 'Bettering children's rights is not a matter of government largesse', Executive Director of UNICEF Carol Bellamy has declared, 'but a fundamental legal requirement' (UNICEF, 1997). Consequently, although the failures to ameliorate the plight of children around the world in the last decade are readily acknowledged by child advocates, the establishment of an international normative and legal framework around children's rights is applauded as a foundation for creating a more humane world.

As Bellamy states:

> While many of the rights established in the Convention remain unrealized for the majority of the world's children, it is an essential touchstone against which to assess the situation of children and a normative frame of reference for strategies and action.
>
> (UN, 2000b: 3)

The moral and practical efficacy of invoking children's rights is taken as given today. Often forgotten is that UNICEF itself originally opposed a children's rights convention, regarding the initiative as a diversion from the strategies it was pursuing to improve child welfare. UNICEF did not in fact become involved in the working groups drafting the Convention until well into the process, while UNESCO and UNDP ignored the initiative (Cantwell, 1992). This is in sharp contrast to the situation today when not only are these organizations championing the Convention, but the international financial institutions too identify increasingly with its approach.

The elevation of the child

Why then have children's rights come to assume so much importance internationally in the last decade, when even the leading international children's organization previously did not see them as relevant to child welfare? Before considering the specificity of children's rights, the special place that children assume in contemporary Western culture and society needs to be addressed.

Children have come to assume international significance through the convergence of particular political, social and economic processes at the end of the Cold War. In essence, the singularity of today's focus on children arises from the profound moral, social and political malaise that characterizes contemporary Western culture and society. That a preoccupation with children should represent an expression of society's anxieties about the future is not novel. The drive for child protection policies arose in the nineteenth century in the context of moral panics over social disorder (Parton, 1985). What is novel, however, is the centrality of the issue of children in policy and ethics.

Underpinning the contemporary elevation of the child as a moral touchstone is the demise of Western belief in humanity as responsible and progressive beings. In the circumstances of disillusion with human progress, the mature rational ego is decried and the childlike instinctual id has come to represent the contemporary ethical ideal. It is the retrieval of the untainted inner child of nature which is to be cultivated and celebrated. Gone is the optimism of postwar belief in science, development and welfarism, replaced by a nervousness and pessimism about humanity's imprint on the planet. Industrialization and material advancement are increasingly eschewed in international policy.

Disenchantment with humanity is accompanied by pessimism about human nature and relationships, but pessimism does not signify the elimination of social concern. Taking an essentially normative approach to social problems, international policy-makers have become preoccupied with the psychosocial functionalism of individuals and their communities. The child–parent relationship has come to assume the heaviest burden of this concern because the origins of psychosocial dysfunctionalism are sought here in the primary relationship, based on the psychological propositions that:

> (a) all socially relevant human behaviour is learnt in intimate social relationships and mostly so in the initial years of life; that (b) the only procedure through which this social learning can be effectively modified is in intimate social relationships in which the origin of the first learning can be retraced and, in light of the day, examined, modified, or replaced.
>
> (Halmos, 1970: 16)

Hence, the psychological development and socialization of children globally has become a key international issue. Article 39 of the Convention codifies the concern over psychosocial functionalism, requiring states to ensure the rehabilitation of child victims:

> State Parties shall take all appropriate measures to promote physical and psychological recovery and social reintegration of a child victim of: any form of neglect, exploitation, or abuse; torture or any other form of cruel, inhuman or degrading treatment or punishment; or armed conflict. Such recovery and reintegration shall take place in an environment which fosters the health, self-respect and dignity of the child.

While Article 39 refers to child victims, it will be seen that the anxieties of international policy-makers over psychosocial functionalism are not narrowly confined to a specific set of children, but encompass children generally. Conflict, poverty and other social problems are blamed on psychosocial dysfunctionalism traced back to childhood. This is evident in the UN Secretary General's *We the Children* report, which links international development to the psychosocial functionalism of children: 'It is children whose individual development and social contribution will shape the world's future – and it is through children that entrenched cycles of poverty, exclusion, intolerance and discrimination can be broken for succeeding generations' (UN, 2001: 139). Regarding the socialization of children as a cause of social problems and a barrier to their resolution, international policy-makers are setting global norms on how children should be brought up.

There is a further dimension to the international focus on children. Alarmed by the lack of social cohesion domestically and state collapse internationally, policy-makers identify a need to find common values to cohere societies. However, it is difficult to agree a set of common values and establish a sense of common interests. Although the collapse of the Soviet bloc created the possibility of international consensus, the post-Cold War era has been marked by a loss of political direction on both the Left and the Right without the old divisions (and therefore the old loyalties and certainties) of the previous era. As one children's rights advocate remarked: 'We live in a time of new hope but also new angst' (Melton, 1994: 27). There is widespread cynicism about politics and a loss of belief in traditional values and institutions. In the place of ideological politics, identity politics or single issues have come to the fore. Policy-makers are searching for common values transcending separate groups' identities around which to cohere societies. The issue of children is of global interest whether for the South with its relatively young population, or for the North with child–parent relations becoming the sole surviving primary relationship as the bonds between adults have weakened (Beck, 1994: 118). The child–parent relationship is to preserve humanity in the face of the relentless logic of capitalism and 'unbearable moral solitude' arising from the disintegration of other ties (Aries, 1962: 406). Symbolizing universal moral concern, the child has become the leitmotif for moral and social renewal in both post-traditional and divided societies, lacking alternative universally integrating symbols.

Yet to what extent may the international children's rights regime act as a universal and inclusionary system? Cultural relativist critiques have criticized international children's rights documents as being based on Western perspectives and failing to reflect other cultures. Sensitive to such criticisms, international children's rights advocates are anxious to accommodate cultural diversity, often recognizing how the drafting of the Convention was dominated by Northern countries (Cantwell, 1995: 23). The positions of advocates of the Convention and those making cultural relativist critiques are not necessarily as opposed as protagonists image. The championing of *children's* rights is in fact related to the importance given to the recognition of difference today and parallels the championing of other rights based on identity. Leading advocate Anne McGillivray, for example, links arguing for children's rights with those of other groups, stating: 'Difference is important in ensuring the realization of rights, whether the rights claimant is a child or an adult, male or female, disabled, a person of colour, a member of a First Nation or anyone else' (1994: 245). Meanwhile, cultural relativist critics do not necessarily challenge the international children's rights paradigm per se, sometimes proposing their own alternative documents to take into account the specificity of the experiences of the Southern child.

Existing international children's rights documents, advocates may argue, do seek to take into account cultural differences. In the preamble, the Convention states how the document takes, 'due account of the importance of the traditions and cultural values of each people for the protection and harmonious development of the child'. Article 30 recognizes a child's right 'to enjoy his or her culture'. An incremental approach, sensitive to existing cultural norms, is propounded under Article 24 by which State Parties are required to 'take all effective and appropriate measures with a view to abolishing traditional practices prejudicial to the health of children'. The desire to accommodate cultural diversity is further illustrated in regional documents; for example, the 'Charter on the Rights and Welfare of the African Child' has a clause on the duties of children towards their families (Article 31). Cultural relativist critiques are therefore misplaced in certain respects.

Nevertheless, the approach of the international children's rights regime derives from the contemporary Anglo-American social risk-management model of childhood whose conceptualization of social justice stresses normative/psychological causations and therapeutic interventions. The particularist and exclusionary character of the normative framework being globalized is easy to overlook because of the disavowed nature of its approach. The normative framework does not espouse a specific set of values. It embraces a pluralist value system and a constructivist approach emphasizing the historically and culturally contingent nature of conceptions of childhood that seeks the reconstitution of individuals (and thereby society) predicated on the dominant Anglo-American therapeutic model of self-actualization.[3] As a model of self-actualization, its particularist and exclusionary character are mystified. Yet when the model is normalized, paths of psychosocial development and behaviour deviating from its norms become pathologized.

The Anglo-American therapeutic model posits the individual as vulnerable, insecure and permanently at risk of psychosocial dysfunctionalism.

As such, individuals' personal development and relations require constant fostering through life-long therapeutic interventions. This therapeutic model is no longer confined to the counselling services, but permeates Anglo-American culture, policy-making and processing (Halmos, 1965 and 1970; Lasch, 1977 and 1985; Nolan, 1998; Rose, 1990; Totton, 2000). International development and social justice policies increasingly resemble forms of therapeutic intervention – manifest not only in the policy recommendations of the 'softer' international institutions such as UNICEF and the UN Committee on the Rights of the Child, but those of the international financial institutions, for example the World Bank in its *Voices of the Poor* series of reports (Narayan et al., 2000a, 2000b and 2000c).

Dealing with poverty is becoming more directly about tackling the personality, intimate relationships, communal networks and cultural attitudes of the poor to ensure their psychosocial functionalism (see Pender, this volume, Chapter 5). Whereas earlier models understood the problem of dysfunctionalism as confined to a residuum, contemporary campaigners see the problem as a general one. Strikingly, children's rights advocacy is accompanied by a profound mistrust of individuals and their relationships, and an imperative to intervene and regulate their psychology and behaviour. At the same time the site of oppression is relocated from political, social and economic relations to intimate relationships. So, whereas earlier development policies saw creating a humane environment as leading to more humane human relations, the relationship has been reversed with the danger that victims of global processes become blamed for their plight.

Intrinsic to this problematizing and professionalizing of the psychological development and socialization of the individual is the requirement for third-party enablers. On the one hand, the misanthropic model of the human personality projects the individual as prone to dysfunctionalism and thereby casts doubt on the moral agency of the individual. On the other hand, the misanthropic model establishes the moral agency of a new caste of professional enablers. Through this dichotomy, between the individual deemed prone to dysfunctionalism and the professional enabler, new hierarchical relationships are also created. The effective denial of the moral agency of individuals counterposed to the affirmation of the moral agency of the professional enabler further belies the apparently inclusive global ethical order. However, since the enabler is engaged in self-actualization of the individual then these hierarchical relationships are also mystified and difficult to disentangle. This mystification of relationships is paralleled in the concept of children's rights, where the moral agency of the individual is likewise questioned.

Redefining the rights of children and adults

Despite the seeming universalism of the contemporary human rights approach, its effect is to codify new hierarchical relationships between individuals and authorized officials, and between the North and the South (Pupavac, 2001a). This effect is not immediately apparent, not least because human rights advocacy is taken up as an emancipatory project to recognize and empower previously excluded groups (Booth, 1995; Federle, 1994; Freeman, 1997; Wheeler, 1996). However, human rights advocacy is distinct from previous progressive rights movements. Underpinned by the Anglo-American therapeutic model of the individual, human rights advocacy approximates a form of therapeutic intervention with rights reconceptualized in therapeutic terms as enablement or protection by authorized officials. In a reversal of the previous position, powers of intervention are not viewed as an infringement of civil liberties domestically or self-determination internationally but empowering and actually constitutive of rights today.

The contemporary international human rights approach is championed as representing a progressive leap away from the classic approach to rights. The latter is condemned by human rights advocates as exclusionary for founding rights on capacity, thereby excluding precisely vulnerable groups such as children most in need of protection (Federle, 1994; McGillivray, 1994). In contrast, human rights advocates seek to provide rights protection irrespective of capacity. Reconceptualizing rights as 'not premised upon capacity but ... powerlessness' (Federle, 1994: 366), an essentially pre-political moral/therapeutic foundation for rights based on human vulnerability and human wrongs is adopted (Chandler, 2002: ch. 4).

At the same time, the children's rights advocacy movement has sought to transcend the moralistic protective model of earlier campaigners and treat children as rights-holders themselves, rather than passive objects of protection and welfare. Contemporary proponents do not deny the immaturity of children and their need for special protection, but, highlighting the socially constructed concepts of childhood, consider extending enabling rights to children as having a transformative effect both on children and how we regard them (Franklin, 1995; McGillivray, 1994). The legal philosopher Martha Minow argues that: 'Including children as participants alters their stance in the community, from things or outsiders to members ... by signalling deserved attention, rights enable a challenge to unstated norms, to exclusion, and the exclusive perspectives' (1990: 297–8). Signalling the aspiration to treat children as distinct rights-holders and facilitate their participation, Article 12(1) of the Convention states: 'State Parties shall assure to the child who is capable of forming his or her own views the right to express those views freely, on all matters affecting the child, the views of the child being given due consideration in accordance with the age and maturity of the child.'

Children's rights advocates reject criticism of paternalism and counter objections that children's rights have not been brought about by children. They note how previous rights struggles have involved members from outside the group and that a children's movement could emerge in the future (Freeman, 1997: 26; McGillivray, 1994: 253–4). There are historical precedents for the courageousness, commitment and leadership shown by young people. It was the Soweto uprising by school children that came to symbolize the struggle against the apartheid regime in South Africa, while Anne Frank's diary has come to symbolize humanism in the midst of the barbarity of the Holocaust. However, to invoke such examples is to make the case for reviewing the appropriateness of the age of franchise on the basis of capacity, that is, to reform when individuals are deemed no longer to be minors but adults under the law. This line of argument is distinct from arguing the case for a specific category of *children's* enabling rights, predicated on their powerlessness and therefore the inherent need of advocacy of their behalf. It is the contradictions that arise from this dichotomy which have led critics to write of 'the fallacy of children's rights' (Lewis, 1998). Indeed, it is not children, but authorized officials under Article 12(1) who determine whether the child is mature enough for the child's views to be heard and heeded. Furthermore, under Article 3, it is what authorized officials deem 'the best interests of the child', rather than the child's views, that 'are to be of primary consideration'.

As a reading of Articles 3 and 12 indicates, there are contradictions with the conception of children's rights under the Convention, which have critical implications for the integrity of children and adults alike and the realization of their rights. The key conceptual problem in children's rights derives from the related dichotomy of the child being the rights-holder but not the moral agent who determines his or her rights. However artificially childhood dependency may be prolonged (O'Neill, 1992: 38), childhood dependency is not merely a social construct, but a biological reality – for at least some period, 'children have interests to protect before they have wills to assert' (Freeman, 1997: 27). That children lack capacity to determine their rights leaves unanswered who is to realize their rights on their behalf. As the children's rights theorist Michael Freeman has perceptively analysed: 'Questions of "by whom" and "how" have not been satisfactorily answered' (ibid.) – namely, who is to represent the child and how a conflict of views, between professionals or between the child's own expressed views and those of his or her appointed representative(s), is determined.

Although the need for advocacy is inherent in the concept of children's rights, the question of the legitimacy and accountability of the moral agent is evaded by children's rights advocates. Nevertheless, it is possible to draw out whose moral agency is considered suspect in children's rights discourse. It is the legitimacy of children's parents or guardians to represent their children's interests that is questioned in the concept of children's rights. While the classical approach deemed that parents or guardians represented the child's interests, the children's rights approach challenges their competence to do so. It is a profound suspicion of their carers that provides the ultimate rationale for children's rights. In the absence of a children's rights framework, the assumption that 'adults already relate to children in terms of love, care and altruism' (Freeman, 1997: 24) is doubted in the children's rights literature. At the same time, these emotional ties are also invoked to disqualify parents' capacity to make decisions about their children's lives. The children's rights lawyer Jane Fortin, for example, argues in relation to bone marrow donations that: 'Parents are not the best equipped to reach such decisions, since their intense emotional involvement may make them less than rational' (1998: 269). Repeatedly, children's rights advocates cite parental authority and influence as hazardous for the child. Parental authority in the children's rights paradigm is associated with notions of ownership, superiority and subordination, and above all violence and abuse (Archard, 1993: 124; Freeman, 1997: 83; McGillivray, 1994: 256). So, although the Convention formally recognizes the rights and responsibilities of parents,[4] their authority is conditional on whether their parenting is considered appropriate.

Contemporary policy-makers assume that parents are incapable of parenting properly without expert guidance (Furedi, 2001; Pupavac, 1999). In line with these perspectives, there is more emphasis on shaping and enforcing the predominant model of parental responsibilities. Article 18 of the Convention indicatively refers to parental responsibilities, not rights. Furthermore, a presumption of a conflict of interest between parents and children is becoming institutionalized under law and social policy as a norm. Meanwhile, the question of a conflict of interest between children and third-party advocates is elided.

One does not need to adhere to a naive, cosy and sentimental view of the family to be concerned about the destructive implications of a systematic problematizing of the child–parent relationship. The very fact that it is a primary relationship not based on 'rights of choice' (Archard, 1993: 124) makes child–parent relations problematic for children's rights advocates. The pathologization of the last primary relationship does not just express mistrust of parents. The boundless alarm expressed over the child–parent relationship is symptomatic of a breakdown of adult solidarity and embodies disenchantment with humanity in general.

How the pathologization of the child–parent relationship has become a feature of the children's advocacy movement can be seen in the UK NSPCC's 'Full Stop' campaign of 2000–1 in which children are portrayed as being at the mercy of any parent. Utilizing the powerful iconography of the mother/father and baby, its billboard advertisements displayed loving child–parent images accompanied by shocking captions such as 'Later she wanted to hold a pillow over his face' or 'That night he felt like slamming her against the cot'. As the sociologist Frank Furedi outlines, the NSPCC's awareness campaign, justified as making parents aware that snapping under pressure was normal and that they needed to learn to cope with the stresses of parenting, suggests that parental 'temporary loss of control "normally" leads to abuse' (2001: 14–15). Such insidious shock tactics advise that one should not be deceived by loving appearances and everybody should be regarded as a potential abuser, thus inciting 'a poisonous atmosphere of suspicion and mistrust' (ibid.).

Criticisms of this sort are almost invariably dismissed by children's rights campaigners as posing the interests of adults above those of children. Yet are these campaigns in the interests of children? As the philosopher Hannah Arendt argues in her essay 'On Violence': 'Where all are guilty then none is' (1972: 128). By treating abuse as pervasive there is a serious danger of not picking up and trivializing actual cases of abuse. The NSPCC itself has been criticized for devoting too great a percentage of its funds in recent years to publicity campaigns and neglecting core child welfare activities (Carvel, 2000; *Guardian*, 2000a and 2000b). Meanwhile, the problematizing and professionalizing of adult–child interactions have a disempowering impact, making individuals hesitant to intervene for fear of doing the wrong thing and causing them to wait for professional intervention. At the same time, professionals are finding themselves swamped with an exponential rise of allegations and referrals, making it increasingly difficult to distinguish serious cases requiring prompt action from trivial or spurious claims. The latter problem directly relates to a professional outlook that regards abuse as the norm and universalizes the need for intervention.

The misanthropic view of the child–parent relationship held by child professionals now pervades society. Awareness campaigns like the NSPCC's 'Full Stop' are not alone in the message they deliver. Contemporary cultural representations popularly depict adults as abusive, dysfunctional or inadequate and child–parent relationships as damaging and treacherous. Typical recent best-selling personal accounts and novels, such as Dave Pelzer's *A Child Called It* (2001), expose the dark child–parent relationship, while others, such as Rachel Cusk's *A Life's Work* (2001), Anne Robinson's *Memoirs of an Unfit Mother* (2001) and Naomi Wolf's *Misconceptions* (2001), depict parents as failures or parenting as an infinitely difficult task. *All Families are Psychotic* (2001) proclaims the title of Douglas Coupland's recent novel, summing up and parodying today's convention of family's relations as dysfunctional. Films and television also express these preoccupations. 'From nightmare kids to abusive parents' declares an advertisement for the UK television Channel 5's Autumn 2001 season of documentaries, characteristic of today's pathologization of the child–parent relationship.

The aim of children's rights has been stated as to protect children so that they can 'mature to a rationally autonomous adulthood and be capable of deciding on their own system of ends as free and rational beings' (Freeman, 1997: 97). The pathologization of the primary relationship, accompanied by the call to regard any relationship with suspicion, effectively denies the possibility that anybody can be trusted with an autonomous adulthood. This mistrust of the moral agency of individuals and their capacity to conduct relationships is resulting in the extension of a paternalistic, protective model of childhood to adulthood. So, although the codification of children's rights is championed as redressing the unequal relations between children and parents, its impact is actually to empower officials in relation to adult individuals and challenge their democratic and ethical freedom to determine the good for their children (Habermas, 1996: 451).

The mistrust of individuals is further leading child advocates to eschew the unfettered democratic determination of policy for the codification of their norms and policies as higher law. The moral legitimacy of their cause is assumed, but general concern for the child does not in itself legitimize the normative framework and strategies of the international children's rights regime. As the socio-legal philosopher Jürgen Habermas outlines, moral universes should not be confused with legal communities, nor moral norms with legal norms (ibid.: 452). Taking morality as the legitimate grounding for the codification of law is problematic today 'in pluralistic societies in which comprehensive worldviews and collectively binding ethics have disintegrated' (ibid.: 448).

In the absence of shared ethics, the democratic process is the only legitimate source of law: 'The modern legal order can draw its legitimacy only from the idea of self-determination: citizens should always be able to understand themselves also as authors of the law to which they are subject' (ibid.: 449). The institutionalization of children's rights as higher law reverses this notion of individuals as law-makers. The autonomy of the legal person, for Habermas, 'includes three different components: the jointly exercised autonomy of citizens, and the capacities for rational choice and for ethical self-realization' (ibid.: 451). In contesting all three components, the children's rights model is transforming the rights-holder into an object of law and inverting rights into externally imposed decrees. Hence children's rights advocacy comes to represent regression to something more reminiscent of *noblesse oblige* than an emancipatory project. Moreover, in challenging the democratic and ethical freedoms of individuals, the codification of children's rights as higher law implicitly denies their inherent dignity as 'free and equal moral person[s]' (Rawls, 1973: 565), ostensibly reaffirmed in the preamble of the Convention.[5]

Analysis of the children's rights framework reveals profound pessimism over people being free and equal moral persons. It is this pessimism which informs children's rights advocates' mistrust of leaving matters up to individuals and to the democratic process which does not presuppose outcomes. What then is to ensure that the resulting positive law does not violate the rights and welfare of individuals, whether they are citizens or non-citizens? How may the rights of unfranchised children be secured? The children's rights model looks to the prescription of higher law, superseding democratic processes, to guarantee their rights and welfare. The anti-democratic impulse of the children's rights approach may be contrasted with that of the humanist tradition and earlier progressive rights movements which have viewed the expansion of human freedoms as key to securing both individual and collective good. From humanist perspectives, it is guarantees of the classical rights to liberty that promote the development of the ethical life and ensure ethical outcomes arise from political contestation. Without private autonomy to allow for a thriving internal life, citizens are unable to develop their capacity for exercising civic autonomy (Arendt, 1959: 54; Habermas, 1996: 455; Rawls, 1973: 161).

The 'colonisation of childhood'[6]

Despite the self-perception of the children's rights approach as representing a shift from dependency to empowerment, rather than enhancing children's autonomy, the model is having the reverse effect. That the children's rights approach should encroach on children's existing autonomy is not accidental since the contemporary focus on children is underpinned by profound misgivings over the moral agency of individuals. Consequently, although today's children's rights campaigners argue that granting children rights affirms their moral worth, the policies proposed by children's rights campaigners demonstrate a preoccupation with children's psychosocial dysfunctionalism akin to the fear of deviancy expressed by the earlier moralistic child salvation approach condemned by today's campaigners.

The erosion of children's autonomy is perhaps best illustrated by the colonization of play by adults, notably in Britain and the United States. The value of play has long been understood and is recognized in the Convention: 'State Parties recognize the rights of the child to rest and leisure, to engage in play and recreational activities appropriate to the age of the child and to participate in cultural life and the arts' (Article 31). Experts on the UN Committee on the Rights of the Child, UNICEF, the World Bank and other international policy-makers are paying more attention to the value of play in children's psychosocial development. For example, as part of the UNICEF-supported parenting initiative in Sri Lanka, a mother is taught 'the importance of play for her children's physical and mental well-being' (UNICEF, 2001). However, it is precisely adult attention to play today that is impoverishing its character and value for children. Therapeutic risk consciousness is leading to the colonization of play by adults for two key reasons: firstly, risk aversion and the precautionary principle; secondly, the imperatives of the therapeutic parenting philosophy.

The anxious, pessimistic therapeutic ethos is creating a besieged climate, which anticipates threats and dangers in every human activity and has become nervous of risk. As a result of the contemporary fearful climate related to the breakdown of adult solidarity there has emerged an overriding imperative to attempt to eradicate even theoretical risk from one's environment. Application of the precautionary principle to children's activities has produced a 'totalitarian ideology of safety' (Furedi, 2001: xv). Panics over strangers, concerns around environmental dangers, potential litigation over accidents (however remote) and fears over bullying are all leading to a constriction of children's play.

The expanded meaning of protecting children from harm has acquired such all-encompassing dimensions that the eradication of risk effectively entails the elimination of children's unsupervised play. Not only are particular traditional games being outlawed from the school playground (skipping in some schools, conkers in others), playtime itself is being reduced because of adult fears over unregulated children's activities. Schools across Britain are adopting a strategy of reducing breaktimes in order to reduce the opportunities for bullying or accidents to occur. Play is increasingly an adult-led activity and more restricted to the confines of the home. Symptomatic of how the scope of their freedom to play outdoors has shrunk are the rising levels of obesity among British and US children, linked to reduced levels of physical activity rather than food intake. A generation of children is now more likely to characterize themselves as indoor rather than outdoor children. One indicative study found that the children symbolically highlighted their bedroom as the main location for their play (Bean, 1999). Children's organizations deplore children not walking and being driven to school, but this is among the many unintended consequences of their alarmist safety campaigns seeking to eliminate risk from children's lives.

Fears over safety only partially account for the colonization of play by adults. Play under therapeutic risk consciousness is now considered too important to be left to children. Adults are seeking to direct the normative, developmental and educational outcomes of play. In effect, play is being instrumentalized by adults to promote specific values, emotional states and educational achievements. However, in instrumentalizing play, play loses precisely what makes it vital in child development. Forgotten in the therapeutic impulse to intervene and secure the benefits from play is all the literature on the limits of education programmes on socialization. In the reinvention of play as an adult-led activity towards adult-set goals, children are thereby denied the autonomous experiences vital for their development into mature independent adults. Instead of play preparing them for the exercise of freedom, children's experience of play today is preparing them for a life of dependency on external mediation.

The therapeutic norms of the children's rights regime are increasing children's dependency on adults. The colonization of play by adults illustrates how the reconception of rights as therapeutic intervention is eroding children's existing freedoms and impoverishing their experiences. Instead of being empowered by experiences, empowerment of children under the children's rights regime entails participation in adult-led role playing or self-esteem initiatives. While therapeutic initiatives favoured by the children's rights approach can give an artificial boost to children's confidence, studies indicate that the self-esteem they have assimilated does not translate into practice (Nolan, 1998: 169). Lessons promoting self-esteem are no substitute for learning through actual experience and the confidence gained from being entrusted by adults with real evolving responsibilities.

The demise of play as an independent child-generated activity serves as a warning of the rapacious therapeutic imperative to regulate individuals. In the context of their constricted lives, it is perhaps not surprising that there has been an apparent explosion of hyperactivity disorders in Britain and the United States. It is not conclusive whether this phenomenon represents a rise of clinical disorders among children or the therapeutic impulse to pathologize challenging behaviour previously regarded as boisterousness. Either way the alarming numbers of children who have been put on behavioural drugs like Ritalin 'in their best interests' is an indictment of the Anglo-American therapeutic approach towards children. Pathologizing their condition is of no benefit to children and is simply reinforcing a vicious circle of therapeutic intervention which is becoming progressively more authoritarian, even imposing therapeutic treatment in the face of objections by both children and parents.

Conclusion

The international children's rights regime holds many lessons and warnings for those seeking to use this approach as a template for extending and protecting human rights. Its conception of rights within the framework of therapeutic intervention holds grave consequences for the rights and freedoms of children and adults alike and is in neither of their interests. The authoritarian implications of the model of therapeutic governance under the children's rights regime need to be highlighted and confronted. In opposition to the bleak vision of humanity of children's rights advocates, the case for the mature rational adult needs to be reasserted. Instead of pathologizing humanity and seeking to limit the scope of human freedom, we need to consider how to promote a future for children globally which is based on expanding their horizons and freedoms. While children in the North are consigned to gilded cages, the policies and politics required to transform the lives of children in the South are even more remote. In neither case is the international children's rights regime offering children the prospects of a more humane childhood or future.

Notes

1. I would like to thank Michael King and Andrew Robinson for their critical comments on an earlier draft. However, responsibility for the arguments outlined here lies with me.
2. For example: Resolution 1261 (S/1999/1261) adopted 28 August 1999; Resolution 1314 (S/2000/1314) adopted 11 August 2000.
3. My discussion of the Anglo-American constructivist approach of self-actualization is informed by Nikolas Rose's *Governing the Soul* (1999a) and *Powers of Freedom* (1999b), James Hunter's *The Death of Character* (2000), and Thomas Popkewitz and Maria Bloch's 'Administering Freedom' (2001) which provide fascinating studies of contemporary policy.
4. Article 14(2) of the Convention states: 'State Parties shall respect the rights and duties of the parents and, when applicable, legal guardians, to provide direction to the child in the exercise of his or her right in a manner consistent with the evolving capacities of the child.' However, there is a certain dissembling in the children's rights regime over this issue when one considers the negative stance of the children's rights literature and trajectory of policy challenging parents' capacity to represent their children's interests.
5. The preamble reaffirms 'recognition of the inherent dignity and of the equal and inalienable rights of all members of the human family'.
6. This section draws extensively upon the compelling analysis of contemporary parenting norms in Frank Furedi's *Paranoid Parenting* (2001) and Sharon Hays' *The Cultural Contradictions of Motherhood* (1996). The phrase 'colonisation of childhood' was coined by Furedi.

Part II
Rights of Empowerment?

4
Devolving Power? Human Rights and State Regulation in Northern Ireland

Chris Gilligan

Introduction

Britain has the dubious distinction of being the European state judged to have been the most consistent violator of human rights throughout the 1970s and 1980s. During this period the UK government 'had more cases taken against it under the European Convention on Human Rights than any other country, and has had more adverse judgements made against it than any other country' (Tomlinson, 1995: 455). The vast majority of the accusations, and associated rulings, have been in relation to the British state's handling of the conflict in Northern Ireland. Concerns about human rights violations in Northern Ireland have been voiced by the United Nations High Commissioner for Human Rights, the UNHCHR's Sub-Commission on the Promotion and Protection of Human Rights, Human Rights Committee and Committee Against Torture[1] as well as the Council of Europe's European Committee for the Prevention of Torture.[2] Human rights abuses in Northern Ireland have also been the subject of criticisms from a range of international NGOs, including Amnesty International (1978), Human Rights Watch (1999b), the Lawyers Committee for Human Rights (1993) and Statewatch (1999), as well as from human rights groups based in Northern Ireland.[3]

Concerns have been raised about the use, by the Royal Ulster Constabulary (RUC) and the British Army, of 'shoot-to-kill' squads, of collusion between the security forces and loyalist paramilitaries in the killing of Irish nationalists (including the killing of Rosemary Nelson, a prominent human rights lawyer) and the army and RUC's use of torture on detainees. The RUC has also come in for criticism for its excessive use of force in policing, including its use of plastic bullet rounds against children. The judicial system has been criticized for its draconian emergency legislation, including extensive powers of detention, the use of uncorroborated evidence from informers to convict suspected paramilitaries, a two-tier justice system in which jury-less courts are used for those accused of 'scheduled' (i.e. paramilitary) offences. The British government has also been guilty of censoring media coverage of the conflict in Northern Ireland.[4]

During the latter half of the 1990s there was a paradigm shift in relation to human rights in Northern Ireland. Since mid-1997 there have been extensive attempts to deal with a wide range of issues that have been the subject of concern for human rights activists. In January 1998 an inquiry was set up to investigate the events surrounding 'Bloody Sunday', when British paratroopers shot and killed 13 unarmed civil rights protestors in Derry. In June 1998 Chris Patten was appointed as head of a Commission to investigate and make recommendations on reform of the RUC. These initiatives were partly designed to encourage the multi-party talks aimed at producing a settlement of the conflict in Northern Ireland. The talks came to a successful conclusion with the signing of an Agreement[5] by the parties to the talks. The Agreement gives prominence to the issue of human rights.

The Declaration of Support for the Agreement, for example, includes a commitment to the 'protection and vindication of the human rights of all'. All legislation passed by the Northern Ireland Assembly is liable to being struck down if it violates the European Convention on Human Rights and a Northern Ireland Human Rights Commission (NIHRC) has been established to 'keep under review the adequacy and effectiveness in Northern Ireland of law and practice relating to the protection of human rights' (NIHRC, n.d.). The human rights provisions of the Agreement have been widely welcomed by human rights groups. The US-based human rights group, Human Rights Watch, for example, welcomed the Agreement by saying that they were 'particularly pleased to note that the new agreement reflects an understanding of the relationship between the protection and promotion of universal human rights and the probabilities for a lasting, just, and durable peace' (HRW, 1998). There is also a consensus among former protagonists that human rights should form an important strand of the new political framework.

Critical questions relating to the prioritization of human rights in the Agreement tend to focus on the British government's commitment to human rights in the new institutional framework for governing Northern

Ireland or on the practical workings of the new framework. Few commentators have posed the question why the British government, formerly so hostile to human rights scrutiny in Northern Ireland, has been keen to promote human rights as a central plank of the new institutional framework for governing the province. This is the key question addressed by this chapter. The analysis of this shift in approach by the British authorities focuses on how the new regulatory framework of human rights represents a change in the *form* of the exercise of British regulatory control in Northern Ireland. This changed form, far from empowering individual citizens in the region, actually promotes new mechanisms of regulation, facilitating the control exercised by the British state in the province. There are a number of reasons for this, including the way that the human rights framework tends to obscure, rather than lay bare, the underlying power relations in society. It will be suggested that the human rights-based construction of Northern Irish society as composed of two distinct and potentially conflicting cultural communities has facilitated government regulation of interpersonal relations and also maintained, in a new form, a lack of democratic accountability. The next section outlines four factors that have led to the prominence that human rights currently enjoy in the new Northern Ireland. The rest of the chapter explores each of these factors in more detail and then highlights how the human rights regime works to strengthen the control of the British state, rather than devolve power downwards to the population of Northern Ireland.

Why human rights now?

Adrian Guelke points out that, before the 1990s, opinion was polarized over the issue of human rights in Northern Ireland (2001). The British government and Ulster Unionists tended to see the human rights agenda as an obstacle to containing the threat to British rule which was posed by Irish Republicans. Irish nationalists, by contrast, tended to see human rights violations as proof of the authoritarian nature of British rule in Northern Ireland. Guelke highlights four factors that have helped to reduce this polarization, and thus create an environment in which human rights provisions could become incorporated into the running of the state in Northern Ireland.[6]

The first factor is the broadening of the scope of human rights scrutiny to include non-state actors. This 'exposed the paramilitary organisations on both sides of the sectarian divide to strong criticism' and thus undermined Unionist perceptions 'that human rights monitoring was ... tantamount to undermining the security forces' (2001: 261). The second factor was the 'paramilitary cease-fires [which] reduced the apparent necessity for the security forces to be equipped with wide-ranging emergency powers' (ibid.). The emphasis on minority rights, the third factor, 'meant that both communities could look to international conventions ... as offering a measure of protection for cultural and other group rights under the general rubric of human rights' (ibid.). The promise of protection for groups, he suggests, helped to maintain ceasefires. The fourth factor was that the human rights provisions lent the Agreement international legitimacy. Guelke suggests that such legitimation was in the interests of Unionists and Nationalists who were pro-Agreement.

It is very likely the case that as long as Unionists and Nationalists were divided over the issue of human rights provisions these provisions could not enjoy the prominent position that they do in the Agreement. The focus on Unionists and Nationalists, however, gives the impression that the conflict has been one between two ethnic groups *within* Northern Ireland.[7] This is peculiar given that the issue of human rights has tended to focus on the British state's actions, not those of Unionists and Nationalists. The cases of human rights abuses by the British state have, in fact, almost exclusively, involved actions directed at Republican paramilitaries. Loyalist paramilitaries have not tended to be the object of human rights abuses. Indeed, on occasion, they have been the instruments through which British-state inspired human rights abuses have been perpetrated (Statewatch, 1999).

The focus on Unionists and Nationalists encourages the impression that the conflict has always been a petty sectarian one between two warring communities. If the dispute has been a local one then the British have been guilty merely of mishandling the situation or, at worst, of taking sides. The main dynamic of the conflict, however, has not been between Nationalists and Unionists, but between Irish Republicans and the British state. Irish Republicans, and the Irish Republican Army (IRA) in particular, with significant support from the Nationalist population, challenged the authority of British rule in Northern Ireland (Burton, 1978; O'Brien, 1993). They did so by use of arms, thus undermining a core aspect of state rule: the monopoly on the legitimate use of force in society (Townshend, 1993: 167–90). Actions such as the bombing of the Conservative Party conference in Brighton in 1984 or the mortar attack on 10 Downing Street in 1991 show that the IRA's military actions were part of a political campaign against British rule in Northern Ireland. These actions are not fully explicable within an internal conflict interpretation. The British state for its part did not adopt a position on the sidelines of the conflict. Actions such as internment, Bloody Sunday, media censorship, shoot-to-kill and no-jury courts were deliberate policies designed to thwart the challenge to British authority posed by Irish Republicans. Human rights abuses by the British state were simply the obviously coercive element in the use of state power to maintain British rule in Northern Ireland.

Focusing on Unionists and Nationalists avoids the question as to why the British government, formerly the focus of human rights criticisms, has been so keen to promote human rights in Northern Ireland. The British government have not simply stood back and accepted an agenda agreed by Unionists and Nationalists. They have, in fact, been actively promoting a human rights framework for running Northern Ireland. Why has their volte-face come about? The four factors that Guelke identifies provide a useful framework for understanding the shift in the British state's position on human rights. The following sections take a critical look at each of the four factors identified by Guelke. I outline the rationale for the shift in the meaning and application of human rights and then critically examine the ways in which each of these shifts operates to strengthen the regulatory control which the British state exercises over Northern Irish society.

The inclusion of non-state actors

The fact that the issue of human rights has gone from being a check on the power of the British state to being openly embraced by the British government suggests that human rights mean something different today. One difference is the extension of scrutiny to include non-state actors. At one level this is understandable. Kevin Boyle and Tom Hadden, two esteemed human rights experts, point out that many of the actions of the IRA 'are clearly contrary to international standards' (1994: 102). They cite the assassination of politicians and civilians as examples of actions that are unlawful under international law and they point out that human rights organizations have traditionally been unwilling to monitor 'violations by non-state bodies on the ground that only states were subject to international human rights law' (ibid.). The violent actions of paramilitaries have been at least as devastating on their victims as the actions of the British state have been on its victims. From the perspective of their impact on victims it makes sense that the actions of non-state actors should be subject to the same international opprobrium as states. There is also a specific local argument in favour of the extension of human rights scrutiny to non-state actors. David and Kimberly Cowell point out that Unionists have traditionally feared that the human rights agenda impeded 'the ability of the state ... to protect law and order' (1999: 6). The extension of human rights scrutiny to non-state actors, such as the IRA, has worked to assuage this fear.

The main problem with the argument advanced by Boyle and Hadden, among others, is that they focus on the act, rather than the regulatory framework within which the act is committed. Some of the actions of non-state actors, such as those of the IRA, are contrary to international standards, but these actions are also subject to domestic law. In fact, these actions have been subject to the 'extraordinary' use of domestic law (the subject of human rights criticisms in the past). From the point of view of the victim it matters little whether the bullet comes from the gun of a paramilitary or a police officer, the effect is the same. The regulatory context, however, meant that paramilitaries were subject to domestic law, whereas the security forces were not, since their actions are carried out as part of an attempt to uphold 'law and order' (Guelke, 1992; Townshend, 1993: 174–85; Walker, 1992). In this context international human rights scrutiny provided a potential counterweight to the exercise of state power.

The logic behind the exclusive focus on states was the recognition that domestic law, in situations where state power was contested, provided inadequate protection to non-state actors. Indeed, in conflict situations, like that found in Northern Ireland, the substance of human rights criticism was that the legal apparatus was being employed as an instrument of state power. States were criticized for violating the rule of law through their use of the legal apparatus to pursue political ends. Actions like the use of internment without trial, no-jury courts, 'shoot-to-kill' and convictions on the uncorroborated evidence of paid informers made a mockery of the idea that justice was impartial. The problem at the heart of this issue, the question of the legitimacy of the British state in Northern Ireland, will be explored in more detail later in this chapter. The main point highlighted here is that the broadening of human rights scrutiny to include non-state actors obscures the underlying power relations by focusing on the effects of the use of force on its immediate victims, thereby excluding a broader framework of analysis. As a consequence, it clouds the issue of power relations and thus opens up the potential for the abuse of power, the very problem that human rights scrutiny has traditionally been designed to keep in check.

The rescinding of repressive powers

The IRA ceasefire has changed the content of the issue of human rights abuses.[8] The ceasefire removed the military threat to the authority of the state, and consequently the need to use 'extraordinary' state powers against the IRA. The promotion of a human rights agenda has without doubt been helped by the fact that the use of repressive state powers has often acted as a destabilizing force, threatening to undermine the British state's authority in the region. The previous crude mechanisms of regulation are no longer suited to today's political context. It is this change in relationships on the ground that has facilitated the restructuring of the British state's relationship to Northern Ireland and enabled the establishment of a political framework with a more efficient set of mechanisms for regulating the province. This new framework has been established through the peace negotiations between the main political actors in Northern Ireland (including the British and Irish governments). It is this context that has provided an opportunity for a human rights agenda to be promoted.

However, an important qualification is necessary regarding the rescinding of repressive powers. The ceasefires may have removed the necessity for repressive powers, but it is the particular *application* of repressive powers, rather than the *principle* of the state using repressive powers, that has been conceded. The Prevention of Terrorism Act, introduced in response to the IRA pub bombings in England in 1974, has actually been extended and its remit broadened to cover animal rights activists, international 'terrorists' and a range of other subversives (Fekete, 2001). It is more accurate to say that what has changed is not the state's repressive powers as such but their form and justification.

Minority rights protections

The new political context created by the IRA ceasefire has also been crucial for the promotion of a human rights regime through the prominence that has been given to minority rights, or, more accurately, group rights. It is important to point out that minority rights are not peripheral to the new institutional arrangements, they are *fundamental* to the Agreement. At the core of the Agreement are the consociational institutions for running Northern Ireland (O'Leary, 1999). Consociational systems of government have been advocated as a means to help stabilize 'territories divided by national, ethnic or religious antagonisms' (O'Leary, 2001: 353–4 and 1989; Lijphart, 1977 and 1996). The Agreement contains the 'four essential features' of a consociation: 'cross-community power-sharing executive', 'proportionality principles', 'community self-government and equality in culture' and 'veto rights' for minorities (O'Leary, 2001: 354). The last of these is the only one that makes explicit reference to rights for minorities, but in fact all four features relate to minority rights. Minorities are included in the power-sharing executive, they are represented in public office in proportion to their number in society and their cultures are to be treated with equal respect by the state.

In the Northern Ireland context both Nationalists and Unionists view themselves as minority groups. Nationalists are, by a small margin, the numerical minority in Northern Ireland. The small demographic margin, and the possibility of a future united Ireland, gives rise to a Unionist fear that they may become a numerical minority within a future Northern Ireland, or all-Ireland state. The emphasis on minority rights thus has an appeal to both Nationalists and Unionists. For Nationalists, it provides some guarantee that there will be no return to domination by Unionists (as happened under the Stormont regime between 1921 and 1972). For Unionists, minority rights provide some protection from 'reverse discrimination' if they were ever to find themselves in the position of being a minority. The protection of group rights also provides both Nationalists and Unionists with some reassurance that their culture and values will be respected and protected in the new Northern Ireland.

The characterization of group rights as a dimension of human rights is a paradox. The notion of human rights would appear to suggest basic core freedoms that are common to all humanity; group rights on the other hand suggest freedoms that are only relevant to specific groups. Or, in other words, the logic of human rights is that they should be universal, but group rights are particular. How can human rights be universal if they conceive of humanity as divided into discrete groups or communities? The way that this particular circle is usually squared is by claiming that there exists a universal human need for 'belonging' or 'identity' and that this need can only be realized within a particular group. This sense of 'belonging' is then coupled to a right to 'recognition', a right to have one's particular identity acknowledged by society (Gutman, 1994).

Brendan O'Leary alludes to this logic when he says that consociations help stabilize divided societies 'by recognising differences, rather than by attempting to eliminate them through the imposition of one identity' (2001: 354). The recognition of differences seems preferable to the imposition of a single identity. An important problem with the consociational approach, however, is that it is achieved through imposing identities. Consociationalism may offer two identities rather than one, but as its critics point out, in doing so it hypostatizes those identities (Rooney, 1998; Cassidy and Trew, 1998). A number of commentators point out that a range of identities are available to any one individual and that the particular identity that a person chooses at any particular moment is highly contextual (Graham, 1997; Trew, 1992).[9] The Agreement operates by elevating one particular identification, the ethno-national one, over all others and institutionalizes this at the centre of the new political arrangements in Northern Ireland (O'Leary, 1999).

There is a consensus among former protagonists that human rights should form an important strand of the new political framework. It is important, however, to recognize that, at least in part, this has been possible because the various parties to the Agreement believe that the human rights framework provides a means through which they can pursue their own, sometimes conflicting, interests. Cowell and Cowell highlight this limitation of the human rights legislation as a means to promote peace, writing that 'the language of human rights in Northern Ireland ... has been employed for ethnocentric purposes' (1999: 1). They argue that in the 1980s 'rights language began to be adopted by Unionists to further Unionists goals' through rights being reconceptualized in a way that precluded 'dissolution of the Union, simultaneously protecting the Unionists and dismissing Nationalist criticism of the government of Northern Ireland' (ibid.: 16). 'Nationalists', and the British government, have in their own ways employed rights language to serve their own ends. The minority rights aspect of the Agreement is therefore also one of the weaknesses of the peace settlement. The minority rights provisions are generally welcomed, but as we have seen, this is more out of fear of 'the other side' than from a commitment to any intrinsic merits that may be claimed for minority rights. Consequently the consent to these provisions is conditional on them protecting the rights of one's own group. Joseph Ruane argues that in this dichotomous framework 'at most only one community can have its expectations fulfilled, and even that will happen only if it is active, vigilant and assertive' (1999: 163). The minority rights dimension of the Agreement promises to protect minorities, but in setting them up against each other it also creates the conditions in which inter-group conflict becomes more likely (for more on the weaknesses of the peace process, see Gilligan, 1997).

The Cowells' acknowledgement of some of the ways that different parties to the conflict use human rights language for instrumental purposes does not lead them to reject human rights. They conclude their analysis of the use of human rights by 'Unionists' in Northern Ireland by saying that 'more work needs to be done in promoting a culture of human rights' (1999: 24), the implication being that there is no problem with the new human rights framework per se, the problem is the use of human rights, by 'Unionists', for instrumental purposes. Despite some reservations, the Cowells concur with Human Rights Watch in their belief that human rights are a useful instrument for bringing peace, commenting that the new framework can usefully channel 'intense communal conflicts by both creating a common and neutral protective legal apparatus and removing the state from the focus of the conflict' (1999: 1). This is a vital point: one effect of the consociational arrangements in Northern Ireland has been to remove the British government from centre stage and to highlight the internal antagonism between 'Nationalists' and 'Unionists'. This removal of the British state from the centre of attention is further facilitated by the devolution of power from Westminster. Devolution means that sovereignty still resides in Westminster, but the majority of the day-to-day workings of state administration now run from Stormont. One commentator has said of devolution in the UK that 'the devolved administrations are treated rather like unruly children, with firm ground rules laid down' (Harvey, 2001: 105). This description, as we shall see, is particularly appropriate for the treatment of Northern Ireland.

International legitimacy

The fourth rationale, mentioned by Guelke, for the inclusion of a human rights component to the new institutional arrangements in Northern Ireland is that it helps to legitimize the new institutions internationally. A number of authors have argued that the peace process has itself been made possible by the declining saliency of national sovereignty. There are a number of different aspects to this. The peace process and the Agreement were enabled through cooperation between two sovereign states, the United Kingdom and the Republic of Ireland (Gillespie, 2000). The Agreement has established two important confederal dimensions to the running of Northern Ireland, the North–South Ministerial Council and the British-Irish Council (O'Leary, 1999). The process of Europeanization has also been considered to have played an important role in changing the context and contours of what had at one time been understood as the 'national question' in Ireland (Cox, 2000; Meehan, 2000), as has involvement by the government of the United States (O'Clery, 1996). If the nation-state is less important then it is logical to suggest that international opinion should be more important.

The greater importance accorded to international opinion, however, can also be seen as a register of the declining importance accorded to the opinion of the citizens of Northern Ireland themselves. As will be considered in the next two sections, the operation of human rights mechanisms of regulation, independently of popular pressures and concerns, constitutes a central factor in the legitimization of the new framework but may also be the source of continuing instability in the province.

The discipline of minority rights

The mutual interest that 'Nationalists' and 'Unionists' have in protecting themselves from domination by a majority provides the basis for the prominence enjoyed by group rights in the Agreement. This mutual interest, however, is simultaneously an expression of an underlying suspicion and antagonism. The promotion of group rights stimulates pressure groups to articulate their concerns through the language of group rights. A good example of mutual antagonism being articulated in the language of rights is the protests over Orange Order parades.

To some extent Orange Order parades have always been a contentious issue in Northern Ireland. Since the mid-1990s, however, they have become a central focus of political contestation in the region. The main focus of contention has been the Garvaghy Road in Portadown where residents of the, mainly 'Nationalist', housing estate have been protesting at an Orange Order parade that marches from Drumcree chapel along the Garvaghy Road (the main arterial route through the housing estate). Before 1997, the RUC forced 'Nationalist' residents off the road to allow the parade to proceed; since then the Orange Order has been blocked from marching down the road. Both groups articulate their demands through the language of human rights.

The Garvaghy Road Residents Coalition (GRRC) justify their protest against the Orange Order march from Drumcree chapel on the grounds that they are victims of sectarian harassment. They characterize their protests as part of a 'struggle for their right to equality [and] freedom from sectarian discrimination and harassment' (GRRC, n.d.). The Grand Orange Lodge of Ireland (GOLI) protest that their right to march and the right to express their cultural tradition is being denied by the banning of parades (GOLI, n.d). The mutual antagonism points to a set of dilemmas. When there is a clash of rights, who decides which right takes priority over the other and on what normative grounds do they decide? In the case of disputes over parades in Northern Ireland the decision is made by a quango, the Parades Commission, but on what grounds do they make their decisions?

In outlining his decision to prevent the Orange parade proceeding down the Garvaghy Road in July 2000, Tony Holland, then Chairperson of the Parades Commission, acknowledged that for the Orangemen: 'The threat to the Drumcree parade is a threat to everything they stand for – for civil and religious liberty and the right to demonstrate faith and culture in a time honoured way' (2000). He highlighted that the Orangemen feared that 'the residents' opposition is politically manipulated [by Sinn Fein and the IRA] and designed to inflict defeat on their political opinions and religious beliefs as well as their rights' (ibid.). The residents of the Garvaghy Road, on the other hand, 'feel isolated and under siege from the effects of the Drumcree dispute and the associated parades and rallies...These are seen as coat trailing, provocative and devoid of any respect for the community on whom they impinge, often at anti-social hours and over long periods' (ibid.). He goes on to note that the Orange Order is also 'seen to represent decades of anti-catholic domination symbolised by the loyal orders' insistence on marching through nationalist areas' (ibid.).

On what grounds did Holland adjudicate between the two sets of rights? Should the Orangemen's right to 'civil and religious liberty' and the traditional affirmation of their faith and culture take precedence over the residents right to freedom from harassment and domination? Or vice versa? Holland decided that the residents' rights outweighed those of the Orange Order. In outlining his decision to ban the parade, Holland explained that the Orange Order, in refusing to engage in dialogue with the GRRC, did not show respect for the concerns of the Garvaghy Road residents.

The ruling is interesting for the insights that it provides into the new regulatory framework shaped by human rights concerns. The first point to note is that the affective needs of the residents take priority over the civil liberties of the Orangemen. It is considered more important to acknowledge and address the feeling of isolation of the residents than to guarantee the freedom of public procession. The elevation of the importance of personal feelings is at the cost of the regulation of public space. It could be argued that the Orange Order's commitment to civil liberties is instrumental rather than principled. In the late 1960s and early 1970s the Order did not object when civil rights marches were banned.[10] It is worth pointing out, however, that the arguments that are applied against Orange Order marches today could have been applied against civil rights parades in the 1960s and 1970s.

The second point about the justification for banning the parade is that dialogue is promoted as something that has intrinsic value. Holland (2000) stated that:

> It is disturbing generally that the organisers of parades and those who oppose them often fail to acknowledge, let alone address, the genuine concerns of the other side. That can be best demonstrated by showing respect. The simplest, and most direct way of showing respect is a willingness at least to speak to those who are most affected...We don't have much evidence of any such efforts by Portadown District [Orange Lodge].

The notion that 'dialogue hurts no one' is found more widely in the peace process (Farren and Mulvihill, 2000; McAllister, 1999). The notion is attractive, but fails to place dialogue in context. Talking for the sake of talking is inane. Meaningful dialogue is never carried out for the sake of talking in and of itself, it is carried out with a purpose in mind. Engaging in dialogue also involves recognition of the legitimacy of both the other party and the process of negotiation. The Orange Order, however, are opposed to negotiation and do not recognize the legitimacy of the GRRC. Their opposition to negotiation is premised on their opposition to the peace process. They fear that the peace process is one of 'appeasement of terrorists'. Holland himself acknowledges the fact that the Orange Order does not recognize the legitimacy of the GRRC when he points to the Orangemen's concern that the IRA is manipulating the GRRC.[11] The presumption that dialogue has intrinsic merit also fails to register the imbalance of power involved in most negotiations. Part of the reason why the Orangemen refuse to engage in discussion is because they are doing so from a position of weakness. Their response is defensive rather than provocative.

One possible way of explaining the favouring of the residents in the Parades Commission ruling would be that it is a logical consequence of the fact that 'Unionists' have an instrumental approach to human rights, whereas 'Nationalists' are committed to human rights as ethical ideals. The Cowells suggest something like this when they say that 'the international profile of the Nationalist community has caused it to develop much more sophisticated language around human rights and to value human rights in themselves rather than as a weapon' (1999: 24). It is undeniable that 'Unionists' have an instrumental view of human rights, but how do we know that 'Nationalists' do not? Dominic Bryan provides evidence that 'Nationalists' may have used the parades issue for instrumental purposes. He cites a GRRC member as saying, in July 1997, that:

> They were probably in a win-win situation. Either the parade was stopped, or, beamed across the televisions of the world, local residents would be dragged, kicked and beaten by RUC men ... to allow Orangemen – the perceived aggressors – down a piece of road. (2000: 173)

Many 'Nationalists' are aware that international opinion is more sympathetic towards them that towards 'Unionists'. The protests against parades are provocative set pieces designed, at least in part, to gain political advantage for 'Nationalists'.

The Orangemen are, in fact, dupes in the peace process. Their traditional Protestantism, with its hostility to the Church of Rome, and their key role in the 'Unionist' dominated state from 1921 to 1972 provides the grounds for their characterization as aggressors. Their role as dominators, however, is largely symbolic. The GOLI is no longer the powerful institution that it once was (Bryan, 2000). It is because they are peripheral to the running of the state that they can become the whipping boy. The focus on the Orangemen's public opposition to the peace process tends to portray any opposition to the peace process as born of intolerance. Such a move, however, obscures the changing power relations in Northern Irish society.

The third point is that Holland, in justifying the banning of the parade, tells the Orangemen how to behave if they want to be accorded rights. The banning of the parade is a way of forcing them to be good citizens. To all intents and purposes the Parades Commission is attempting to institutionalize a new etiquette for public conduct. Rights, in this view, are not freedoms from state intervention but are rewards for good conduct. From this perspective human rights in Northern Ireland are a complete inversion of what they have traditionally been held to be. Rather than being a counterweight to the coercive powers of the state, human rights have become something that are gained as a *consequence* of the deployment of the coercive powers of the state. The promotion of minority rights treats the population of Northern Ireland as if they are squabbling children and allows the British state to re-enter the picture, but this time as the parental figure, teaching the population how to behave as good citizens.

Legitimacy and the exercise of state power

The exercise of power is a necessary feature of the operation of the state. It is the abuse of power, rather than the exercise of state power, that has traditionally been the focus of human rights scrutiny. The exercise of power is normally relatively unproblematic for the state because it is accepted as legitimate. Or, in other words, in liberal democratic societies those who are the object of the exercise of power normally accept the justification for its exercise and consent to power being exercised (Beetham, 1991). The exercise of state power is only a major problem for the state under conditions, such as Northern Ireland, where those over whom it is exercised do not accept it as legitimate.

The human rights framework has enabled the British state to reassert its legitimacy in Northern Ireland by problematizing 'Nationalist' and

'Unionist' groupings on the grounds of human rights protection and questioning the capacities of both elected representatives and their voters. In fact, it is notable that many of the most vocal advocates of the peace process and the new institutions established by the Agreement are suspicious of the 'masses' in Northern Ireland. This suspicion of the Northern Ireland electorate can be seen in the explicit attempts to insulate the new institutions from popular protest. O'Leary, for example, argues that 'a referendum on Northern Ireland's Bill of Rights is not necessary' and explains his view on the grounds of 'the danger of a referendum on the Bill of Rights becoming a second referendum on the Agreement itself' (2001: 363). The fear that fresh Assembly elections would become a de facto referendum on the Agreement was an important factor in the decision of John Reid, the Secretary of State for Northern Ireland, to go through successive temporary suspensions of the Assembly in the summer of 2001 (Cowan, 2001; Simpson, 2001). A suspicion of ordinary people can also be seen in Cowell and Cowell's favourable view of the informal diplomacy that preceded the negotiation of the Agreement. They argue that: 'Removing the public element tends to produce more honest debate and less political posturing' (1999: 20). Gordon Lucy, a 'Unionist' critic of the new institutional framework, has complained that the process of forming the Executive of the Assembly, the prime representative body in the region, operates to disenfranchise ordinary people. The consociational formula for electing the Executive, he points out, 'has deprived citizens of the fundamental democratic right – the ability to hold ministers to account by throwing them out of office' (2001: 19).

Related to this anti-democratic tendency is the shift in the locus of state power away from representative institutions toward judicial and quasi-judicial ones. The lack of embarrassment about this shift is striking. Holland extols the virtues of the quango as a means for governing Northern Ireland. Responding to a question about the anti-democratic nature of the Parades Commission he said that:

> The Parades Commission is not responsible to an electorate, and therefore we can be more objective … Being unelected means we can be more judicial. If we had to be elected again, then frankly what you'd get is what the majority wanted winning through every time, and others wouldn't be heard.
>
> (O'Neill, 2001)

Against the backdrop of widespread elite suspicion of ordinary citizens it is hardly surprising that Cowell and Cowell detect that the language of human rights 'remains an elite issue lacking widespread grass-roots support' (1999: 1).

The lack of widespread grassroots support is an issue not just for the human rights aspects of the Agreement, but for the new institutional framework as a whole. An institutional set-up that relies on resisting popular pressure will experience difficulties trying to gain active consent for the exercise of power by those institutions. The centrality of minority rights to the new regulatory framework also harbours potential problems for the future. The promise of protection for minority rights has helped to provide a justification for the new framework but, as noted earlier, the appeal of the minority rights dimension rests on a suspicion of the 'other' community. Consequently the consent to these provisions is conditional on them protecting the rights of one's own group. There is a danger here that gaining legitimacy for British rule among Irish 'Nationalists' could be at the expense of losing legitimacy in the eyes of Ulster 'Unionists'.

A high-profile example of this process occurred in the latter half of 2001 when the world's media broadcast pictures of Loyalist protestors hurling bricks and abuse at infants and their parents who were attempting to get to their school in north Belfast. Events such as this are an example of the way that the new human rights framework helps to institutionalize cross community conflict. The parents, Irish 'Nationalists', objected that the 'Unionist' protestors were denying their children the human right to an education. The Loyalist actions represented a defensive response to fears that their right to housing and other amenities were being denied by Irish 'Nationalists' in the area. Both responses are consistent with the new regulatory framework, which ensures claims are posed in the language of inter-community division, rather than as claims of individual rights to be upheld on the basis of legal and political equality. In this way the British state is recast as the enforcer of human rights which are threatened or abused by the actions of the 'other' community. In fact, for the parents it was only through the exercise of state power, in the form of police officers in riot gear, that ensured that their children were able to exercise their right to education.

This example illustrates the way in which the new framework tends to obscure the underlying power relations in society. Through the incorporation of the state's opponents into government, and through the shift in the locus of power from representative institutions to judicial ones, the issue of state power has been depoliticized. One effect of this is to give the exercise of state power, in this example the use of police in riot gear, a judicial appearance. State power is simply the enforcement of law and order. As long as both sides accept the new framework then the exercise of state power loses its coercive appearance. By contrast, the actions of the protestors appear as naked aggression. In this way the new regulatory framework makes the abuse of power appear as if it is as an attribute of the 'other' community.[12]

Conclusion

The British state supports a human rights framework in Northern Ireland today for essentially the same reason that it opposed human rights scrutiny in the past: it makes the task of governing Northern Irish society easier. The peace process has neutralized the threat to British rule posed by Irish Republicans, it has also helped to legitimize British rule in Northern Ireland in the eyes of Irish 'Nationalists'. There is nothing inherently wrong in the exercise of and legitimization of state power. From the allocation of resources in the health sector to the deployment of the Army, every state needs to exercise power in order to get things done. The worrying aspect of the new human rights framework is the way that it constructs Northern Irish society as composed of two mutually hostile cultural communities. This has the effect of institutionalizing social and political divisions while at the same time focusing on these divisions as the locus for state regulation. This process of creating new regulatory mechanisms of human rights adjudication has recast the role of the British state in Northern Ireland, allowing regulatory control while at the same time isolating the process of political control from the pressures of democratic decision-making and accountability to the electorate. The analysis outlined in this chapter suggests that the new regulatory framework, rather than helping to bring peace to Northern Ireland, may well ensure that inter-communal conflict continues to be a central political focal point, despite the fact that the IRA's military campaign against British rule is over. The new framework helps to legitimize British rule in the region, but at the expense of the development of democratic and accountable regional ownership of the peace process which is necessary for a sustainable and long-term settlement.

Notes

1. For the range of concerns raised by the UNCHR and its sub-committees between 1991 and 1999 see reports available from the Committee for the Administration of Justice (available from: <http://www.caj.org.uk/keydocs/ CAJSubmUNHRC.html>).

2. See, further, Committee for the Prevention of Torture reports on visits to Northern Ireland in 1993 and 1999 (available from: <http://www.cpt.coe.int/en/states/gbr.htm>).

3. See for example, reports by the Committee for the Administration of Justice (available from: <http://www.caj.org.uk/>), Pat Finucane Centre (available from: <http://www.serve.com/pfc/>) and Relatives for Justice (available from: <http://www.relativesforjustice.com>).

4. For academic studies of the various issues see, for example: Boyle, Hadden and Hillyard (1975), Dickson (1995), Ellison and Smyth (2000), Foley (1998), Hillyard (1997), Jennings (1990), Miller (1994), Townshend (1993: 167–90).

5. The formal title of the document is the Agreement; so as to distinguish it from other documents also known as the Agreement (e.g. Anglo-Irish Agreement 1985), it has been referred to variously as the Belfast Agreement (where it was signed), the Good Friday Agreement (the day it was signed on) or the British-Irish Agreement (in acknowledgement of the transnational dimension of the conflict). In this chapter it is referred to simply as the Agreement. A copy of the Agreement can be accessed on the web at: <http://cain.ulst.ac.uk/events/peace/docs/agreement.htm>.

6. Guelke outlines these four factors only briefly and in the context of a chapter that focuses more broadly on the international dimensions of the Agreement. I focus on the same four factors because it provides a useful framework through which to develop this analysis.

7. This understanding of the conflict is often referred to as an 'internal conflict' interpretation (for more on this see Whyte, 1990).

8. A full explanation of how the new human rights regime has come to prominence would also include an outline of shifts within the Republican movement. Due to limitations of space this dimension is not included here. (For a good analysis of shifts within Republicanism see Ryan, 1994 and 1997.)

9. I agree with Trew, Graham and others that identities are hybrid and highly contextual. In order to acknowledge this fact the terms 'Nationalist' and 'Unionist' will be placed inside inverted commas for the rest of the chapter. This is done in order to remind the reader that these are not monolithic constructs but are constituted as such in relation to particular events and contexts established by the peace process (and, before that, the conflict).

10. In the late 1960s and early 1970s in Northern Ireland the Unionist government banned a series of civil rights marches. The marches called for an end to the discriminatory practices of the 'Orange' state and, later, the use of emergency powers by the state. The justification given for the banning was that the marches were a threat to public order (Farrell, 1980: 243–91; Purdie, 1990).

11. Breandán MacCionnaith, one of the main spokespersons for the GRRC, was convicted and imprisoned for IRA activities.

12. For more background on events in north Belfast see O'Neill (2002).

5
Empowering the Poorest?
The World Bank and the
'Voices of the Poor'

John Pender

> Essentially, [the new development consensus] says that in evaluating an economy's state or progress, we must focus primarily on how the poorest people are faring.
>
> Kaushik Basu, 'On the Goals of Development'

> [The *Voices of the Poor* study] argues for a reorientation of development priorities, practice and thinking. It reinforces the case for making the well-being of those who are worse off the touchstone for policy and practice.
>
> Deepa Narayan et al., *Voices of the Poor: Crying Out for Change*

Introduction

World Bank intervention in the world's poorest countries has undergone a dramatic transformation in less than a decade. In the name of the world's most marginalized and vulnerable people, World Bank regulatory intervention has become more detailed and far-reaching than ever before. Simultaneously, World Bank development policy has been substantially modified to elevate the perceived needs of the poorest. Today, it is hard to find a major World Bank study that does not defer to what it has termed the 'voices of the poor'. The World Bank has gone to great lengths to seek out the most impoverished and isolated people in poor countries to solicit their views on development. These consultations have most notably been brought together in the World Bank study

97

Voices of the Poor, which synthesizes the experiences of over 60,000 people from 60 countries.[1]

It is primarily on the basis of this work that the World Bank suggests that the relationship between itself and poor countries has been qualitatively transformed. No longer does the Bank regard itself as prescriptive, imposing tight conditions as a precondition for the receipt of desperately needed finance. Rather, the Bank presents its relationship with poor countries as one of partnership. In terms of World Bank buzzwords, 'conditionality' is out and 'country ownership' is in. Reflecting the new basis of the relationship between the World Bank and the poor countries which receive funds from it, the favoured World Bank instrument of intervention for most of the 1980s and 1990s, the Structural Adjustment Programme, and the prescriptive conditionality associated with it, has been replaced. The Poverty Reduction Strategy Paper (PRSP), drawn up by the borrowing country government, is now the basis upon which lending decisions are made.

In parallel, the content of World Bank development policy has changed. The overall thrust of rolling back the state and minimizing restrictions on the free play of market forces has gone. The economic policy instruments associated with structural adjustment – notably summed up in John Williamson's 'Washington Consensus' synthesis – have less prominence (Williamson, 1990). While controlling inflation and trade liberalization, for example, are today regarded as essential aspects of a sound macroeconomic policy framework, much greater emphasis is placed on the potentially positive benefits of 'market friendly' state intervention and regulation. Nicholas Stern, the current World Bank chief economist, has suggested that 50 per cent of GDP could be regarded as an acceptable level for state intervention in a developing country (Stern, 1997: 153–4).

The new emphasis of World Bank development policy is 'poverty reduction', and is captured in its Comprehensive Development Framework (CDF). This framework combines extensive regulatory intervention across many aspects of society previously ignored by the development policy associated with structural adjustment. This chapter elaborates and critiques these developments. It is suggested that the claim to be acting on behalf of the poorest, and the poverty reduction agenda itself, have had important negative impacts on both democracy and development. Increased legitimacy has been given to the World Bank's regulatory intervention in the policy-making processes of poor countries, which has undercut the role of elected representatives, effectively giving people in poor countries less of a say in development issues. Perhaps more damaging, in the long term, the relentless focus on new World Bank anti-poverty measures will have the paradoxical effect of institutionalizing the international poverty divide between rich and poor countries.

The claim of country ownership

Launching the *Voices of the Poor* study, Nicholas Stern was at pains to emphasize that 'we are taking country ownership very seriously' (World Bank, 2000b). For Stern, country ownership is about empowerment, participation and community-driven development. Similarly, James Wolfensohn, World Bank Group president, and Clare Short, UK Secretary of State for International Development, stressed in their foreword to the *Voices of the Poor* study: 'What can be more important than listening to the poor and working with our partners all over the world to respond to their concerns?' (Narayan et al., 2000a: ix).

This new emphasis on 'country ownership' is a graphic break from the World Bank's previous approach of conditionality. Conditionality was first proposed in the late 1970s by World Bank president Robert McNamara as the idea of encouraging economic growth and development by linking the provision of World Bank financial assistance to the adoption of a particular set of policies recommended by the World Bank. Conditionality has been more broadly defined by Collier as 'the idea that international public resources should be used to induce policy reform' (2000: 299). Conditionality was implemented as an integral aspect of Structural Adjustment Programmes. During the 1980s and into the 1990s, loans from the World Bank, International Monetary Fund and regional development banks, aid from bilateral donors and even private finance became effectively conditional on agreement by the recipient to implement often far-reaching economic policy reforms along the lines of the World Bank model.

A very particular model of development, and a narrow set of economic policy instruments, was therefore externally imposed on developing countries through Structural Adjustment. This heavily constrained the capacity of these countries to experiment with any other models or policies. As Brown notes: 'These conditions, and the declining availability of alternative sources of finance, have meant that there has been precious little leeway for experimentation with heterodox policies at odds with the [International Financial Institutions'] prescriptions' (2000: 120). However, these stringent regulatory mechanisms were at least formally confined to the economic arena. The World Bank consistently deferred to the notion of national sovereignty on many matters which it would perhaps have liked to use its leverage to influence. As Williamson states:

> Washington certainly has a number of other concerns ... besides furthering economic well-being. These include the promotion of democracy and human rights, suppression of the drug trade, preservation of the environment, and control of population growth. For better or worse, however, these broader objectives play little role in determining Washington's attitudes to the economic policies it urges ...
>
> (1990: 8)

Today, the World Bank has renegotiated the notion of conditionality and the mechanisms of projecting its influence into poor country societies. Joseph Stiglitz, one of the key initiators of this shift, has suggested that changing 'the process of the development dialogue' was one of his central objectives when he took up the post of World Bank chief economist (cited in Brauer, 2000: 26). His successor Stern has stated that: 'We are working to simplify conditionality so that countries themselves describe, select and implement the policies which are necessary to promote the reduction of poverty' (cited in World Bank, 2000b). As Collier suggests of the Comprehensive Development Framework:

> Its main innovation is its emphasis upon partnership, both between donors and the government, and between the government and civil society. The CDF is thus a clear departure from the narrow and coercive conditionality appropriate for crisis management.
>
> (2000: 323)

The World Bank therefore suggests that today it is committed to country ownership. It claims that it does not dictate to poor countries, rather that the World Bank is a 'knowledge bank' – 'defining and propagating a model of development best practice' (Gilbert and Vines, 2000: 19). It asserts that it works in partnership with countries to assist them in determining their own approach to development, which poor countries formulate in Poverty Reduction Strategy Papers.

Several initial reservations can be highlighted at this point regarding these claims. Most notably there is an implicit assumption that poor country governments should choose to pursue a development policy within the clear parameters of the World Bank's own approach. The idea that poor country governments could legitimately devise or formulate a substantially different approach is not entertained. Today, the World

Bank will not accept a lending application from a poor country government which it deems not to have a 'good policy environment'. The World Bank has a clear and pre-determined view of what it understands this to be – a clearly demonstrated commitment to controlling inflation and pro-market reform. In this sense the policy environment is not subject to country ownership. No allowance is made, outside the strictly defined parameters set down by the World Bank, for government decision-making (World Bank, 1998; Stiglitz, 2000: 4).

The World Bank exerts influence over poor country governments, where there is a perceived lack of a commitment to a suitable good policy environment or lack of agreement on the development policy priorities, through 'financing the overseas education of policymakers' and sponsoring political movements supportive of World Bank views (nurturing a 'strong domestic movement for change') (World Bank, 1998: 8–9). Poor country governments, which are not fully compliant with the Bank's policy recommendations, are to face the externally sponsored cultivation of political opposition movements. We can therefore see the development of a highly prescriptive and coercive framework, imposing externally determined policies and priorities on to poor countries. The claim of country ownership, in this light, appears a questionable one. The main factor obscuring the restrictions on poor country policy independence and meaningful 'country ownership' is the World Bank's justification that it is acting on behalf of the poorest. The claim to be acting on behalf of the most marginalized and the most vulnerable in poor societies has had considerable currency in legitimizing greater regulatory powers for the World Bank. The most comprehensive work outlining the World Bank's claims to be acting on behalf of the poor is the seminal study *Voices of the Poor*. The key aspects of the study are outlined below. The limitations of the study in its own terms are then examined before discussing the broader context of the recent reorientation of World Bank development policy.

The 'Voices of the Poor'

The World Bank's new orientation towards the poorest and most marginalized has been justified extensively through the 'Voices of the Poor' initiative. James Wolfensohn and Clare Short have commended the study for its 'authenticity and significance' (Narayan et al., 2000a: ix). The once-a-decade World Bank *World Development Report* addressing poverty was published in 2000 and was strongly oriented around the findings of the *Voices of the Poor* study. The main thrust of the study is that development policy should be clearly focused on the poorest. The study concludes that it 'reinforces the case for making the well-being of those who are worse off the touchstone for policy and practice' (Narayan et al., 2000b: 264). It is the poorest and most marginalized people in poor societies who should determine the overall development priorities for that society. Indeed, the knowledge of the poorest is championed over and above that of those who have traditionally formulated development policy. 'There are 2.8 billion poverty experts', the study suggests, 'the poor themselves'. However: 'the development discourse about poverty has been dominated by the perspectives and expertise of those who are not poor – professionals, politicians and agency officials' (Narayan et al., 2000b: 2). The study's findings reflect a new approach to how development policy should be formulated.

First, the study reports that, on the basis of its consultations with the poorest, the World Bank should 'revisit the meaning of development'. While 'historically many development professionals have given priority to the material aspect of people's lives' (Narayan et al., 2000b: 264), the study finds that, for the poor, material aspirations are modest. 'Materially', the researchers claim, 'enough for a good life is not a lot'. A young man from Ecuador is reported as saying: 'I would like to live simply ... I don't like big houses with too much inside ... I would like a simple house ... not big, or luxurious ... a simple house with a floor' (Narayan et al., 2000b: 24). 'Money itself', the report notes, 'is mentioned less frequently than one might expect' (Narayan et al., 2000b: 25). The poor, it is claimed, repeatedly distinguish between wealth and well-being, viewing them as 'different, and even contradictory' (Narayan et al., 2000b: 21). A 26-year-old woman from Ethiopia reports: 'A better life for me is to be healthy, peaceful and to live in love without hunger ... Love is more than anything. Money has no value in the absence of love' (Narayan et al., 2000b: 22).

Well-being, not wealth, is, for the poor, the desired outcome of development. Well-being is described as a concept that has 'a psychological and spiritual dimension as a mental state of harmony, happiness and peace of mind' (Narayan et al., 2000b: 21). Similarly, poor people's definition of poverty includes 'vulnerability, powerlessness, the shame of dependency, and social isolation' (Narayan et al., 2000a: 274). The study emphasizes that interventions to improve people's sense of well-being do not necessarily have to result in any material improvement in their lives. It notes that 'psychological well-being is independent of economic well-being' (Narayan et al., 2000a: 146) and that 'tranquility and peacefulness are important to poor people, even when poverty does not decrease' (Narayan et al., 2000a: 267). The report goes on to draw attention to the frequent observation by its study teams that many poor communities are welcoming and hospitable and have well-developed social networks. From this it concludes that some people, for example those in indigenous rural populations, 'appear happier despite greater poverty' (Narayan et al., 2000a: 146). The study claims that the poor are calling for a reconceptualization of the meaning of development. That they call for multifaceted non-material considerations to be introduced into development policy and, in fact, object to primacy being placed on material development.

Secondly, the researchers actively press the case for an expansion of regulatory development policy intervention in order to address the new issues raised by the poor. For example, in order to meet poor people's need for 'social and psychological support' (Narayan et al., 2000a: 205). The most pressing arena for intervention, the researchers argue, is the household: 'There may be no other domain than gender relations that suffers such neglect by governments, international agencies and the private sector' (Narayan et al., 2000b: 276). The *Voices of the Poor* studies 'capture the silent trauma going on within households that has yet to be factored in to poverty reduction strategies' (Narayan et al., 2000a: 175). The poor, it is claimed, tell us that more detailed and extensive regulatory intervention is required to deal with their perceived problems. 'Poor people's experiences', concludes the report, 'urge an expansion of poverty measures to include voice and power, vulnerability and accumulation of assets' (Narayan et al., 2000a: 274). Appropriate targets for World Bank policy intervention are held to include poor country government agencies, community organizations and the dominant socio-cultural norms.

Finally, the researchers raise a central concern with the effectiveness of the institutions dealing with development. The study notes: 'The poor usually experience formal institutions as ineffective, inaccessible, and disempowering' (Narayan et al., 2000a: 83). A priority is therefore to bring pressure to bear on these institutions to modify their priorities and their policies: 'To bring about change requires changing the strength and nature of the institutional connections among the poor, civil society, and the state' (Narayan et al., 2000a: 13). The researchers argue for the cultivation of social movements and development entrepreneurs who can effectively press the case for the reorientation of development policy to prioritize the well-being of the poorest:

> Transforming a government department or ministry through social movement ... requires empowering development entrepreneurs with

authority, finances, and supportive resources to implement programmes and to deliver results both in changed social norms and in
services.

(Narayan et al., 2000a: 282)

They suggest: 'It is only when poor people can draw on the strength of
their numbers and organize themselves that their voices can be heard'
(Narayan et al., 2000a: 277). The researchers claim that this will take
considerable external resources and a protracted period of intervention:
'Developing organisational capacity of the poor is a long-term process
that may take 10 to 20 years. It requires long-term financing, trust and
flexibility' (Narayan et al., 2000a: 277).

The *Voices of the Poor* study claims to accurately reflect the perspective
of the poorest. It argues that the perspective of the poor should be ele-
vated as the basis of a dramatic reorientation of development policy.
These findings are repeatedly justified on the basis of the authenticity of
the views of the poor people who participated in the study. The study
claims that it 'simply offers a view of the world from the perspective of
the poor', and that 'this book is about their voices' (Narayan et al., 2000a:
3). But does this claim to reflect authentic voices stand up to scrutiny?
Serious flaws in the approach of the study throw into question exactly
whose 'voices' have shaped the study's findings. The study claims to be
participant-driven. Based on a participatory approach, the study actively
engaged participants in the research process by using 'open-ended and
participatory methods'. This, it is claimed, 'allows for the emergence of
issues and dimensions of poverty that are important to the community
but not necessarily known to the researchers' (Narayan et al., 2000a: 16).

Yet the research agenda was not set by the participants. Rather, it was
predetermined by World Bank staff and the study researchers. For example, the theme of well-being was one of four predetermined aspects of
inquiry. The researchers had decided to explore the theme of well-being
by asking the participants for their ideas about security, risk, vulnerability, opportunities, social exclusion, crime and conflict. Researchers noted
the difficulty of adequately conveying terms such as these to people who
were not fully conversant with the latest Western intellectual buzzwords.
The participants were not even directly asked whether they regarded
more income as integral to determining their well-being. Further, the
researchers actively intervened in the study process to elicit answers that
they regarded as more desirable. For example, while the study claimed to
ask the poor, impartially, for their problems and priorities, the study
report notes that they 'changed the sequencing of methods as needed'

(Narayan et al., 2000b: 14). Changing the sequencing to first asking about problems rather than priorities, for example, was justified on the ethical grounds of not unreasonably raising the hopes of the participants. But the impact of taking everyday problems as the discussion's starting point, rather than broader hopes or ambitions, would certainly be to marshal answers informed by lower expectations.

The study was also hostile to the idea of quantifying results, favouring instead the 'documentation of what was said in poor people's own words' (Narayan et al., 2000b: 16). After interviewing 60,000 people, on what basis were the relatively few quotes, cited in the report, selected? How, scientifically, can we regard them as anything other than personal, unrepresentative opinions? The clearest example of the distorting impact of the researcher's preconceived framework relates to the study's finding that the need for material development was consistently downplayed by the poor. One group of participants in Takhtakupyr, Uzbekistan, remembered:

> The absence of bread and the necessity to send the children to the neighbour, since they had already gone to ask for bread several times before and hesitated to go again ... The relative who died in the hospital because they could not buy the required medicine in time ... Their children had forgotten the taste of sugar and meat ... Their children could not go to school due to the absence of clothes and shoes.
>
> (Narayan et al., 2000b: 13)

The study report notes: 'All this caused tears of despair' (Narayan et al., 2000b: 13). Yet a central finding of the researchers was that material wealth is not as important as a sense of well-being. But there is no indication that any of the above problems could be resolved by a better sense of well-being rather than by more money – a higher per capita income across the region or country, and a society which was able to develop in a more all-rounded fashion.

The report is packed with examples of the material desires of poor people, yet the study chooses to reinterpret the dominant desire as for 'not a lot' of material development and for well-being over wealth. The participants repeatedly emphasize their need for food, housing, clothes, jobs, land, and for access to schools and health facilities. They aspire for infrastructure such as roads, transport, water and electricity. A substantial degree of material development is implicit if not explicit in these expressed needs and desires. The overall unreliability of the study methodology contrasts with the brash confidence of the study report in asserting that the poorest should become the object of development policy and that the poorest desire a sense of well-being more than material development. This suggests that the reconceptualization of development could be 'driven' more by the researchers' own preconceived agenda than by the poor themselves. In the following sections the broader reorientation of World Bank development policy is considered. The approach of downgrading the importance of material economic development and extending the regulatory remits of the World Bank appear to have developed some time before the 'voices of the poor' were consulted. These sections strengthen the suggestion that the 'voices' of the poorest are in fact being used to legitimize a pre-existing World Bank agenda.

Poverty reduction?

For the World Bank, development policy in the poorest countries is now focused on the most deprived sections of society. It is through this focus on the most marginalized and poorest people that the World Bank has been able to gain substantial legitimacy for its regulatory interventions. This is in sharp contrast to the situation in June 1995, when James Wolfensohn became World Bank Group president. At this time, the credibility of the Bank's policies and interventions was at an all time low and the Bank was facing a serious crisis of credibility. The World Bank model had failed to account for the success of the 'Asian miracle', structural adjustment had failed to deliver high and sustained levels of growth in the least developed countries, the free market was seen to be failing in Eastern Europe, and in 1994–95 economic crisis hit the Bank's star performer Mexico. These developments all called into question fundamental tenets of the World Bank's approach to development. The economic policies, which had for a protracted period been confidently prescribed by the Bank, were seriously compromised.

The Bank was also facing serious criticism from without. The protests of the various non-governmental organizations in the '50 Years Is Enough' campaign made a critical presence felt precisely at the time when the World Bank's uncertainty was at its peak. Probably more decisively, powerful figures within Western governments and international institutions were voicing harsh criticism, even proposing the abolition and, perhaps ironically, the privatization of the World Bank. At this moment, as Martin Wolf noted in the *Financial Times* (1995: 8), the Bank was 'neither confident nor popular' (see further, Pender, 2001a). The appointment of James Wolfensohn was widely regarded as a reaction to the loss of confidence in the World Bank as an effective international institution. His mission was to carve out a new role for the Bank, to build a new legitimacy for its interventions. It was he who had, as Michael Prest noted in *Prospect*, the job of overseeing the redefinition of the Bank's mission and renewing its sense of purpose (1996).

Wolfensohn immediately embarked on a fundamental overhaul of the Bank's policy outlook and mode of operation. A central aspect of this was the refocusing of the Bank's mission away from any association with society-wide development towards a focus on the poorest most marginalized people in poor societies. This was justified through a thorough revision of the Bank's approach to development and its understanding of poverty. An important influence in the reshaping of World Bank development policy was the deliberations of the High-level Group of Experts on Development Strategy and Management of the Market Economy. Initiated by the United Nations Secretary General in 1993, these deliberations took place over five meetings held between 1994 and 1996. The purpose of these discussions was 'to analyse key aspects of development policy in the light of the new thinking on economic and social issues that has evolved over recent years' (Malinvaud, 1997: ix). These deliberations were highly significant for the future direction of World Bank policy. Three of the experts involved – Joseph Stiglitz, Amartya Sen and Nicholas Stern – had a pivotal influence on the reorientation of the Bank with the integration of 'new thinking' into the World Bank's development approach.

The exponents of the new development consensus uphold a new terminology reflecting the changed values underpinning development policy. James Wolfensohn recently suggested that: 'The Bank, commentators from all horizons, and the Prime Minister of France agree with Amartya Sen's view that development is freedom', before arguing that 'today, people are the true ends of development' (2000b). Development as freedom, as quality of life, as well-being, is strongly and self-consciously counterposed to 'narrow' economic development. There are two key aspects to this reorientation, initially conceptualized by Amartya Sen and subsequently integrated, in modified form, into World Bank development policy. Indeed, Sen's recent important contribution to the development debate, 'Development as Freedom', is based on a series of speeches delivered to the World Bank in 1996 and 1997, at Wolfensohn's invitation.

Sen, firstly, upholds a reorientation of development policy from a focus on achieving rapid economic growth, to a focus on the most deprived in the present generation (1997a: 9). His concern is with 'placing the appropriate valuation on the terrible deprivations that exist right now (even when balanced against very large gains to the more prosperous future generations)'. Ameliorating the misery of today takes priority over a development strategy that initiates measures focused on the overall material improvement of society. This focus on immediate deprivation implies a radical shift in the tempo of the development process. Sen criticizes a 'fierce', 'blood, sweat and tears' approach which, he argues, unacceptably neglects 'the well-being and quality of life in the present' (1997a: 5). He upholds an approach to development which is an essentially 'friendly' process, with a focus on 'helping each other and oneself' and 'getting by with a little assistance'. Secondly, he is at pains to emphasize that there is more to well-being than wealth. 'Comparisons of real incomes', he argues, 'can ... be very deceptive in examining the quality of life'. He notes that, despite a much greater level of real income, residents of Harlem, USA, have 'systematically lower chances of surviving to a ripe old age' than residents of China, Sri Lanka or Kerala, India. Sen concludes that: 'It would be a mistake to base a development strategy only on the enhancement of real incomes' (1997b: 39).

Since the mid-1990s, the World Bank has given a qualitatively new emphasis to poverty reduction, described by Wolfensohn as a 'new, sharply focused approach' (2000a). As Stiglitz states, there is 'an increased focus on whether, taken as a whole, the government's actions and the institutional environment support the goal of poverty reduction' (1999: 580). Kanbur and Vines note 'the current crusade within the Bank to make poverty reduction the core issue in the Bank's agenda at the beginning of the century' (2000: 88). 'Our mission', declares the World Bank's website, 'is a world without poverty'.[2] However, mirroring Sen's reconceptualization of the development process, the World Bank has sharply reoriented its use of the concept of poverty. As Kanbur and Squire highlight, the common usage of the term 'poverty' has traditionally related to material deprivation (2001: 185). They quote the definition of 'poverty' in Merriam-Webster's Collegiate Dictionary as 'the state of one who lacks a usual or socially acceptable amount of money or material possessions' and emphasize that the World Bank's has redefined the meaning of 'poverty'. They suggest that the World Bank's (1999) definition:

> ... represents a marked difference from conventional definitions in that it does not mention income or expenditure but focuses on well-being as revealed by nutritional status, educational attainment, and health status. To be sure, income may be important to the realisation of these outcomes, but there is no universal or guaranteed transformation of income into these outcomes.

Kanbur and Squire note that the additional themes of literacy, risk, vulnerability and voice have been incorporated into the World Bank's conception of poverty. As the *World Development Report 2000/2001* elaborates:

> This report accepts the now traditional view of poverty as encompassing not only material deprivation but also low achievements in education and in health ... This report also broadens the notion of poverty to include vulnerability and exposure to risk – and voicelessness and powerlessness.
>
> (World Bank, 2000a: 15)

The World Bank has also reconceptualized the process of development. Replacing the 'blood, sweat and tears' approach focusing on the achievement of rapid economic growth is a 'friendlier' one that declares holism its guiding principle. The World Bank suggests there is a need to 'reach beyond economics to address societal issues in a holistic fashion' (1999: 14). For Wolfensohn (1998b):

> Development is about getting the macroeconomic right – yes; but it is also about building the roads, empowering the people, writing the laws, recognising the women, eliminating the corruption, educating the girls, building the banking systems, protecting the environment, inoculating the children ... Development is about putting all the component parts in place – together and in harmony.

Wolfensohn emphasizes how far perspectives have shifted and argues that, in today's World Bank, 'there is very little talk about macro-economic theory in the traditional sense' (1998a: 59). Similarly, Ravi Kanbur, the initial director of the World Bank's *World Development Report 2000/2001*, notes the 'complete flip around', over the course of the 1990s, in the World Bank's approach to development (Kanbur et al., 2000: 95). The Comprehensive Development Framework emphasizes the importance of addressing all aspects of deprivation together. As Wolfensohn writes:

> We have learned that traditional elements of strategies to foster growth – macroeconomic stability and market-friendly reforms – are essential for reducing poverty. But now we also recognise the need for much more emphasis on laying the institutional and social foundations for the development process and on managing vulnerability and encouraging participation to ensure inclusive growth.
>
> (World Bank, 2000: vi)

New regulatory controls

A central aspect of this shift is the far greater scope of development policy. As Hoff and Stiglitz note: 'Development is no longer seen primarily as a process of capital accumulation but rather as a process of organisational change' (2001: 389). Development policy now has something to say about the most appropriate way to organize virtually every aspect of society. It is in this sense that the 'comprehensive' aspect of the CDF marks a clear departure. Comprehensive development incorporates a broader set of objectives that have taken primacy over and above economic and formally non-political objectives. Regarding these broader objectives, Stern and Stiglitz have concluded that: 'while all of these may be summarised within the rubric of "raising living standards", they go far beyond the standard objective of increasing GDP per capita' (1997: 254). 'Far beyond' is no understatement. The objectives of World Bank development policy are virtually all encompassing, reflecting a vision of extensive social regulation. As Wolfensohn (1998b) argues:

> In a global economy it is the totality of change in a country that matters…Too often we have focused too much on the economics, without a sufficient understanding of the social, the political, the environmental, and the cultural aspects of society.

This theme was taken up by Joseph Stiglitz when he suggested that: 'Views of development have changed from a more narrow focus on solving certain technical problems, like lowering tariffs, to a broader one of the transformation of society' (1999: 582). The reorientation of World Bank development policy towards the poorest, and the expansion of the development agenda to address multiple aspects of deprivation, have contributed significantly to a relegitimization of the capacity of the World Bank to dictate the policy agenda in the world's poorest countries. Tanzania's Poverty Reduction Strategy Paper is a good illustration of how many poor countries now acquiesce to the World Bank agenda of focusing resources towards the poorest.

Tanzania's PRSP, which was initiated in August 2000, commits the country to confine its development strategy to meeting the needs of the poorest. It commits state spending to be sharply focused towards basic education, primary health, rural roads, the judiciary, agricultural research and HIV/AIDS. It is envisaged, for example, that basic education alone will consume around a quarter of discretionary government expenditure by financial year 2002/3 (United Republic of Tanzania, 2000: 25). Within the education sector, basic education is strongly prioritized over secondary education. Whereas the government plans to increase funds for the development of basic education from 173.3 billion Tanzania shillings in 2001/2 to 215.5 billion in 2003/4, it plans to decrease the funds available for the development of secondary education from 8.4 billion in 2001/2 to 2.6 billion in 2003/4 (United Republic of Tanzania, 2001: 22). Funds to develop secondary education will be around 1 per cent of the funds available to develop basic education. Tanzania's limited government resources are to be focused single-mindedly on the perceived needs of the very poorest.

Such is the strength of the consensus today that poor countries should confine their activities to addressing the concerns of the poorest people that in 2001 Tanzania's proposal to spend $40m on a BAe Systems air traffic control system with civilian and military capacity was met with outrage (Pender, 2001b). Oxfam attacked the proposed purchase of an air traffic control system as immoral when problems of basic health and education remained. The *Guardian* in its editorial 'Britain must block the Tanzania deal' suggested that it was 'barely believable' that the UK government, which in the past had emphasized its commitment to poverty reduction, should allow such a deal to go through (2001b). The *Financial Times* in its editorial 'Controlling Tanzania' opposed an export licence on the grounds that 'spending $40m on a state-of-the-art air traffic control system is ... difficult to square ... with the eradication of poverty' (2001).

Tanzania's Poverty Reduction Strategy highlights how the 'Voices of the Poor' consultations have been used to legitimize World Bank priorities over and above those of the people consulted. The notable finding of the *Voices of the Poor* study in Tanzania was that basic education was not perceived to be a major priority. The report states that: 'Despite the fact that the poor recognise the value of education and make much effort to send their children to school, the PPA [Participatory Poverty Assessment] found that lack of education was not seen by them as an important cause of poverty' (Narayan et al., 1997: 16). Education was regarded as the number one problem by 2 per cent of men and 1 per cent of women. However, as noted above, basic education has been prioritized and is set to consume 25 per cent of public spending. When the views of the poorest conflict with the views of the donors, they are overridden by the donor agenda which takes precedence.

The World Bank's claim that poor countries own the poverty reduction process is challenged by the air traffic control controversy. While a joint International Monetary Fund/World Bank report suggests that 'the PRSP process is strongly owned domestically' (IMF et al., 2001), the government of Tanzania came under intense pressure from the World

Bank and the international community to change its decision. The World Bank indeed won plaudits for openly criticizing the purchase as inappropriate for Tanzania's needs – 'too expensive and not adequate for civil aviation' (cited in *Guardian*, 2001a). Whatever the outcome of the furore, it is clear that the external priorities imposed on Tanzania undermine any genuine country ownership. The UK government, while granting the export licence, failed to mount an effective defence of its decision, and promised to introduce legislation to ensure that future deals with poor countries were subject to stringent sustainable development criteria, preventing any such deal going through in the future. While technological systems such an air traffic control system would be considered as essential for any modern state, poor countries will effectively be restricted to investment projects that are deemed to fit in with the 'basic needs' straightjacket increasingly imposed on poor countries.

Conclusion: empowering the poor?

The World Bank has successfully legitimized the extension of regulatory intervention in the poorest countries of the world. This has been achieved by championing the cause of the poorest people in poor societies. The World Bank has used their 'voices' to gain a powerful moral credibility that has allowed it to dictate the developmental agenda to poor country governments. The World Bank has gained legitimacy for greater regulatory interventions in poor country society than even during the now discredited regimes of structural adjustment. The World Bank's claim that poor countries 'own' their development strategy is false. Poor country governments have to demonstrate a commitment to a World Bank determined 'good policy environment' and to poverty reduction. If they do not, development finance will be withheld and the World Bank will cultivate political opposition forces through support for individual 'development entrepreneurs' and alternative 'social movements'.

The focus on the poorest adds considerable weight to this external coercion. By deploying the moral force associated with the argument that development policy should be directed to the needs of the poorest, the World Bank gains credibility for regulatory coercion. The poor may be extensively consulted and consistently given 'voice' by the World Bank, but they are far from empowered by this process. The World Bank claim to authentically reflect the views of the poorest is a false one. The example of Tanzania highlights how the expressed priorities of both the poor and poor country governments can be easily manipulated and overridden by the priorities of the international institutions. More importantly, as their government has a diminished capacity to formulate and implement its own development strategy, the poor are deprived of any effective opportunity to autonomously 'voice' their own social, economic and political interests through the democratic process.

The poor are not only disempowered by the World Banks's marginalization of the political process, the World Bank's focus on the poorest will also have the paradoxical effect of institutionalizing poverty. In poor societies the deprivation of the poorest is inextricably linked to the overall lack of development of society. The focus on the poorest prioritizes amelioration over development, and in this sense institutionalizes poverty and non-development. Indeed, the moral force associated with the focus on the poorest has obscured a serious retreat in the scope of the development agenda for the poorest countries in the world. Development used to imply society-wide material transformation. For a low-income country this would perhaps be the achievement of middle-income country status as a step towards fully realizing the possibilities of material development. Mkandawire and Soludo describe a serious 'lowering of expectations' and note that: 'After 1994 "development" disappeared from the adjustment discourse to such an extent that the success indicators were confined to the movement of policy instruments, rather than the real economy' (1999: 91). Today, as considered above, for the world's poorest countries, 'development' is being redefined in such a way as to downgrade the significance of material improvement.

A focus on the needs of the poorest is strongly counterposed to an approach which focuses on achieving high and sustained economic growth. Yet achieving consistently high economic growth is surely a key aspect of the resolution of the pressing problems of underdevelopment in the world today. As Robert Wade notes of recent trends in the World Bank:

> There is a dangerous tendency in development thinking ... to shift attention from growth towards non-income aspects of poverty and from hard-nosed technical subjects such as industrial technology policy and irrigation investment towards 'soft-nosed' issues – education, health, participation, legal reform and cultural projects ... The growth crisis is itself an important proximate cause of the rising numbers in poverty and should be right at the forefront of the development debate ...
>
> (2001: 135–6)

The World Bank has used the 'voices of the poor' to claim that well-being is independent of growth and material development. The Bank's success in promoting this approach illustrates a growing ambivalence about economic growth, and the importance of reasserting the right to development. The first step in this process should be to question the moral authority which the World Bank has gained by manipulating the 'voices of the poor' to legitimize its regulatory control. The argument that the poorest can somehow be empowered without overall societal development should be firmly rejected.

Notes

1. The *Voices of the Poor* study has been synthesized in three volumes (Narayan et al., 2000a, 2000b and 2000c). Each is favourably prefaced by James Wolfensohn, World Bank Group president. For examples of major World Bank studies which consistently defer to the 'voices of the poor' see World Bank (2000a and 2002). The influence of the *Voices of the Poor* study on development policy thinking can be seen, for example, in Easterly (2001).
2. More information available from: <http://www.worldbank.org>.

6
The Limits of Human Rights and Cosmopolitan Citizenship

David Chandler

Introduction[1]

This chapter addresses the question of how to assess the trend towards increasing prominence for individual rights in the international sphere and the restricted interpretation of traditional rights of sovereign independence and self-government. Over the last decade, many leading international relations theorists have developed a cosmopolitan perspective, which sees current trends as benign or potentially positive.[2] Cosmopolitan international relations theorists envisage a process of expanding cosmopolitan democracy and global governance, in which for the first time there is the possibility of global issues being addressed on the basis of new forms of democracy, derived from the universal rights of global citizens. They suggest that, rather than focus attention on the territorially-limited rights of the citizen at the level of the nation-state, more emphasis should be placed on extending democracy and human rights to the international sphere.

This chapter highlights problems with extending the concept of rights beyond the bounds of the sovereign state, without a mechanism of making these new rights accountable to their subjects. It argues that the emerging gap between holders of cosmopolitan rights and those with duties tends to create dependency rather than to empower. It suggests that, while the new rights remain tenuous, there is a danger that the cosmopolitan framework can legitimize the abrogation of the existing rights of democracy and self-government codified in the UN Charter framework. The following section raises some theoretical questions about the essence of the cosmopolitan perspective: the extension of democracy beyond states and the development of the global citizen as a subject of international law. Further sections will develop the theoretical and practical implications of the cosmopolitan framework for questions of state sovereignty and the relationship between states and international institutions.

Cosmopolitan democracy?

Leading cosmopolitan theorists seek to challenge the inter-state framework of the UN Charter, established in the aftermath of the Second World War, which prioritized the principles of sovereign equality and of non-intervention. They argue that these principles need to be replaced by new ones based on a higher level of public accountability, which make the universal individual rights of members of 'global society' the primary focus. Rather than the rights of states being the founding principle of international society it should be the rights of individual citizens. Today, a new consensus is forming that 'there is a pressing need to rethink the concept and practice of sovereignty' (Camilleri and Falk, 1992). Andrea Bianchi argues that the values and principles governing international law are under challenge:

> The two opposite poles of the spectrum are evident. On the one hand, there stands the principle of sovereignty with its many corollaries ... on the other, the notion that fundamental human rights should be respected. While the first principle is the most obvious expression and ultimate guarantee of a horizontally-organized community of equal and independent states, the second view represents the emergence of values and interests ... which deeply [cut] across traditional precepts of state sovereignty and non-interference in the internal affairs of other states.
>
> (1999: 260)

Geoffrey Robertson QC, a leading advocate of individual rights and author of *Crimes Against Humanity: the Struggle for Global Justice*, argues:

> Customary international law is in the human rights field anachronistic, to the extent that it is an emanation of agreements between sovereign states ... [M]illions of ordinary men and women ... do not talk about *jus cogens* and *erga omnes*: they believe in the simple language of the Universal Declaration, and they are not bound by Article 2(7) of the UN Charter to avert their eyes from repression in foreign countries ... These citizens, of global society rather than the nation state, cannot understand why human rights rules should not rule.
>
> (1999: 82)

Cosmopolitan democrats argue that democracy and accountability can no longer be equated with sovereignty and non-intervention: 'democracy must transcend the borders of single states and assert itself on a global level' (Archibugi, 2000: 144). To meet the needs of cosmopolitan or global citizens it is necessary to extend democracy beyond the nation-state. David Beetham argues that in a world of nation states 'the *demos* that is democracy's subject has come to be defined almost exclusively in national terms, and the scope of democratic rights has been limited to the bounds of the nation state' (1999: 137). He suggests that in the same way that democracy was extended from the level of the town to that of the state in the eighteenth century it should, in the twenty-first century, be extended from the nation to humankind as a whole.

The reason for this new and more expansive institutionalization of democracy is held to be the impact of globalizing processes, which have created a 'democratic deficit' at the national level. Daniele Archibugi and David Held assert that decisions made democratically by citizens of one state or region can no longer be considered to be truly democratic if they affect the rights of 'non-citizens', i.e. those outside that community, without those people having a say. Held argues that, for example, villagers in sub-Saharan Africa, who live at the margins of some of the central power structures and hierarchies of the global order, are profoundly affected by the policies made in these inter-state forums (1998: 14). Archibugi stresses that the inequalities of global power relations mean that decisions democratically restricted to the nation-state cannot be considered democratic from a cosmopolitan perspective:

> ... few decisions made in one state are autonomous from those made in others. A decision on the interest rate in Germany has significant consequences for employment in Greece, Portugal and Italy. A state's decision to use nuclear energy has environmental consequences for the citizens of neighbouring countries. Immigration policies in the European Union have a significant impact on the economic development of Mediterranean Africa. All this happens without the affected citizens having a say in the matter.
>
> (1998: 204)

Cosmopolitans highlight that, for democracy to exist in a globalized world, it is necessary to have the consent of the entire community which will be affected by a particular decision. To this end, new political constituencies need to be created to address these questions. These constituencies may be smaller or larger than the nation-state, depending on the issue at stake. For Held, in a cosmopolitan democratic system:

> People can enjoy membership in the diverse communities which significantly affect them and, accordingly, access to a variety of forms of political participation. Citizenship would be extended, in principle, to membership in all cross-cutting political communities, from the local to the global.
>
> (1995: 272)

In order to address this 'democratic deficit', cosmopolitans propose replacing the territorially-bounded political community of the state as the subject of international decision-making by new flexible frameworks based on the rights of the global citizen, freed from territorial restrictions. To quote Archibugi:

> If some global questions are to be handled according to democratic criteria, there must be political representation for citizens in global affairs, independently and autonomously of their political representation in domestic affairs. The unit should be the individual, although the mechanisms for participation and representation may vary according to the nature and scope of the issues discussed.
>
> (1998: 212)

Ken Booth similarly asserts the centrality of the individual for cosmopolitan democracy, rooting this in the acceptance of universal human rights:

> In 1948, with the Universal Declaration of Human Rights, the individual was potentially brought back to the centre. A building block was constructed for the possible development of a cosmopolitan democracy in a world of post-sovereign states ... This is the hope of progressively leaving behind the politics of the concentration camp – the ultimate sovereign space – for a cosmopolitan democracy aimed at reinventing global human being – being human globally – based on the politics of the-I-that-is-an-other, and badged with common humanity.
>
> (1999: 65–6)

Cosmopolitans argue that there is still an important role for the state and for representative democracy, but that these institutions cannot have the final say in decision-making. In certain circumstances, where this is not democratic enough it must be possible for sovereignty to be overridden by institutions which are 'autonomous and independent' and whose legitimacy is derived from the universal rights of the global citizen, unconstrained by the nation-state framework. This limitation on state-based mechanisms of democracy and accountability, and on states as the subjects of international law, relies on the possibility of a 'higher law' derived from the individual global citizen as a new, and prior, subject of international relations. It is at this point that the theoretical underpinnings of the cosmopolitan project appear fragile. The citizen-subject of international decision-making appears overburdened with theoretical (let alone practical) problems.

Cosmopolitan theorists accept that there is no global state or global federation or institutional framework and also argue that, if there were, it would be a bad thing. They are clear that the establishment of democratic institutions on a global level would meet the opposition of nation-states and that, even if this could be brought into existence, it would involve such a high level of homogenization, through social, economic and cultural regulation, that it could only be imposed through war and repression.[3] In this case, there can be no cosmopolitan framework of formal political rights in which individual citizens would be represented as political equals. The global citizen cannot have the same sorts of rights as the citizen of a nation-state. The formal rights of the global citizen are a thorny issue for cosmopolitan theorists and for many the question falls 'outside the scope' of their immediate concerns (Kaldor, 1999a: 148). Archibugi states: 'World citizenship does not necessarily have to assume all the demands of national citizenship. The real problem is to identify the areas in which citizens should have rights and duties as inhabitants of the world rather than of secular states' (1998: 216).

The rights of the global citizen are certainly 'less demanding'. For cosmopolitan theorists, the new institutions through which the cosmopolitan citizen can exercise his or her rights must exist independently of states and their governments. Theorists who develop the implications of this approach go further, and add that national political parties, which are orientated around national questions rather than global ones, also cannot be vehicles for cosmopolitan citizenship, capable of representing individuals on global issues (Archibugi, 2000: 146). For this reason the global citizen can only be represented through global or transnational civil society, which it is argued can hold governments to account, through campaigning and media pressure (Beetham, 1999: 142).

There are several difficulties with this perspective. Firstly, there is little agreement on the extent to which civil society groups can influence government policy-making and thereby create a new mechanism of political 'accountability' (Forsythe, 2000: 169; Charnovitz, 1997). Secondly, and most importantly, even if civil society groups did wield influence over policy-makers, this has little relationship to democratic accountability, precisely because civil society operates outside the sphere of formal politics. Civil society organizations – whether they are community groups, single issue pressure groups, NGOs, grassroots campaigns, charities, media organizations, research groups, or non-government-funded policy advisers – operate, by definition, outside the political sphere of democratic equality and accountability. While it is often possible for individuals to participate in the organizations of global civil society, it is difficult to accept the assertion that 'signing petitions for and donating charitable contributions to such organisations must surely count as acts of world citizenship' (Heater, 1999: 144).

The opportunity for participation depends on the organization concerned. For example, many of the NGOs most active and influential in defending rights, like Human Rights Watch, the International Crisis Group or the International Commission of Jurists, have no mass membership and concentrate on elite advocates to enable them to gain admittance to government and international officials (Forsythe, 2000: 167–8; Charnovitz, 1997: 270; de Waal, 1997b). The extent of any participation differs between individuals and generally stops short of having any say over policy. As Jenny Bates, at the Progressive Policy Institute, states: 'NGOs are not elected and, unlike governments, need not answer to the broad public they claim to represent' (cited in Bosco, 2000). There is no direct link between (non-)participation and any conception of citizenship rights which can be given content through formal mechanisms of democratic accountability. We are not all equally involved in civil society, we do not vote for civil society policies and we cannot hold civil society to account.

Thirdly, global civil society is no less shaped by national governments and state-based political structures than national political parties and other representative institutions. Without a global state or a global political framework, it is debatable whether it is possible to talk about a 'global' civil society beyond the nation state. Martin Köhler, for example, argues that it is misleading to talk of a 'global' or 'transnational civil society' in the same way as the independent realm of civil society within the domestic sphere:

> [T]he transnational public sphere itself cannot be conceived of simply as the extension of the national one. The very concept of the public

sphere is intrinsically bound up in structures of authority and accountability which do not exist in the transnational realm ... [A]s long as the state continues to be the only site of political authority in international relations, it is impossible for a transnational public sphere ... to emerge.

(1998: 233)

In the cosmopolitan framework, it would appear problematic to talk about the exercise of rights, or of democracy, outside the framework of nation-states. As Steve Charnovitz highlights, even the involvement of international NGOs in policy-making cannot make nation-states more accountable. The establishment of NGO advisory committees actually gives nation-state governments greater control over decision-making as the real power belongs to the international officials who determine which NGOs to appoint (1997: 283). This reality of dependency is acknowledged in the frameworks articulated by Archibugi and Held, and in similar reform proposals forwarded by the Commission on Global Governance. These allow citizens and civil society groups to participate in global or regional institutional forums where they have specific competencies, for example in those that deal with the environment, population issues, development or disarmament. However, this participation 'would supplement but not replace existing inter-governmental organizations'. As Archibugi stresses: 'Their function would be essentially advisory and not executive' (1998: 219).

Despite the desires of cosmopolitan advocates, there appears to be little evidence of the claims of any 'new' levels of democracy or political accountability promised to the global citizen, as opposed the humble citizen of the nation-state, who can formally hold his or her government to account. In fact, any search for the formal democratic rights of the cosmopolitan citizen would be a fruitless one. The new rights that the cosmopolitan citizen possesses cannot be located within the liberal rights tradition, which equates the rights-holder and the duty-holder within the same legal subject. These 'new' rights do not manifest themselves at the level of the citizen but rather at the level of international institutions:

Rights ought to relate, in the first instance, to the sphere of survival and to issues which cross national boundaries. In relation to these rights, world citizens undersign certain duties which enable global institutions to perform a function of temporary replacement, subsidiarity and substitution *vis-à-vis* national institutions.

(Archibugi, 1998: 217)

The new 'rights' of global citizens are not exercised by the rights-holders but by international institutions, which have new 'duties' corresponding to the new rights created. This equation of the 'right' of the global citizen or global civil society with the 'duty' of international institutions creates a new level of rights on paper but is problematic in practice:

> The institutions of global civil society would exercise direct control in one essential area: the prevention and impediment of acts of genocide or domicide. To do so they would be entitled to demand the immediate intervention of the governments of all states.
>
> (Archibugi, 1998: 219)

The exercise of this right of protection or prevention is dependent on the actions of international institutions and major powers, which have the economic and the military resources to intervene. The new rights of cosmopolitan citizens, additional to their territorial citizenship rights, are ones which they cannot act on or exercise themselves, and in this crucial respect the new rights are highly conditional. While there may be a duty to protect the new rights of the cosmopolitan citizen the cosmopolitan framework provides no mechanism of accountability to give content to these rights. There is no link between the 'right' and the 'duty' of its enforcement. The additional rights upheld in the cosmopolitan framework turn out to be a chimera. As David Beetham notes: 'the weak point in this regime of course remains enforcement' (1999: 140). Archibugi concedes:

> There is undoubtedly a contradiction here: the cosmopolitical project would delegate to structures devoid of coercive powers (... institutions of the world's citizens) the job of establishing when force should be used, while asking states, who monopolize the means of military might, to acquiesce in their decisions.
>
> (2000: 149)

As Neil Stammers writes, the imperative of action to defend the human rights of cosmopolitan citizens ironically entails a realpolitik which is highly state-centric (1999: 992). Rather than exercising 'direct control' the cosmopolitan citizens and cosmopolitan civil society groups are dependent on nation-states to accede to their claims. The rights of democratic accountability remain restricted to the 'limited' sphere of the national *demos*.

The ethical approach

While the previous section considered the limited and conditional nature of the new rights of the cosmopolitan citizen, this section seeks to outline the consequences of this approach for the rights of state sovereignty and representative democracy. If the cosmopolitan framework merely held out the promise of additional rights, but still needed to develop the theory further to establish mechanisms through which these rights could be realized, there would be little problem. In this case, one could perhaps sympathize with what Held terms the 'embedded utopianism' inherent in the project, or with Mary Kaldor's defence of the need for a 'ridiculously utopian project', and with Archibugi's advocacy for the 'politics of cosmopolitan dreams' (Held, 1995: 286; Kaldor, 1999b: 212, Archibugi, 2002: 38). However, what makes the cosmopolitan project important is not so much the chimera of empowering global citizenship but the consequences which this framework has for the defence of existing civil and democratic rights. While the new rights may be difficult to realize, the cosmopolitan cause has helped cohere a powerful consensus on the need to recast the relationship between international institutions and the nation-state.

Far from a utopian theory of hope for progress and the development of democracy, cosmopolitan theory appears to be a reflection of a growing disillusionment with politics at the international level. Cosmopolitan theorists are disappointed that after the end of the Cold War the resources of international society have not been devoted towards resolving outstanding 'global concerns'. Liberal international relations theorists often display a teleological or idealistic view of progress at an international level, assuming that the creation of international society in itself established a framework through which differences could be put aside and new means developed for the resolution of global problems. It appears that the only thing stopping progress today, after the 'diversion' of the Cold War, is the narrow preoccupation of nation-states with appeasing their electorates as opposed to addressing global concerns.

This disillusionment with the narrow or selfish interests of realpolitik, and its legitimization through democratic mandates, has resulted in a growing attention to the prioritization of ethical or moral approaches. Philip Allott, for example, argues that traditional international relations theory is based on Machiavellism: 'the overriding of general moral duty by *raison d'état*', a paradoxical 'morality of immorality' (1999: 34). For Allott, this privileging of the political sphere over the ethical meant that international relations theory tended to be innately conservative and uncritical:

> Machiavellism was ... a calculated negation of a long tradition which conceived of values that transcend the power of even the holders of the highest forms of social power. Those ideas – especially ideas of justice and natural law, but also all those philosophies which speak of 'the good' or 'the good life' – were transcendental and aspirational and critical in character; that is to say they were conceived of as an *ideal* which could not be overridden or even abridged by the merely *actual*, and in relation to which the actual should be oriented and would be judged. The ideal makes possible a morality of society.
>
> (1999: 35)

In contrast to realist approaches to politics and international relations, which have been accused of justifying the status quo, ethical international relations theory sets out a radical agenda of criticism. Booth asserts that the narrow focus on the political sphere of state interests and inter-state rivalry in international relations theory has become a barrier to developing new approaches which can address the problems of the international arena: 'What is needed must have *moral* at its centre because the fundamental questions of how we might and can live together concern values, not instrumental rationality' (1995: 110). He argues:

> To my mind the twenty-first will be the century of ethics, and global ethics at that. What I would like to see is a shift in the focus of the study of international relations from accumulating knowledge about 'relations between states' (what might be called the 'dismal science' of Cold War international relations) to thinking about ethics on a global scale.
>
> (1995: 109–10)

Andrew Linklater, similarly, argues that international relations theory needs to develop a 'bolder moral standpoint' (cited in Wheeler, 1996: 128). Richard Falk, drawing on Held and Archibugi's emphasis on the agency of global civil society, suggests that 'normative democracy' may be the best description of a unifying cosmopolitan ideology which can galvanize social change. He states that: 'I prefer normative to substantive democracy because of its highlighting of ethical and legal norms, thereby reconnecting politics with moral purpose and values ...' (2000: 171).

This chapter suggests that the utopian aspects of cosmopolitan theory stem from the fact that there is more attention paid to the ethical ends of cosmopolitan democracy than there is to the mechanisms and means of ensuring these. The irony is that, despite the talk about extending and deepening democracy, cosmopolitan theory is not really concerned with establishing new frameworks for democracy on the international level. The question that cosmopolitans seek to address appears to be rather how to legitimize moral and ethical policy ends against the 'narrow limits' of democracy and sovereign government. The cosmopolitans and global governance advocates are hostile to sovereignty, and strongly in favour of international regulation of the sovereign sphere, but not in order to strengthen the mechanisms of democratic accountability. They challenge the existing order because they represent a growing belief that progressive ends – such as the protection of human rights, international peace or sustainable development – would be more achievable without the constraints of popular democracy and universal state sovereignty.

In fact, the moral and ethical premises of cosmopolitan democracy necessarily lead advocates of this perspective to degrade the rights framework of democracy and political equality. For cosmopolitans, the artificial construction of the global citizen-subject is the key concept in their attempt to privilege the sphere of morality and ethics over that of politics. The cosmopolitan, or non-national, democratic subject is defined through being freed from the political framework of representative democracy based on the nation-state. The cosmopolitan citizen, by definition, has no fixed territorial identity and so tends to be 'represented' on a particular issue through the campaigning work of international NGOs which are not tied to a particular nation-state. Mary Kaldor argues that 'the role of NGOs is not to be representative but to raise awareness', adding that the 'appeal is to moral conscience' not to political majorities (2001). Johan Galtung, similarly, gives support to this form of 'empowerment', which he terms 'democracy by articulation, not by representation' (2000: 155).

In this respect, cosmopolitan theorists reflect broader political trends towards the privileging of normative claims. Political activity is increasingly undertaken outside of traditional political parties and is becoming a sphere dominated by advocacy groups and single-issue campaigns who do not seek to garner votes but to lobby or gain publicity for their claims. Today, groups which campaign on a minority cause often support their case by exaggerating their moral claim to make up for political weakness. For example, if a group opposes the construction of a hydro-electric dam in another country or the construction of a motorway or the building of an out-of-town superstore closer to home, they do not say they are just representing the personal views of those involved. Instead, they argue that they have a greater claim, not as individuals but as advocates for the rights of others, such as the rights of rare butterflies or the natural diversity that would be destroyed if these developments went ahead. They are, in fact, arguing against formal democracy, and suggesting that democracy should come second to the ethical or moral concerns which they champion.

Groups that disapprove of mass production today often argue that democracy must be overridden by the 'rights' of the environment or the 'rights' of future generations. These rights are fictitious. The subjects of these rights cannot speak or act for themselves. Often it is radical critics, who oppose the injustices of the world, who bolster their cause through the reliance on fictitious rights. Cosmopolitan theorists start from a radical critique of existing norms in international relations, but it is a critique based on moral advocacy. The essence of cosmopolitan democracy vis-à-vis traditional views of liberal democracy, is that the new citizenship 'rights' it calls for are not democratic rights but moral claims. These 'rights' are considered to be so important that on a moral or an ethical basis they 'trump' democracy or sovereignty. Moral or ethical rights are claims which cannot be legitimized politically through democracy and universal equality.[4] In this context, to talk of the rights of global citizens or of cosmopolitan democracy is to create fictitious rights.

New rights for old

The problem with fictitious rights is that they are not as radical as they sound. In fact, fictitious rights are at the core of new mandates for international institutions to intervene against sovereignty. Fictitious rights separate rights from their subject. The rights of the cosmopolitan citizen are outside the control of their subject in much the same way as animal rights or environmental rights cannot be acted upon by their subjects. The problem with rights without subjects is that they necessarily become a licence for undermining real existing rights, such as democracy and self-government. The proposed framework of cosmopolitan regulation, based on the fictitious rights of global citizenship rather than the nation-state, recognizes neither the democratic rights of citizens nor the collective expression of these rights in state sovereignty.

There is a fundamental difference between the liberal-democratic approach, which derives rights from self-governing human subjects, and the cosmopolitan approach of claiming rights on behalf of others. The central component of all democratic systems of rights or legal systems, and their theoretical starting point, is the individual's capacity for self-government. The subject of modern law is a person assumed to be a moral agent or self-willing actor. As a rights-bearing subject the person is not simply coerced into accepting the law by forces outside his or her influence. The law is seen to be freely accepted and to derive from his or her own will. The framework of regulation of the modern democratic system is historically and logically derived from the formal assumption of equal self-governing individuals, responsible and accountable for their actions and capable of rational decision-making. All modern doctrines of the enforcement of contract, the punishment of crime, the election of governments and the state system of international law rest on this core assumption (Heartfield, 1996). This can be usefully highlighted by a brief consideration of the different facets of a modern state's 'rights framework' or legal system.

Civil law is the clearest expression of the derivation of the law from the will of the self-governing subject. In enforcing the law of contract, civil law does not impose an alien or external goal onto individuals. In fact, the civil law only binds individuals to their word; this is an expression of the will of the legal subject as the contract is voluntarily made. There is no compulsion to higher policy goals or ends; the only object of the law is the contract between two equal contracting parties. Criminal law also assumes the equality and free will of the legal subject. The accused is represented at the court in the same way as for breaches of civil law and has the right to defend his or her interests in court equal to any other citizen. The law is binding on the individual as if it were a contract, although there is no formal contract beyond the assumption of assent to membership of a law-bound community (mythologized in social contract theory). This is clearly only notional assent, but it is through this fiction of consent that the equal rights of defendants before the law are enshrined. In constitutional law, the notional social contract is given content. For all its limitations, the principle of popular sovereignty is a thoroughly radical conception of authority from the people. It argues that the state's authority derives exclusively from the people, without any external source of either power or legitimacy.

This idealized picture reveals the centrality, to all aspects of the modern framework of rights, of the rights-bearing individual with the capacity for self-government. The source of democratic rights is the citizen, as an autonomous legal subject, rather than the abstraction of the cosmopolitan or global human individual. As Hannah Arendt noted, the concept of rights, separated from a specific political framework, would mean claimants falling back 'upon the minimum fact of human origin' (1979: 300). For Arendt:

> Equality, in contrast to all that is involved in mere existence, is not given us, but is the result of human organisation ... We are not born equal; we become equal as members of a group on the strength of our decision to guarantee ourselves mutually equal rights.
>
> (1979: 301)

The universal human subject of cosmopolitan rights may be identifiable as an individual, but unless that individual can act within a political or legal framework he or she will be unable to exercise equal legal or political rights. Norman Lewis notes:

> Placing the concept 'human' in front of 'rights' may represent a quantum leap up. But this is only in the abstract. No matter how these rights are presented, what they have in common is the fact that they are not derived from legal subjects.
>
> (1998: 85)

This central distinction in approach to the rights-subject explains why the two different rights approaches have an opposing conception of the importance of the political sphere and its institutions at the level of the state and international society. In the work of cosmopolitan theorists this distinction, and the consequent undermining of traditional liberal democratic rights, is clear. In reinterpreting rights as a moral category, as opposed to a legal and political one, a contradiction appears between the enforcement and guarantee of cosmopolitan rights and the formal equality of the liberal democratic legal and political framework. Within the ethical normative framework of cosmopolitan theory, every area of democratic accountability and formal equality is criticized while every area without formal institutionalized accountability is seen to be positive.

Firstly, the formal right of sovereign equality under international law is denigrated. The UN Charter regime was a radical break from the pre-World War Two system in which Great Power domination was accepted as legitimate. For the first time non-Western states had the same legitimacy and international rights as the more developed Western states, despite the inequality of economic and military power. Unlike the UN, which recognizes the equality of nation-states regardless of political regime, cosmopolitans argue that many regimes are illegitimate. The right to equality under international law, the central pillar of the post-colonial international system, would be a conditional or residual right under the cosmopolitan framework. As Held notes, 'sovereignty *per se* is no longer a straightforward guarantee of international legitimacy' (2000: 24). Archibugi argues that it is a matter of urgency that 'democratic procedures should somehow be assessed by external agents' (1998: 210). Beetham has developed a 'democratic audit' framework to undertake such assessments (1999: 151–94). States that fail the assessments of their legitimacy will no longer have equal standing or full sovereign rights and could be legitimately acted against in the international arena.

Cosmopolitan regulation is in fact based on the concept of sovereign inequality: that not all states should be equally involved in the establishment and adjudication of international law. Ironically, the new cosmopolitan forms of justice and rights protection involve law-making and law-enforcement, legitimized from an increasingly partial, and explicitly Western, perspective. Held, for example, argues:

> In the first instance, cosmopolitan democratic law could be promulgated and defended by those democratic states and civil societies that are able to muster the necessary political judgement and to learn how political practices and institutions must change and adapt in the new regional and global circumstances.
>
> (1995: 232)

Martin Shaw explains that behind the language of cosmopolitan universals lies the reality of legitimization through 'economic, political and military resources' which gives the Western powers a new 'duty' or 'right' to assert 'global leadership':

> This perspective can only be centred on a new unity of purpose among Western peoples and governments, since only the West has the economic, political and military resources and the democratic and multinational institutions and culture necessary to undertake it. The West has a historic responsibility to take on this global leadership...
>
> (1994: 180–1)

Secondly, the right of sovereign autonomy or self-government is undermined. Cosmopolitans assert that despite adherence to all internationally accepted formal democratic procedures, a state's government may not be truly democratic. For Archibugi: 'The governments of states do not necessarily represent global interests. On the contrary, they tend to privilege the particular interests of their own political quarter' (1998: 213). Because of this 'bias' of self-interest a decision or choice made by the *demos*, or the people, even with full information and full freedom of decision-making, would not necessarily have democratic legitimacy. In the cosmopolitan framework any decision by popular vote would be as flawed as national governments having the final say. The *demos* cannot necessarily be the final arbiter of democracy because:

> ... the choices of a people, even when made democratically, might be biased by self-interest. It may, for example, be in the interests of the French public to obtain cheap nuclear energy if they manage to dispose of radioactive waste in a Pacific isle under their control, but this will obviously be against the interests of the public living there.
>
> (Archibugi, 1998: 211)

For cosmopolitan theorists the ethical ends for which they advocate are privileged above the sphere of democracy. In this framework a small minority may be more 'democratic' than a large majority, if they have an outlook attuned to cosmopolitan aspirations. Kaldor draws out the implications of the argument when she suggests that the international community should not necessarily consult elected local representatives but seek 'to identify local advocates of cosmopolitanism' where there are 'islands of civility' (1999a: 120). Just as states cannot be equally trusted with cosmopolitan rights, neither can people. Instead of the 'limited' but fixed *demos* of the nation-state there is a highly selective '*demos*' identified by international institutions guided by the cosmopolitan impulse.

Good governance

If governments and people cannot be trusted to overcome their narrow 'political' differences and prejudices, then a new authority is needed to act in important international situations. This authority must be 'independent' of established political mechanisms of democratic accountability. Cosmopolitan theorists favour an independent and 'higher' mechanism of international regulation in the belief that under such a system the ethical ends of cosmopolitan liberalism can be enforced. The authority they wish to establish, without democratic accountability but with the legitimacy to overrule popular opinion and elected governments, is that of cosmopolitan governance. The essential attribute of 'governance' is that it is regulation freed from the formal restrictions of 'government'. Cosmopolitan governance, the less accountable power of international regulation, is the ideological counterpart to the cosmopolitan citizen, who has less rights of democratic accountability. In exchange for new 'rights' for the global individual, the cosmopolitans want to sacrifice the old rights of sovereignty, which are seen to restrict the benign and protective actions of international institutions. Kaldor suggests:

> [T]he term cosmopolitan, when applied to political institutions, implies a layer of governance that constitutes a limitation on the sovereignty of states and yet does not itself constitute a state. In other words, a cosmopolitan institution would coexist with a system of states but would override states in certain clearly defined spheres of activity.
>
> (cited in Archibugi, 1998: 216)

For Held, the framework of global governance is 'cosmopolitan democratic law', a 'domain of law different in kind from the law of states and the law made between one state and another, that is, international law' (1995: 227). This law 'transcends the particular claims of nations and states' and would be upheld by a framework of 'interlocking jurisdictions' (1995: 232). While there is no world state that is constituted politically, there are international and transnational institutions which have the authority to undermine sovereignty when the need arises regarding an issue of 'global concern'.

Held's prescription of a new form of flexible law-making, no longer formally restricted by traditional domestic or international frameworks of accountability, reflects the evolving practice of leading Western states in international intervention. Over recent years the legitimization of intervention through claims of protecting the universal rights of citizens has clashed with traditional international law restrictions on interference in the internal affairs of sovereign nation-states. The report of the Independent International Commission on Kosovo acknowledged the gap between international law and the practice of leading Western states and suggested 'the need to close the gap between legality and legitimacy' (IICK, 2000: 10). However, rather than proposing to extend the formal reach of international law, the Commission sought to justify a new moral conception of 'legitimacy', one which differed from formal legality. They described their doctrinal proposal for humanitarian intervention as 'situated in a gray zone of ambiguity between an extension of international law and a proposal for an international moral consensus', concluding that 'this gray zone goes beyond strict ideas of *legality* to incorporate more flexible views of *legitimacy*' (IICK, 2000: 164).

This international commission was followed by the International Commission on Intervention and State Sovereignty which held further discussions on the question throughout 2001.[5] These discussions indicate that formal legal equality will be undermined by current 'developments' in international law. In a typical panel, leading policy-advisor Adam Roberts noted that it would be a mistake to 'focus mainly on general doctrinal matters' regarding rights under formal international law:

> The justification for a particular military action, if it is deemed to stand or fall by reference to the question of whether there is a general legal right of intervention, is likely to be in even more difficulty than it would be if legal considerations were balanced in a more *ad hoc* manner.
>
> (2001: 2)

He recognized that in the current international context where 'there is no chance of getting general agreement among states about the types of circumstances in which intervention may be justified', it was necessary to counterpose 'powerful legal and moral considerations' (2001: 3; 13). The attempt to resolve the clash between the partial demands of Western powers and the universal form of law means that the advocates of cosmopolitan forms of international law assert the need for new, more flexible legal forms:

> It may be for the best that the question of a right of humanitarian intervention, despite its undoubted importance … remains shrouded in legal ambiguity. While there is no chance of a so-called right of humanitarian intervention being agreed by a significant number of states … answers to the question of whether in a particular instance humanitarian intervention is viewed as legal or illegal are likely to depend not just on the circumstances of the case … but also the perspectives and interests of the states and individuals addressing the matter: in other words, they are not likely to be uniform.
>
> (Roberts, 2001: 113–14)

Whether a military intervention is 'legal' is held to be a matter of 'the perspectives and interests' of those involved. This viewpoint, which seems certain to be adopted by the Commission, is an open argument for law-making by an elite group of Western powers sitting in judgement over their own actions.

The cosmopolitans allege that this 'ethical' framework can lead to a more equal society, as any state can be intervened in if it breaches moral or ethical norms. However, larger and more powerful states will have the resources and opportunities to intervene whereas weaker states will be unable to take up the interventionist duties on behalf of the 'global citizen'. The Independent International Commission on Kosovo, for example, stated that 'not only is the interventionary claim important, but also the question of political will, perseverance, and capabilities' (IICK, 2000: 169). The question of will and capacity are commonly highlighted as crucial to the legitimacy of military intervention, as Ramesh Thakur, vice rector of the United Nations University in Tokyo, argues, if there is no normative consensus on intervention there has to be 'realistic assessments of our capacity to coerce recalcitrant players' (2001: 43). This approach sets up the scenario where intervention is the prerogative of the powerful against the weak.

This flexible and multi-layered framework, where the strict hierarchies of international law are absent and there are no established frameworks of accountability in decision-making, undermines the UN Charter protections for non-Western states. The realities of unequal power relations mean that the more flexible decision-making is, and the less fixed international law, the easier it is for more powerful states to dictate the international agenda. International regulation, which is no longer based on sovereign equality, means excluded states will no longer have the opportunity to have a say in or consent to international regulation, abolishing the universal equality of international law (Chandler, 2000c).

The restrictions of formal equality in the international sphere and of non-intervention in the affairs of weaker states will have disappeared but no other constitutional framework will have replaced it. This does not mean that we will have international anarchy, but it does indicate a return to the days of 'might equals right' where the only limits on the capacity of major states to exert their influence internationally will be their ability to enforce their wishes. Smaller and weaker states were always under the influence of larger powers. The difference today is that it is increasingly difficult to call on international law as a formal barrier to direct intervention and domination. Whereas the new 'rights' created by 'globalized interconnectedness' take on an ephemeral form and are difficult to pin down, the new powers of intervention of international institutions become ever more concrete. Beetham stresses the 'duties to strangers that we all owe' arguing that global interdependence means we must 'expand our definition of the stranger who merits our concern' (1999: 138–9). Kaldor takes the point to its logical conclusion, stating

that 'there is no such thing as non-intervention'. We are so intercon-
nected that we have a duty to take responsibility for events which affect
citizens in any country in the world: 'The failure to protect the victims
is a kind of tacit intervention on the side of those who are inflicting
humanitarian or human rights abuses' (1999a: 118).

The cosmopolitan argument comes full circle. The starting point was
that democracy was too restrictive because it excluded non-citizens who
would be affected by decisions of foreign national governments. Now,
however, the affairs of these non-citizens can be directly intervened in
by foreign powers. While the non-citizens have gained no more power
to influence the policy-making of the major Western states they have
lost the right to hold their own governments to account. Rather than
being more democratic, the framework of universal cosmopolitan rights
can easily result in the rights people do have being further restricted.

Conclusion

It would appear that, far from empowering individual global citizens,
the cosmopolitan rights discourse has had the opposite effect, empowering the dominant international institutions and world powers, who
have acquired a new set of rights of interference in and regulation over
the affairs of non-Western states. Many writers and commentators on
international relations argue precisely for such a framework of more
direct Western domination.[6] They argue that the majority of states cannot be trusted to look after their citizens and that their citizens cannot
be trusted to elect good rulers. They maintain that major Western democratic powers have a 'duty' to interfere and take over if necessary, in
order to safeguard international peace and to capacity-build and educate
citizens and governments in the ways of democracy and civilization,
and openly see democracy and sovereign equality as barriers to enlight-
ened intervention by Western powers.

Cosmopolitan theorists, on the other hand, distance themselves from
this openly elitist perspective. They emphasize democracy on the international level and even pay lip-service to self-government or 'endoge-
nous democracy' and to sovereign equality, alongside the perspective of
limited rights of sovereignty and self-government dictated by the needs
of global civil society and the cosmopolitan citizen. In this way they
equate the new 'rights' of intervention with the old rights of self-
government, under the framework of extending and deepening the
operations of democracy at the international level. This approach would
appear to be a highly misleading one, which promotes the duty of

Western 'responsibility' as a development of democracy rather than its negation.

Notes

1. The theme of this chapter emerged from a debate with Daniele Archibugi on 'Cosmopolitics' organized by the European University Institute, Florence, Italy, on 15 May 2001. The author would like to thank the organizers and those present for their comments and also the unnamed reviewers of *Political Studies* who commented on an earlier draft of this chapter.
2. The work of cosmopolitan theorists, for example that of David Held, Daniele Archibugi, Mary Kaldor, Richard Falk, Ken Booth and David Beetham, differs in focus and emphasis. However, for the purposes of this brief survey, the similarities in their approach to the questions of democracy and rights are highlighted.
3. See, for example, the Commission on Global Governance (1995: xvi), Kaldor (1999a: 148) and Held (1995: 230).
4. Because ethical or moral rights are held to institute safeguards, against the democratic 'tyranny of the majority', ethics committees, which deal increasingly with many areas of life and work, are inevitably selected from the 'great and the good' rather than elected.
5. For further information, see the Commission's web page: <http://www.iciss.gc.ca/>.
6. For example, Max Boot (1999), Michael Ignatieff (2000c), Robert Cooper (2001) and Niall Ferguson (2001).

7
Humanitarian Intervention and the Recasting of International Law

Jon Holbrook

Introduction

International law since the Second World War has been built upon a respect for the sovereignty of nation-states. States, as the legal subjects of international law, have been treated as equal under international law regardless of economic and social power. This principle of sovereign equality was codified in international law by the United Nations' Charter that provides at Article 2(1): 'The Organization is based on the principle of the sovereign equality of all its Members.' However, since 1990 the sovereign equality of nation-states has been challenged and international law is being recast in the face of a humanitarian agenda which asserts that the rights of individuals should take priority over the rights of state sovereignty. From the imposition of no-fly zones over Iraq in 1991 to the bombing campaign over Kosovo in 1999, international actions which have undermined state sovereignty have been justified on a humanitarian basis.

This chapter considers the changing international context in which humanitarian interventions have gained a moral and legal respect that they lacked previously. It then analyses the effect of humanitarian interventions on international law and the efforts made by international lawyers to justify intervention from a legal standpoint. It is argued that sovereign equality is a vital legal principle that enables international power to be exercised fairly, accountably and legitimately. The chapter concludes by considering the problems that humanitarian interventions in Iraq, Somalia, Bosnia and Kosovo have caused by rejecting the sovereign equality of nations.

A new international context

In April 1991 thousands of troops from 13 countries, under a no-fly zone declared by the United States, initiated a large humanitarian relief operation in northern Iraq. This action was novel in that it took place in a country without the consent of the government of that country and its professed objective was a humanitarian one (to avert suffering by the Kurds of northern Iraq). This intervention displayed the three key features of a humanitarian intervention: coercive action, the absence of indigenous consent and a declared humanitarian objective. At the G7 summit in London, in July 1991, the seven most powerful nations in the world urged 'the UN and its affiliated agencies to be ready to consider similar action in the future if the circumstances require it'. The declaration went on to observe that: 'The international community cannot stand idly by in cases where widespread suffering from famine, war, oppression, refugee flows, disease or flood reaches urgent and over-whelming proportions' (cited in DUPI, 1999: 91). The international community, or at least the most powerful part of it, did not stand idly by. In August 1992 the United States, the UK and France added to the no-fly zone of northern Iraq by declaring a no-fly zone in southern Iraq in response to Iraqi oppression of the Shi'ite community.

The no-fly zones in Iraq were not authorized by the United Nations. UN authorization for a humanitarian intervention was first given in December 1992 when the Security Council authorized action in Somalia. Resolution 794 provided for the use of 'all necessary means to establish as soon as possible a secure environment for humanitarian relief operations in Somalia'. US marines then entered Somalia and a UN Task Force (UNITAF) of 38,000 was formed to oversee the delivery of humanitarian aid. These troops were unable to control more than 40 per cent of the country and so, in March 1993, the Security Council authorized another force of similar size (UNOSOM II) to take more resolute action. Resolution 814 mandated the American-led troops to take action to ensure that 'all Somali parties desist from all breaches of international humanitarian law' (Slim, 1995: 160).

While military force was being used in Iraq and Somalia, coercion was also deployed in the Federal Republic of Yugoslavia. Comprehensive economic sanctions were imposed in 1992 (Resolution 757) in an effort to force Serb forces to withdraw from Bosnia-Hercegovina and to permit the 'unimpeded delivery of humanitarian supplies'. Shortly afterwards, UN forces (UNPROFOR) were authorized to use force to carry out their humanitarian mandate (Resolution 770). In June 1993 the Security

Council specifically authorized the use of air power in and around the six 'safe areas' that the UN had declared in previous months (Resolutions 819 and 836) (Griffiths et al., 1995: 53). But it was not until the summer of 1995 that force was actually used when NATO launched air strikes in the Federal Republic of Yugoslavia (Chandler, 2000b: 19).

The Federal Republic of Yugoslavia was later the subject of further NATO intervention. In March 1999 NATO forces began a bombing campaign of Serbia and Montenegro that lasted 78 days until the Yugoslav government signed an agreement with the G8 that permitted an international military presence in Kosovo. Although the UN did not sanction the Kosovo campaign, Secretary-General Kofi Annan gave it his blessing in an April 1999 press release in which he noted that an international norm was emerging 'against the violent repression of minorities that will and must take precedence over concerns of State sovereignty' (Annan, 1999a).

Humanitarian interventions seem set to remain a feature of international relations. NATO forces are stationed in Bosnia and Kosovo for the foreseeable future and Anglo-American planes continue to enforce the no-fly zones in northern and southern Iraq as part of a strategy of isolating Iraq that has now lasted for over ten years. It appears that this new 'international norm' is not just to be enforced by NATO firepower, the European Union is preparing to assume similar responsibilities. The EU Rapid Reaction Force will have an autonomous capability, 'where NATO as a whole is not engaged, to launch and conduct EU-led military operations in response to international crises' (European Parliament, 2000a: 43). By 2003, the European Union is aiming to be able to deploy a force of up to 60,000 within 60 days and to sustain it for at least one year (European Parliament, 2000b: para 24).[1]

Since the objective of humanitarian interventions is the alleviation of human suffering it might be thought that these have developed in a world where suffering has increased. The twentieth century saw 160 million lives lost by war and state killings (Robertson, 1998). But, only a tiny fraction of these were lost during the last decade of that century. The century witnessed significant loss of life in two world wars and wars in Korea (1950–53), Vietnam (1965–73), Cambodia (1976–79) and the Persian Gulf (1980–88). Against this background of mass slaughter, it can be said that the last decade of the twentieth century, during which humanitarian interventions have developed, was one of the least violent in human history (Holsti, 1996). As the Secretary-General of the UN, Kofi Annan, observed:

During the 1990s, ... the number of armed conflicts in the world declined – from 55 in 1992 to 36 in 1998. That may seem surprising, when each of us can reel off a list of horrific conflicts, from Bosnia to Sierra Leone to East Timor. But the truth – so far entirely missed by the media – is that more old wars have ended than new ones have begun.

(Annan, 1999b)

The point is not that there are no humanitarian crises: there are. But that the existence of human suffering cannot explain the phenomenon of humanitarian interventions. Other factors to explain this phenomenon need to be considered. UN Secretary-General Kofi Annan is not alone in pointing to globalization as the explanation for humanitarian interventions:

Satellite communication, environment degradation, and the globalization of markets are just a few of the contemporary phenomena that are bringing into question the extent of state authority. The starving child on television screens around the world has generated global constituencies and pressure for action that governments cannot ignore.

(Annan, 1998: 57)

Global communications have increased. But the argument that new global constituencies are forcing governments to act is not straightforward. Pressures on Western governments to respond to humanitarian crises existed before the 1991 relief operation in northern Iraq. What needs to be explained is why Western governments did not, until 1991, translate these pressures into coercive action that breached national sovereignty. In the 1970s, for example, there were significant humanitarian disasters in Bangladesh (1971), Uganda (1971–79), Ethiopia (1973), Sudan (until 1972), East Timor (1975) and Cambodia (1975–79).[2] The images of starvation and war that were seen on television screens by Western populations in the 1970s were considerably more powerful than the images of homeless Kurds seen in 1991. The power of those earlier images may have resulted in the delivery of humanitarian aid but they did not result in any military intervention from Western governments. As an explanation for humanitarian interventions in the 1990s, the 'global constituency created by media images' argument does not work. It is not that the world's population is now seeing things that it has not previously seen. It is that what the world is now seeing, even though less disturbing that in previous decades, is sometimes stirring the world's most powerful states to take action that breaches national sovereignty.

In order to understand why the world since 1990 has sometimes been stirred into humanitarian action it is necessary to consider the issue of power. Before the 1990s, the West's power to use coercion abroad was impeded by the influence of the Soviet Union. The Soviet Union was not as powerful as the West but it could tempt states, disaffected with the West, into its orbit. The Soviet Union's willingness to play a global role that was antagonistic to the West ensured that Western actions were tempered by the concern that coercive action would drive foreign states into the Soviet sphere of influence. As Russia's willingness to act as a counterweight to the West's power faded, so the West's ability to intervene in the rest of the world increased. In 1991 the UN sanctioned the use of force to expel Iraq from Kuwait. Until then the UN's ability to sanction war had been neutered for over forty years by the Soviet Union's willingness to veto Security Council resolutions.[3] The humanitarian intervention into Iraq that started after Iraq's expulsion from Kuwait was a further example of the dominant role that America and its allies were then able to play on the world stage.

This is not to say that in 1991 and subsequently there was no opposition to Western incursions against the sovereignty of other states. Even before force was used against Iraq, Security Council Resolution 688, which required Iraq to provide access for humanitarian organizations but did not authorize the use of force, was opposed in the Security Council by Cuba, Yemen and Zimbabwe, while China and India abstained (Griffiths et al., 1995: 49). However, the international weakness of the three states that voted against this resolution showed the extent to which, by 1991, the West's power was no longer constrained. On subsequent occasions, Russia, China and other states have been prepared to flex their diplomatic muscles on the international stage. This was evident in 1998 and 1999 when Russia and China would have both vetoed any Security Council authorization for military intervention in Kosovo. But diplomatic protest by these states could no longer fetter the power of the West to intervene in affairs which had hitherto been regarded as the preserve of the sovereign state. The shift from a bipolar world to a unipolar world with only one superpower was crucial to the capacity of America and its allies to exercise authority abroad under the banner of humanitarian action.

Changing law

Until recently there was a consensus among states, if not lawyers, that humanitarian interventions were not lawful. The view of the British Foreign Office, as recently as 1986, was admirably clear:

> ... the overwhelming majority of contemporary legal opinion comes down against the existence of a right of humanitarian intervention,

for three main reasons: first, the UN Charter and the corpus of modern international law do not seem specifically to incorporate such a right; secondly, state practice in the past two centuries, and especially since 1945, at best provides only a handful of genuine cases of humanitarian intervention, and, on most assessments, none at all; and finally on prudential grounds, that the scope for abusing such a right argues strongly against its creation.

(UKFCO, 1986)

But in recent years Western states have been prepared to justify their interventions on the basis that there is a humanitarian right of intervention that exists outside of the UN Charter framework. In order to justify NATO's Kosovo operation, leading cabinet ministers were forced to overturn the traditional Foreign Office opinion. Foreign Secretary, Robin Cook, told the House of Commons on 1 February 1999: 'We are clear we have legal authority for action to prevent humanitarian catastrophe' (*Hansard*, 1999a). Defence Secretary, George Robertson, stated on 25 March 1999: 'We are in no doubt that NATO is acting within international law. Our legal justification rests upon the accepted principle that force may be used in extreme circumstances to avert a humanitarian catastrophe' (*Hansard*, 1999b).

Over time, the British government also revised its legal justification for flying over Iraqi air space. Initially, UN Resolution 688 was the preferred justification (Roberts, 1999), but in recent years the British government has relied increasingly on humanitarianism to justify its actions. Giving evidence to the Select Committee on Defence in 2000 the Defence Secretary, Geoffrey Hoon, said of the no-fly zones: 'There is a clear justification in international law for the international community to respond to protect people where they are threatened by an overwhelming humanitarian catastrophe. That is precisely the same legal justification that was used in relation to Kosovo' (UKSCD, 2000: para. 30).

In 1986 the Foreign Office believed that humanitarian interventions were unlawful. Now it believes they are lawful. How is this reversal of opinion to be explained? And in particular, to what extent can the about turn be attributed to the development of a unipolar world? The concern that the principle could be abused will be considered first.

Between 1945 and 1990 there were a number of interventions in sovereign states by countries acting without Western backing. In the 1970s alone, breaches of sovereignty occurred due to: India's intervention in East Pakistan in 1971;[4] Turkey's intervention in Cyprus in 1974; Indonesia's invasion of East Timor in 1975; Vietnam's intervention in Cambodia in 1978; and Tanzania's intervention in Uganda in 1979. Each of these interventions in the affairs of a neighbouring state showed that in the bipolar world of the Cold War it was possible for a state to use military force independently of Western interests. It was under these circumstances that the Foreign Office had reason to fear that a right of humanitarian intervention would have given less powerful states a lawful right to wage war.

By the 1990s, less powerful states had lost their ability to act independently of Western interests. Saddam Hussein was to discover this when Iraqi tanks rolled into Kuwait in 1990 and provoked an international response, the like of which had not been seen in previous decades. National conflicts in the 1990s, in the Balkans, East Timor and Sierra Leone, have all been met with an international response led by Western powers. In recent years even a civil conflict in Chechnya, in a country as powerful as Russia, has received considerable international comment and censure. It is now highly unlikely that states like India, Turkey, Indonesia, Vietnam and Tanzania could intervene militarily in other states, as they did in previous decades, unless they had prior Western support. It is not that the right of humanitarian intervention can no longer be abused; it is that only a select few major powers are in a position to impose their will on other states. As the previous decade of humanitarian interventions has shown, it is only the NATO countries that have the political and military clout to utilize the newly claimed right.

The second reason given by the Foreign Office in 1986 for denying that there was a right of humanitarian intervention was that state practice over 200 years, and especially since 1945, did not show that such a right existed. Many legal scholars have supported this opinion. Malanczuk found that nineteenth-century state practice did not persuasively establish that such a doctrine had become part of customary international law and Pape was more forthright in his rejection of the doctrine (Malanczuk, 1993: 11; Pape, 1997: 85). After analysis of a much longer time-frame, Ian Brownlie concluded that state practice, with one possible exception (the occupation of Syria in 1860 and 1861), offered no genuine case of humanitarian intervention and furthermore found it 'extremely doubtful' whether the doctrine had survived condemnations of intervention in international declarations of the twentieth century (1963: 338). By 1974, Brownlie was certain that even if such a right had ever existed it had not survived the legal regime of the UN Charter (1974).

It is generally accepted by international lawyers that a change in international law may come about from a change in state practice but only if that change has been clearly stated and accepted by the vast majority of states as uncontroversial. In the absence of a global state power, which states and their populations would consider to be legitimate, international law has developed on the basis of consensus. It is for this reason that international law has historically been founded on the mutual respect of state sovereignty. In fact, with the developing use of international treaties international law has developed, not by state practice, but by ratification of international treaties on a state-by-state basis. International treaties have been regarded as binding only on those states that ratify them. So even if every state in the world, save for America, signed up to the Kyoto Protocol few would argue that America was bound as a matter of international law to abide by its provisions.

Those who argue that international law has evolved over the last decade to establish or revive a right of humanitarian intervention are reneging on the principle that international legal norms can only be formed where there is a consensus. In effect they are saying that the novel actions of powerful states can create an international norm that is binding on less powerful states. Ruth Wedgwood, for example, has suggested that the war over Kosovo may mark the emergence of a limited and conditional right of humanitarian intervention (1999: 828). She assumes that most of the world supported NATO's action. Even if this dubious assumption were accepted, the ramification of Wedgwood's argument is profound: it means that one military intervention that many non-Western states were strongly opposed to may have established a new international legal norm. Wedgwood premised her argument by claiming that: 'The lack of any single source of rules or ultimate arbiter of disputes in international affairs means that state practice remains key to the shaping of legal norms' (1999: 828). But why should international law be determined by state actions? Can there not be any principles to international law that take precedence over state practice? If there are no principles to international law then international law readily accommodates to the actions of powerful states.

The primary reason given by the Foreign Office, in 1986, for rejecting the right of humanitarian intervention was that the 'UN Charter and the corpus of modern international law' did not seem to provide for such a right. In fact, the situation has become less straightforward since 1986 as lawyers have devised arguments for departing from the previously held consensus against the existence of such a right. At the outset it should be noted that, during the last decade, humanitarian interventions took one of two legal platforms: those that were sanctioned by the UN Security Council and those that were not. Some lawyers deny the legality of both forms of humanitarian intervention whereas some accept the legality of only UN-sanctioned interventions and others accept the legality of all 'legitimate' humanitarian interventions.

Of the humanitarian interventions of the 1990s, several, including those in Somalia and Bosnia, proceeded with the sanction of the UN Security Council. Commentators who support the legality of these interventions therefore need only pray in aid the UN Charter. In Iraq and Kosovo the actions did not have Security Council authorization, despite attempts by some Western governments sometimes to claim the contrary. UN Resolution 688 of 5 April 1991 had called on Iraq to 'allow immediate access by international humanitarian organizations' but it did not authorize the use of force in pursuit of this demand. In fact, the resolution reaffirmed 'the commitment of all Member States to respect the sovereignty, territorial integrity and political independence of Iraq'. In these circumstances it cannot be claimed that the resolution sanctioned any coercive action in Iraq, least of all that it authorized the imposition of any no-fly zones over Iraqi air space. In Kosovo, UN Resolution 1199 of September 1998 had envisaged specific Security Council authorization for any subsequent military action. Yet none was sought before or during NATO's 78-day bombing campaign because NATO members knew the Security Council would refuse it. Supporters of the actions in Iraq and Kosovo therefore look to customary international law, rather than to the UN Charter, to establish the legality of these humanitarian interventions.

Dealing first with UN sanctioned interventions, the most relevant provisions of the UN Charter are Articles 2(4) and 2(7), which fetter the UN's ability to intervene:

> 2(4). All Members shall refrain in their international relations from the threat or use of force against the territorial integrity or political independence of any state, or in any other manner inconsistent with the Purposes of the United Nations.

> 2(7). Nothing contained in the present Charter shall authorize the United Nations to intervene in matters which are essentially within the domestic jurisdiction of any state or shall require the Members to submit such matters to settlement under the present Charter; but this principle shall not prejudice the application of enforcement measures under Chapter VII.

These provisions preclude the threat or use of force unless the UN Security Council sanctions it under Chapter VII of the Charter. Articles 39 and 42, of Chapter VII, set out the circumstances in which force may be sanctioned:

> 39. The Security Council shall determine the existence of any threat to the peace, breach of the peace, or act of aggression and shall make

recommendations, or decide what measures shall be taken in accordance with Articles 41 and 42, to maintain or restore international peace and security.

42. Should the Security Council consider that measures provided for in Article 41[5] would be inadequate or have proved to be inadequate, it may take such action by air, sea, or land forces as may be necessary to maintain or restore international peace or security. Such action may include demonstrations, blockade, and other operations by air, sea, or land forces of Members of the United Nations.

It can be seen from Article 42 that the power for the Security Council to authorize collective military action only exists when there is a threat to 'international peace or security'. On the basis of the plain meaning of words it is difficult to see how a civil war or systematic repression within a state is capable of posing a threat to 'international peace or security'. Moreover, the Charter was drafted when the horror of two world wars was in people's minds. This background supports the view that Chapter VII was intended to enable the Security Council to authorize a collective response to wars between states. It was never intended to enable the Security Council to take action against states on the grounds of humanitarian necessity (Österdahl, 1998: 12). On this basis, the UN Charter does not empower the Security Council to authorize a humanitarian intervention.

But in recent years the Security Council has seen it differently. It has passed resolutions relating to Somalia, Iraq and the Balkans, noting that the humanitarian situation posed a threat to international peace or security. In law it is possible to support these findings by interpreting the words 'international peace and security' loosely. Hans Kelsen, for example, concluded in 1951 that the word 'international' was probably of no importance (1950: 12). Michael Reisman went further and concluded that humanitarian interventions could be lawful even without the sanction of the Security Council. He came to this novel 'interpretation' by claiming that a humanitarian intervention is not directed against the 'territorial integrity' or 'political independence' of a state and so the constraint on the use of force in Article 2(4) does not apply (Reisman and McDougal, 1973: 171). However, Reisman's rejection of the plain reading and clear intention of the Charter remains a minority perspective.

Other lawyers have found in favour of a humanitarian right of intervention by looking to customary international law. These lawyers have concluded that a Security Council resolution to authorize a humanitarian intervention is not required. Their reasoning is that the UN Charter has not established a binding and all-encompassing framework for international law and that there is a right of humanitarian intervention that exists outside of the UN Charter. Richard Lillich has reached this conclusion by relying on his 'link theory'. This means that UN member states have a responsibility to maintain international peace and security (Article 1(1) of the UN Charter) and that when the Security Council is unable to fulfil its responsibilities by taking enforcement action under Chapter VII the prohibiting provision of Article 2(4) is suspended (Lillich, 1967: 34; Jessup, 1948: 170). In other words, when the veto power is exercised in the Security Council states may take humanitarian action to maintain international peace and security. Marc Weller has reached a similar conclusion by relying on the legal doctrine of 'representation'. He argues that the authority to govern must be based on the will of the people. Where governmental authority breaks down entirely, forcible international action can, under certain circumstances, be taken on behalf of the unrepresented population. He claims that the right to intervene is triggered when the government cannot claim to represent its people or a segment of it such as when the results of a democratic election are overturned (as in Haiti) or when it actively exterminates or displaces its population (as in Kosovo) (Weller, 1999a: 20; Reisman, 1990: 866). Geoffrey Robertson QC relies on a more straightforward assertion of customary international law. He argues that there is an evolving principle of humanitarian necessity, whereby force of a proportionate kind may be used to prevent a humanitarian catastrophe. This principle, he says, existed before the UN Charter and there is nothing in the Charter to say that the Charter has abrogated the right of humanitarian intervention (2000: 404–8).

Sovereignty and international relations

Robertson, unlike Wedgwood, does not explicitly base his argument on state practice; no doubt he realizes that state practice is against him. Robertson's 'evolving principle of humanitarian necessity' is based on principle: that states 'must override the rule about not intervening in the affairs of other states' so as to protect human rights. What Robertson describes as 'the Good Samaritan paradigm' leads him to quote with approval Václav Havel, when addressing the Canadian parliament six weeks into the Kosovo campaign:

> ... although it has no direct mandate from the UN, it did not happen as an act of aggression or out of disrespect for international law. It happened, on the contrary, out of respect for a law that ranks higher

than the law which protects the sovereignty of states. The alliance has acted out of respect for human rights as both conscience and international legal documents dictate.

(Robertson, 2000: 407)

If humanitarian interventions could undermine state sovereignty without negative consequences few would object. But humanitarian interventions challenge basic rights of self-government and sovereign accountability. Humanitarian interventions are by definition carried out without the consent of the state that is being intervened in. Sovereignty is a quality that a state either has or does not have. Either a state makes and enforces its own laws or it does not. Either a nation-state decides how to respond to a famine, insurgency or claim for more minority rights or a section of the international community decides for it. As power has been centralized in the West over recent years so the ability of the West to coerce a state by economic and diplomatic means has increased. The Yugoslav government, for example, decided to hand Milošević to The Hague war crimes tribunal only after America, the European Union and World Bank made it a precondition for the release of $1.3 bn of much needed aid (*The Times*, 2001). In other words, sovereignty can be breached by economic and diplomatic coercion as well as military intervention.

As noted above, lawyers who advocate a right of humanitarian intervention tend to justify their case by looking at state practice and precedent or by interpreting, often loosely, the meaning of the UN Charter. It is the job of lawyers to interpret laws and it is for the legislature to make them. But, when it comes to international law there is no legislature. It is easy for the international lawyer to fill this void by straying beyond interpretation of the law into the arena of advocating it. If a law is to be advocated, the principles underpinning that law should be put to the fore. In other words an open debate about the principles that should underpin international law is required rather that an exclusive debate between lawyers about state practice, precedent and interpretation of the UN Charter.

This author believes that a 'right' of humanitarian intervention would be wrong in principle because it would undermine the one principle that should underpin international law: sovereignty. Sovereignty is a principle worth defending because (a) it is a bulwark against the abuse of international power, (b) it enables those who exercise power to be accountable for it, and (c) it permits power to be exercised in a way that is seen as legitimate. An international 'law' that permits states to breach another's sovereignty will merely enable powerful states to exercise their power unaccountably and in a way that may well be seen as illegitimate by the recipients of the intervention.

Without the restraining influence of sovereignty, power would be easy to abuse on the international stage. Economic and social power and military strength are not evenly distributed between states and, in truth, only a handful of major Western industrialized powers have the ability to influence world affairs. As illustrated above, the end of the Cold War has heralded a new era of unipolar international relations where the influence of America and its allies is untrammelled. Respect for the sovereignty of smaller or less powerful states inhibits the ability of the more powerful ones to intervene in their internal affairs. The sovereign equality of states, which is enshrined in Article 2(1) and expressed in Article 2(7) of the UN Charter, means that every nation-state, no matter how small or economically or politically weak, has the right to govern its own affairs.

In theory a right of humanitarian intervention gives the powerful states of the world an unfettered ability to intervene in less powerful states as and when they like. Faced with this prospect those who advocate a right of humanitarian intervention suggest criteria that would separate the 'legitimate' from the 'abusive' humanitarian intervention. Most commentators suggest that the intervention would only be legitimate if there were 'gross and massive violations of human rights' (DUPI, 1999: 106; Robertson, 2000: 409; Cassese, 1999: 23; Charney, 1999: 838). But, no matter how the trigger for intervention is defined, there is still the problem of which authority has the right to decide whether the definition is satisfied. On this issue, the Danish Institute of International Affairs concludes that 'the state(s) intervening must initially make the assessment' (DUPI, 1999: 107). The conclusion of the Danish Institute, that the intervening states must decide for themselves whether human rights abuses are so gross that they are entitled under international law to intervene, is an inevitable one in these circumstances.

The idea that the interveners may determine the legality of a humanitarian intervention offends a fundamental principle of justice: that one may not be a judge of one's own cause. Moreover, if the interveners are empowered to determine the legality of their own actions then international law is subverted to the opinion of the world's most powerful states. The practical illustration of this problem is the continued bombing of Iraq by Anglo-American forces. The protagonists insist that they are acting lawfully even though the actions are taken without international sanction and with the disapproval of an increasing number of states.

The bombing of Iraq also draws attention to the second problem raised by humanitarian interventions: that of accountability. Neither America nor Britain is accountable for its continued bombings, either to the people of Iraq or to the international community. As long as power is exercised by a sovereign state it is exercised subject to a degree of accountability to its citizens. If a regime acts oppressively towards its people then this creates a pressure against the regime's continued existence. This accountability is most clearly expressed in democratic states where a popular mandate to govern is required. But even in non-democratic states the will of the people is a force that cannot be ignored, as the demise of many autocratic and despotic regimes over the decades has shown.

Those who advocate the abandonment of the UN Charter protections for state sovereignty do so with honourable intentions. Geoffrey Robertson states that: 'The moral imperative must be to stop crimes against humanity whenever they occur, not merely when the five permanent members of the Security Council have unanimously resolved to act' (2000: 410). British prime minister Tony Blair was also keen to seize the moral high ground when justifying the Kosovo campaign as a war 'fought for a fundamental principle necessary for humanity's progress: that every human being regardless of race religion or birth has an inalienable right to live free from persecution' (cited in Shawcross, 2000: 325). Using less emotive language to make a similar point, Professor Cassese[6] has sought to justify the development of a right of humanitarian intervention, post-Kosovo, on the basis that human rights are and should be at the top of the world's agenda:

> Human rights are increasingly becoming the main concern of the world community as a whole. There is a widespread sense that they cannot and should not be trampled upon with impunity in any part of the world ... [T]he idea is emerging in the international community that large-scale and systematic atrocities may give rise to an aggravated form of state responsibility, to which other states or international organizations may be entitled to respond by resorting to countermeasures.
>
> (1999: 26)

After more than a decade of humanitarian interventions it is important to ask whether the new mandates for intervention, which the major powers have granted themselves, have contributed to the humanitarian cause. The problem with externally imposed solutions is that they have tended to lack legitimacy. In the absence of domestic support, humanitarian interventions have often done little to resolve humanitarian problems.

More than ten years after the no-fly zones were imposed over Iraq, as part of 'Operation Provide Comfort', it can be seen that they have done little to provide comfort for the Kurds and Shi'ites of Iraq (Keen, 1995: 170). If anything, the coercive military action and stringent sanctions have enabled Saddam Hussein to gain a degree of legitimacy by standing up to foreign aggression. According to one expert, American policy in Iraq has left George W. Bush and his foreign policy team their 'most intractable international problem' (Dodge, 2001: 5). Similarly, the Somali intervention failed to live up to its title: 'Operation Restore Hope'. The objective of bringing peace to a war-torn country faded as the interventionist forces alienated a growing section of the population and increasingly demonized Somali leader General Aideed in an attempt to reduce an ugly civil war into a simple struggle between good and evil. The forces pulled out hastily after an attempt to arrest General Aideed, on 3 October 1993, left 18 US soldiers and thousands of Somalis dead (Slim, 1995: 147).

The international imposition of Balkan settlements has met with similar disappointments. In 1995 President Clinton assured his doubting population that American troops would be out of Bosnia within a year. Seven years on, they are still there, serving as part of the 20,000 NATO (SFOR) presence. Their withdrawal is less likely now than it was in 1995 because it is only the presence of these troops that prevents unresolved conflicts from erupting. Under the Dayton Accord Bosnia is officially composed of two 'entities' – the Muslim-Croat Federation and the Republika Srpska – in practice there is not a single state because each entity has veto rights over actions of the central government. The state has now effectively broken down into three entities as the Croats have become more assertive of their own separateness. Democracy in Bosnia is stifled by international officials who find it necessary to 'skew elections, disqualify candidates [and] close down radio and television stations' in order to prevent further political fragmentation (Betts, 2001: 53). As William Shawcross, a supporter of the principle of humanitarian interventions, observed towards the end of 2000:

> ... the fighting, mercifully, had been stopped, but almost nothing had been achieved in terms of building a democratic multi-ethnic state. The original, well-intentioned concept of Dayton 'one state, two entities and three peoples', had failed. Dayton's electoral system had confirmed the power of the Muslim, Serb and Croat blocs.
>
> (2000: 364)

The situation in Kosovo is similar to that in Bosnia in that self-government or genuine democracy are postponed to the indefinite future. To make matters worse, the expulsion and killing of non-Albanians has happened apace since NATO troops were deployed. It is estimated that some 180,000 Serbs have left Kosovo during and since the war, while the Serbs who remain live in enclaves heavily guarded by NATO troops (Chandler, 2000a: Afterword). Yet even these troops have been unable to prevent the disappearance of 1,300 Serbs and over 800 Romany who have either been killed or abducted in Kosovo since the UN took over control of the region in June 1999 (EIN, 2001a, 2001b). William Shawcross, writing shortly after NATO troops entered Kosovo, observed:

> ... by the end of July it seemed that the province which Milosevic had tried to empty of Albanians was now likely to be virtually emptied of Serbs. One cleansing had replaced the other. There was reason to fear that NATO would have to remain in Kosovo at least as long as it was in Bosnia, which probably meant decades, not years.
>
> (2000: 352)

What Shawcross could not then foresee was that within two years Kosovo would have become a focal point for the export of instability to neighbouring Macedonia.

Yet, unbowed by the negative experiences, advocates of humanitarian interventions often argue that the failings are borne out of a 'too little, too late' approach. William Shawcross blames a failed Iraqi policy not on the policy itself but on 'the appeasement of Saddam by some of the Security Council's prominent members' (2000: 368). After acknowledging that the intervention in Somalia had served to disempower and frustrate Somali society and had exacerbated the conflict, Hugo Slim and Emma Visman conclude that the UN should have been more involved in 1991 and 1992 (1995: 164). Former High Representative in Bosnia, Carlos Westendorp, argues, on the basis of his experience, that Kosovo should be a full international protectorate – in other words, that NATO's denial of Yugoslav sovereignty has not gone far enough and it is necessary for the international community to do more to impose a respect for human rights on the people of the Balkans. He states that: 'Yes, this disregards the principles of sovereignty, but so what? This is not the moment for post-colonial sensitivity ... The problems of the region will only be solved when we have introduced a general respect for democracy and the rule of law' (Westendorp, 1999). The advocates of international intervention see the problems as caused by the people of the regions intervened in and fail to question their own role in the unravelling of political settlements and the institutionalizing of insecurities in post-conflict regimes.

Conclusion

Diplomatic supporters of humanitarian interventions, such as UN Secretary-General Kofi Annan, do not suggest that sovereign equality should be undermined. He seeks to reconcile humanitarian interventions with sovereignty on the basis that 'sovereignty is undergoing a significant transformation'. As was noted above, he claims that the transformation has come about due to the world's greater interdependence, 'globalization' for short, which is 'bringing into question the extent of state authority' (1998: 57). But it is questionable whether globalization has either weakened state authority or increased the pressures on states to conform to global norms. Annan has confused 'isolationism' with 'sovereignty'. Isolationism, states cutting themselves off from the world community of nations, differs from sovereignty, states being permitted to govern themselves. Annan would be right if he contended that global pressures made it impossible for a state to isolate itself from all contact with other states but he is wrong to contend that these same pressures have changed the nature of sovereignty. Global communication networks and markets do not prevent a state from having control over its own internal affairs. As we have seen from humanitarian interventions since 1990, it has been the use of military force by powerful Western states, rather than any forces of globalization, that have denied the people of Somalia, Iraq and Yugoslavia the ability to govern themselves.

Basing international relations upon a respect for sovereignty does not mean that states should withdraw into themselves. In fact, humanitarian interventions developed in the 1990s at the same time as a great many countries were being internationally isolated. With the end of the Cold War competition for influence, Western states had less reason to look for friends and allies in order to preserve their geostrategic interests. Much post-11 September analysis has drawn attention to the extent to which Western nations ignored and isolated Afghanistan after the Soviets withdrew in 1989. Isolating and shunning Afghanistan did much to turn it into a pariah state and hence laid the basis for Afghanistan to be the first arena for the Anglo-American 'War on Terrorism' (Holbrook, 2001). The 'War on Terrorism' illustrates the extent to which isolationism and disregard for sovereignty can coexist. Making respect for sovereignty the central principle of international relations could encourage powerful states to engage constructively with less powerful ones. Trade, untied aid and diplomatic and political respect are the hallmarks of an international order built upon the sovereign equality of nation-states. Sanctions, embargoes, ultimatums, tied aid, diplomatic and political isolation and military intervention are the hallmarks of an international society that does not respect the sovereign equality of states. Fundamentally, this is a challenge for politicians and statesmen but international law could provide a framework within which constructive engagement can prosper. Those who advocate a legal right of humanitarian intervention are serving to create an international framework in which isolationism and intervention can flourish and where constructive engagement is sidelined.

'Something must be done' is the usual rallying cry of those who advocate humanitarian interventions. What these advocates fail to appreciate is that the actions they advocate for can undermine the international framework, established after 1945, which prioritizes the principles of consent and cooperation and codified them in the UN Charter. The undermining of this universal framework through humanitarian interventions over the last decade has, in fact, made bad situations worse. This consequence is not because the international community has done 'too little, too late', but because it has acted erroneously in principle in undermining sovereignty as the cornerstone of international relations. Sovereignty should not be respected due to any 'post-colonial sensitivity' but because it provides people the best opportunity to decide how to resolve difficult situations for themselves. Sovereignty is not a guarantee of an immediate solution to every problem, but only those with a colonial notion of their own superiority would want to argue that the award of unaccountable powers of intervention to powerful states is a more viable approach. Unaccountable, externally imposed solutions, through the force of economic sanctions or military intervention, are less likely to help resolve humanitarian crises than assistance and cooperation with locally and regionally accountable authorities who have a lasting interest in a sustainable and long-term solution. After more than a decade of failed humanitarian interventions, it is time for America, Britain, NATO, the EU, the OSCE, the G8, the World Bank, the UN and other international institutions, bloated by the power they have assumed in a post-Cold War world, to rethink their cavalier approach to intervention. They should begin by respecting the sovereign equality of nation-states.

Notes

1. The European Parliament resolution of 30 November 2000 was adopted by 326 votes to 119 with 49 abstentions.
2. In November 1971 Pakistani forces had committed large-scale human rights violations and had forced some 10 million people to flee to India; during Idi Amin's reign of terror an estimated 300,000 people lost their lives in Uganda; between 1975 and 1979 Pol Pot's Khmer Rouge killed close to two million people in Cambodia (DUPI, 1999: 35).
3. The UN intervention in Korea in 1950 was owed to happenstance, as the USSR was absent from the Security Council when the vote was taken (Robertson, 2000: 169).
4. India initially appeared to justify its intervention on humanitarian grounds but then changed the record of its submission to the UN Security Council to one of self-defence (Griffiths et al., 1995: 42).
5. Article 41 provides that the Security Council may decide upon measures 'not involving the use of armed force'.
6. Professor Cassese was President of the ICTY between 1993 and 1997.

Part III
Human-Centred Rights?

8
New Wars and Old Wars?
The Lessons of Rwanda

Barrie Collins

Introduction

Since the tragic events of April–July 1994, when between 500,000 and 800,000 people were slaughtered (Kuperman, 2001: 19–21), Rwanda has been an important reference point for the discourse of international action to protect human rights. Given the scale and intensity of this killing of civilians, this is hardly surprising. Much has been written about the failure of the international community to recognize the extent and genocidal nature of the killings, and about its reluctance to intervene to save lives. Laudable efforts have been made to examine the reasons for this failure and to offer strategies based on the lessons that Rwanda provides. There are widely opposing views on how effective intervention would have been in saving lives even if there had been a prompt response to the reports of the killings (for example, Melvern, 2000; Kuperman, 2001). However, advocates of international intervention to protect human rights generally assume that the problem is of a domestic nature and that the international community is an indispensable part of the solution. A near unanimous consensus has it that the problem in Rwanda's case was Hutu extremism (see, for example, Rothchild, 1997: 37–8). Graphic accounts of machete-wielding Hutu militia murdering Tutsi civilians would seem to be a stark illustration of this, leaving little doubt that 'the culture of violence', essentialist attitudes or 'blind obedience to authority' were at the root of the killings (Sisk, 2001: 67–89; Collins, 1998).

Contemporary conflicts, especially in less developed non-Western countries, tend to be understood less as struggles for state power, involving a clash of political or ideological interests, and more as violations of human rights by 'extremists' who are defined in terms of identities rather than ideologies. The 'lessons learned' from Rwanda have informed this discourse to a significant extent. Analysts of these 'New Wars' stress the irrational and uncontrollable nature of modern conflicts, alleged to be driven by a dangerous internal dynamic:

> These internal conflicts are characterized by a highly unpredictable and explosive dynamic of their own, as well as by a radicalization of violence, the irrationality of which stands in stark contrast to the politically guided and systematically escalated use of military force for which the mechanisms and instruments laid down in the UN Charter ... were designed.
>
> (Thurer, 1999)

Rather than consider the causes of conflict, the 'New Wars' thesis focuses on the victims of war to highlight the widespread abuse of human rights. From this perspective, it is a short step from focusing on human rights abuses to presenting these abuses as the explanation of the conflict, as the aim of the war itself. In this manner, modern conflicts become seen as a 'crime against humanity, masquerading as a war' (Gutman, 2000). While all wars are barbaric, 'New Wars' appear in a particularly degraded light. These conflicts are apparently 'less a noble clash of soldiers than the slaughter of civilians with machetes or firing squads, the mass rape of women in special camps, the cowardly execution of non-combatants' (Cassese, 1998: 5). As a human rights campaigners' handbook, *Crimes of War: What the Public Should Know*, asserts in its introduction:

> Wars today increasingly are fought not between armies where officers are bound by notions of honour but by fighters ... who are not soldiers in the conventional sense of the word. The goal of these conflicts is often ethnic cleansing – ... not the victory of one army over another.
>
> (Gutman and Rieff, 1999: 10)

No longer connected with international relations of power, it appears that conflict has a dynamic of its own. Martin Shaw makes the point that in these cases 'genocide may be discerned, therefore, in relatively limited mass killing' (2000). He argues that 'the concept of "genocidal massacre" should be proposed to cover smaller incidents, which are often a prelude to a larger-scale genocide' (2000). The use of the emotive term 'genocide' to describe these conflicts establishes 'New Wars' as qualitatively different from earlier conflicts, predominantly understood within a framework of state competition and Great Power rivalries. Mary Kaldor's *New and Old Wars: Organized Violence in a Global Era* exemplifies this approach:

> The goals of the new wars are about identity politics in contrast to the geopolitical or ideological goals of earlier wars ... By identity politics, I mean the claim to power on the basis of a particular identity – be it national, clan, religious or linguistic. In one sense, all wars involve a clash of identities – British against French, communists against democrats. But my point is that these earlier identities were linked to a notion of state interest or to some forward-looking project – ideas about how society should be organized.
>
> (Kaldor, 1999a: 6)

Kaldor argues that the politics of these 'New Wars' fought on the basis of identity are backward-looking and exclusivist. She also argues that a second aspect of new wars is that they are not fought for territorial gains but to 'sow fear and hatred', to terrorize the population:

> The aim is to control the population by getting rid of everyone of a different identity (and indeed of a different opinion). Hence the strategic goal of these wars is population expulsion through various means such as mass killing, forcible resettlement, as well as a range of political, psychological and economic techniques of intimidation. This is why, in all these wars, there has been a dramatic increase in the number of refugees and displaced persons, and why violence is directed against civilians.
>
> (ibid.: 8)

This chapter suggests that the 'New Wars' perspective, which in the case of Rwanda focuses on domestic factors, particularly the ethnic essentialism implicit in Hutu extremism, not only fails to explain the dynamics of what took place but does little to protect and promote the human rights of those in conflict-torn and post-conflict societies. The following section highlights the domestic–international dynamics from the end of the 1980s which reveal that far from non-intervention in Rwanda, the major Western powers shaped the context in which the Rwandan state disintegrated and wholesale slaughter ensued. Individual Western powers, international financial and other institutions, were closely involved in the political reforms which prefigured war and invasion and the subsequent Arusha peace process, as Rwanda's peace talks were known.

The next section considers how the externally imposed settlement could not resolve the war between the Rwandan state and the Rwandan Patriotic Front (RPF) and was responsible for exacerbating a deteriorating situation and creating the conditions that accelerated the descent into mass slaughter. In conclusion, the chapter highlights how the 'New Wars' thesis has rewritten the failure of international interference in Rwanda, casting responsibility onto the Rwandan people themselves, by portraying them as irrational and unable to break free from conflicting ethnic identities. By questioning the moral and political capacity of the majority of Rwandan people, the 'New Wars' thesis has legitimized the denial of their democratic rights and ignored the human rights abuses under the unelected postwar military regime.

Good governance?

Whereas, in the past, 'structural adjustment' was the centrepiece of World Bank and International Monetary Fund policy, the watchword of the post-Cold War era is 'good governance', a term embracing transparency, democracy and respect for human rights. According to Michael Bratton and Donald Rothchild, the concept of governance arose in the 1960s in response to requests by newly independent African governments for assistance in setting up government agencies and training public officials to implement public policy. It began to disappear from aid portfolios as recipient countries became more self-reliant in skilled personnel. 'By the 1980s, however, with special reference to Africa, it was revived under the leadership of the World Bank, as an institutional "capacity-building" initiative under the rubric "governance for development"' (Bratton and Rothchild, 1992: 264–5; World Bank, 1989). With further input from institutions like the Carter Center and the Ford Foundation, the initiative became less technocratic and more directly political. Among Western powers, the United States was the first to introduce an explicitly political conditionality in its foreign policy, signalled by Assistant Secretary of State for Africa Herman Cohen in April 1990. Although Bratton and Van de Walle warn against overstating the impact of political conditionality on events (1992: 48), all African governments and most opposition movements responded to this changed international environment. As far as governance and democracy were concerned, however, the results were certainly mixed.

In Rwanda's case, it was France which signalled the post-Cold War shift in Western policy toward Africa. In a landmark speech to the June 1990 Franco-African Summit, President François Mitterrand explicitly linked future French aid with moves toward democratization. This had a decisive effect on the Rwandan President, Juvénal Habyarimana. Whereas, two months earlier, he had defended the virtues of the one-party state in a speech to Rwandan exiles in Paris (EIU, 1990a), one month after the June 1990 Summit Habyarimana committed himself to revising the constitution and separating the party from the state, conceding that: 'it is no longer normal these days to subordinate the institutions of the state to a political organisation' (EIU, 1990b). By September 1990 Habyarimana had established a national commission to produce a charter on multi-party government.

The US and France both assisted in framing Rwanda's new constitution, funding 'conferences on constitutional reform and even [paying] for the printing of much of the government's constitutional literature' (EIU, 1991). When the new constitution was signed into law in June 1991, Western diplomats were said to be 'deeply satisfied' (ibid.). America was quick to reward Habyarimana's efforts. In July 1991, Herman Cohen announced an increase in US aid from 11.6 million dollars in 1990 to 20 million dollars in 1991, stating that on 'both the plane of politics and economics, Rwandans are doing very well' (ibid.).

As well as responding to this international agenda, Habyarimana also hoped the new constitutional arrangements would silence the RPF's accusations of systematic discrimination against ethnic Tutsis by the Rwandan state. Habyarimana claimed the new constitution conceded everything the RPF asked for: it ended the one-party system which had excluded Tutsis from Rwandan politics, and gave exiled Rwandans the right of return. The RPF was free to return under amnesty, form its own political party and compete in future elections (*Africa Confidential*, 1991).

Having neutralized the substantive elements of the RPF's grievances, Habyarimana felt able to mount a direct challenge to the RPF and thereby expose its lack of political support within Rwanda. As *Africa Confidential* remarked, as an 'almost wholly Tutsi organisation, a political version of the RPF will present no serious challenge in national elections' (ibid.). Catherine Newbury argues that with these moves toward democratization, Habyarimana had undermined the RPF's political case and prompted its decision to invade Rwanda on 1 October 1990:

> The timing of the invasion, however, may have been more affected by initiatives within Rwanda, as the Habyarimana regime moved – very cautiously – toward a more open political system and a new position on refugee issues. Both policies – the move to 'political liberalization' and the move to address the 'refugee problem' – undercut

RPF claims to moral superiority. So the RPF attack on October 1, 1990, carries the appearance of an attempt to pre-empt two issues on which the Rwanda government had indicated a willingness to act. By attacking when they did, the RPF seemed intent on maintaining the moral 'high ground'.

(1995: 13–14)

The RPF leadership was also responding to pressures within Uganda. This leadership had emerged in the course of a guerrilla movement that had brought Yoweri Museveni to power in Uganda in 1986. Faced with harassment and insecurity, many Rwandan Tutsi refugees had volunteered with Museveni's National Resistance Army (NRA). Some, including future RPF leaders Paul Kagame and Fred Rwigyema, played key roles. With the NRA's accession to power in 1986, several of these refugees gained senior positions in the government and military. However, as Ugandan political analyst Mahmood Mamdani shows, these individuals subsequently found themselves passed over for promotion in favour of indigenous Ugandans. A dispute between ranchers and squatters in southwestern Uganda brought national anti-Rwandan feeling to the surface. Museveni responded by prohibiting non-indigenous Banyarwanda (Rwandans) from owning land or holding state positions and demoted several Rwandan officers. Rwigyema was transferred from Deputy Commander of the Army to the largely ceremonial Deputy Minister of Defence. In 1988 he was also removed from this position. In a letter to Human Rights Watch, Uganda's ambassador to the United States, Katenta-Apuli, cited the prohibitions on land ownership and on holding public office as the key reasons for the RPF's desertion from the NRA and its decision to invade Rwanda (Mamdani, 2000: 335–6).

The invasion took place while presidents Habyarimana and Museveni were both in America attending a conference on children's rights. It resulted in five hundred civilian deaths and the displacement of another 350,000 (Uvin, 1998: 61). Although Museveni denied supporting the formation of the Rwandan Patriotic Army (the armed wing of the RPF) at the time (officially, they were called 'deserters'), there is evidence to the contrary, and also of tacit American support for the invasion. For example, Marwitz cites telegrams to the State Department from military observers documenting Ugandan support for RPF attacks. There were at least 56 'situation reports' in State Department files in 1992 (Marwitz, 1994). Eight years later, Museveni admitted his support. He told other heads of state that, while the Banyarwanda in the NRA had informed him in advance 'of their intention to organise to regain their rights in

Rwanda', they had launched the invasion 'without prior consultation'. Significantly, he continued, even though 'faced with [a] *fait accompli* situation by our Rwandan brothers', Uganda decided 'to help the Rwandan Patriotic Front materially, so that they [were] not defeated because that would have been detrimental to the Tutsi people of Rwanda and would not have been good for Uganda's stability' (cited in Mamdani, 2000: 336).

Western conditionality toward Rwanda effected a change in that country's constitution. The political pluralism enabled by the new constitution, together with the response of the Museveni regime in Uganda to its first major political crisis, precipitated the RPF invasion. Having successfully complied with the terms of Western conditionality, the Rwandan government was shocked that the invasion was not condemned by the international community outside of France. The suspicion that the RPF enjoyed discreet American approval in addition to significant Ugandan support placed a question over the sincerity of the stated motivations behind political conditionality.

The invasion was successfully repulsed. The Armed Forces of Rwanda (Forces Armées Rwandaises (FAR)) were backed by Zairian troops, President Mobutu's Division Spéciale Présidentielle, and by French forces. Three days after the invasion, 300 French paratroopers arrived in Kigali, officially to protect French nationals and not to engage in combat. According to Melvern, the French had operational control of the counter-insurgency campaign and used two companies of parachutists and paramilitaries from the secret service – the Direction Générale de la Sécurité Extérieure (2000: 30). After the 1990 invasion, France assisted Rwanda in rapidly building up the FAR, with technical and military assistance and credit for arms purchases. By the time of the Arusha Accords, in August 1993, the FAR had trebled in size to 30,000 (Millwood, 1995: II, 22).

The war was sustained largely due to the extent to which both sides received external backing: the FAR most significantly from France; the RPA from Uganda, which was in turn reliant upon military and economic support primarily from the United States and Britain.

The peace process?

The invasion had set off a flurry of diplomatic activity. Habyarimana flew to Paris and obtained pledges of military support. The French moved 4,300 troops from Bangui, Central African Republic, to evacuate 200 French residents and man the airport, provide arms, set up communications facilities and supervise interrogation of RPF prisoners

(Klinghoffer, 1998: 16). Museveni, meanwhile, went to Brussels and got Prime Minister Wilfried Martens to agree to mediate. Martens, Foreign Minister Mark Eyskens and Defence Minister Guy Coeme travelled to Kenya and Tanzania for talks on 15–18 October, with regional leaders including Habyarimana, Museveni, Mobutu and Mwinyi of Tanzania (ibid., 16–18). This was the start of what later became officially known as the Arusha peace process (hereafter referred to simply as 'Arusha').

While France had initiated Rwanda's democratization, Belgium had initiated the peace process. The United States then gradually took on a more direct role. In May 1991 Herman Cohen engaged in shuttle diplomacy between Habyarimana in Kigali, and Museveni and the RPF in Uganda's capital, Kampala. According to the Economist Intelligence Unit: 'This was a less than subtle nudge to the Rwandan government that Western nations want it also to meet the RPF and to stop dismissing it ... France and the USA have expressed a strong desire to expedite peace talks' (EIU, 1992). The talks began officially on 10 August 1992 (Mamdani, 2001: 210).

Yet, even while direct talks got underway, the RPF renewed its offensive in order to strengthen its bargaining power. Instead of establishing administrative structures in areas it controlled, the RPF sought to increase the political and financial costs of the war for the Habyarimana regime by displacing the local population and halting production. Between 1991 and 1992, such policies resulted in the flight of hundreds of thousands of civilians into camps near Kigali (Reed, 1995: 50). According to Human Rights Watch:

> Between 1990 and 1993, RPF soldiers killed and abducted civilians and pillaged property in north-eastern Rwanda. They attacked a hospital and displaced persons' camps. They forced the population of the border area to flee either to Uganda or to displaced persons camps further in the interior of the country.
>
> (1999a: 701)

During the same period, Hutu militia forces and members of the army killed civilians suspected of being RPF sympathizers. Given the RPF's predominantly Tutsi membership, Tutsi civilians tended to be targeted. Between 7 and 20 January 1993, an international commission of NGOs comprising Human Rights Watch, the International Federation of Human Rights, the Inter African Union of Human Rights and the International Centre for Human Rights and Democratic Development conducted a mission into Rwanda: hundreds were interviewed and graves were excavated. Their report published in February stated that over 2,000 Tutsis had been murdered since the RPF invasion for the sole reason that they were Tutsi. It documented massacres in northwest Rwanda by civilian groups with the support of the regime (Uvin, 1998: 83). Alison Des Forges demonstrates the report's influence:

> In March 1993 we submitted a 160-page report documenting the involvement of the Rwandan government in the killing of its citizens. We submitted to the US government, where it did produce some change in policy. For instance, there was a reduction in US government aid, and the remaining aid was taken from the governmental channels and funnelled through non-governmental channels. Belgium recalled its ambassador within two hours of publication of the report.
>
> (1997: 127–9)

In January 1993 a power-sharing agreement was made. The following month a conference entitled 'Democratization in Africa – The Role of the Military' was held in Burundi, hosted by the American embassy and sponsored by the US Departments of State and Defense (Foltz, 1993). A subsequent Department of State report claimed that 'we believe that a dialogue that begins by using the American experience in this field can greatly enhance our contribution to African thinking' (*Africa Confidential*, 1993a).

Yet, by this stage the RPF had just completed its largest offensive to date. As was its custom, the RPF justified it as a reaction to human rights abuses by the regime. But, according to Human Rights Watch:

> The RPF, critical of international inaction, claimed that they had to attack to halt the late January massacres of Tutsi and others. In fact, the slaughter of the Tutsi had stopped more than a week before the RPF moved, suggesting that the real motive for the attack had been to force progress on the negotiations...
>
> (1999a: 109)

The offensive had displaced a million people. By now popular resentment against the RPF was manifest across much of the country, especially as news spread of arbitrary killings (Uvin, 1998: 62). Lemarchand points out how the camps for these displaced people generated prime recruits for militia in much the same way as the Tutsi refugee camps in Uganda had proved fertile recruiting ground for the RPF (1996: 78). On 20 February the RPF stopped 30 kilometres north of Kigali and announced a ceasefire. Prunier describes how support for Habyarimana increased at this point:

> By then their agents were also bringing back from the capital information on the very negative psychological and political effect of the offensive on the Hutu population. Everybody, including the most resolute opponents, was prepared to fight. President Habyarimana could count on massive popular support...
>
> (1995: 177–8)

Prunier also shows how the offensive destroyed the alliance between the opposition parties and the RPF: 'The Hutu opposition now had a problem. It had supported RPF as wanting to restore rights of exiled Tutsis versus a regime depiction of RPF as bloodthirsty and power seeking. The latter view now seemed more credible' (ibid.: 180). Indeed, the offensive had made the Mouvement Démocratique Républicain (MDR), the Parti Social Démocratie (PSD), and the Parti Libéral (PL) feel 'betrayed' (HRW, 1999: 109).

The resumption of war and massive population displacement revealed the fact that the prospects for peace could not have been worse, and yet 'the peace process' was presented by the US as still on track. In March, the US greeted the resumption of the Arusha talks with a 20 million dollar aid package 'in recognition of progress on democracy and economic reform' (EIU, 1993). The offensive had in fact strengthened the hand of the RPF at Arusha at a most crucial point, when the leadership and composition of a proposed united Rwandan army were being negotiated. The RPF had initially been offered a 40:60 ratio with government forces for leadership positions. After the February offensive, the ratio was amended to 50:50. Arusha had rewarded the RPF for an offensive that had wreaked havoc upon Rwanda and driven the last nail in the coffin of reconciliation. The battle-hardened and exuberant RPF could now set its sights on a complete military takeover of the country. It simply had to ensure that it continued to enjoy the moral high ground by capitalizing on the intensifying attacks upon Habyarimana by human rights NGOs.

With the army humiliated, severe economic deterioration and a threat of famine (the February offensive had depopulated one of Rwanda's key food producing regions), Habyarimana was in no position to counter the moves made by the RPF and its backers in negotiations. When the Accords were put before him, they resembled a suicide note. Knowing the extent of disaffection with Arusha within Rwanda and the violent backlash it was certain to invite, Habyarimana did everything possible to stall. This brought down upon him an impressive display of coercive power by Western leaders. Western nations (including France) and the World Bank, informed Habyarimana that international funds for his government would be halted if he did not sign the treaty by 9 August (HRW, 1999: 123). With no other source of funds available, Habyarimana was obliged to sign along with the other parties, on 4 August 1993 (ibid., 124).

Des Forges was clear about the way in which the accords were signed: 'This peace agreement had come about largely as a result of the active intervention of the international community, particularly the United States and various other actors through the United Nations' (1997: 129). At a House of Representatives hearing on Rwanda a year later, she again referred to this act of coercion:

> We are dealing with a situation where Rwanda is highly dependent upon international assistance. We know that, and the Rwandans know that. Everyone who is a major player here knows that no regime established in that country is going to be able to make it without significant international assistance ... there is a precedent for this. There have been on any number of occasions joint actions among the donor nations and involving also the World Bank. For example, last August when it was getting very difficult to get the Arusha Accords signed, there was a deadline of August 9 that said no more foreign aid unless this accord is signed. The accord was signed.
>
> (USC, 1994: 22)

Reference to this is also made by Donald Rothchild, professor of political science at the University of California (1997: 265). It was precisely these 'joint actions' which played the most decisive part in shaping the 'peace process', and, as Des Forges indicates, in the acceptance of the final documentation. Lemarchand also remarked upon it: 'The democratisation process was forced on Kigali by outside powers who largely dictated the form of this political crisis' (1998: 80). A report commissioned by the Danish foreign ministry was in no doubt as to which party had emerged strongest from the signing of the Accords: 'The Arusha Accords represented a veritable coup d'etat for the RPF and the internal opposition' (Millwood, 1995: II, 46). Newbury concurs, stating that they 'consolidated so many gains that they seemed proof to many that once again the Tutsi were to be the winners' (1995: 46).

Newbury highlights three ways in which the Arusha Accords contributed to the polarization of political tensions in Rwanda. Firstly, the allocation of ministries indicated a preference for the RPF. While

Habyarimana received a largely ceremonial position and his party five relatively insignificant posts out of twenty, the RPF received five as well, including the important Ministry of the Interior. Secondly, provisions on merging the two armies stipulated that in the new army RPF elements would fill 40 per cent of the rank and file positions and half of the officer corps. As a result, few RPF personnel would be dismissed, while large numbers of Rwandan government soldiers faced demobilization and an insecure future. Thirdly, the stipulation of a right to return for refugees contained inadequate provision to allay real fears and anxieties among the population as to the impact of this policy, especially on the issue of land reclamations (ibid.: 15).

The untenable nature of the Arusha Accords was evident on the day they were signed. There were no celebrations in Kigali. Two leading 'moderate' participants, Faustin Twagiramungu, who had been designated prime minister for the transitional period, and Agatha Uwilingiyimana, the party premier, were both expelled from their party, the MDR, for exceeding the mandates given them (*Africa Confidential*, 1993b). The MDR had allied itself with the RPF in the mistaken belief that combined pressure upon Habyarimana would hasten the advent of elections. As the largest alternative to the former ruling party, the MDR was confident it would emerge the winner. But once it began to dawn on it that the RPF was aiming for an outright victory on the battlefront, its enthusiasm for the Arusha Accords dissipated and serious tensions erupted. Human Rights Watch had recognized the precarious state of affairs at Arusha:

> The carefully calibrated three-part division of power in the government made it unlikely that any one group could dominate and thus be able to disrupt the movement toward elections and real peace. But the hope of progress depended on each of the three groups remaining coherent and able to act as a counterweight to the others. As the negotiators all knew, that was a doubtful premise given the divisions of the MDR just three weeks before the signature of the treaty.
>
> (HRW, 1999a: 125)

Similar considerations led to the fracturing of the Liberal Party (ibid.: 139). However, most other commentators failed to understand these tensions and expressed them instead in terms of a crude extremist–moderate caricature.

These rapidly rising tensions within Rwandan society were clearly evident. Human Rights Watch stated that 'two days after the treaty was signed, Belgian military intelligence reported much dissatisfaction among both soldiers and civilians, warning that 'a wave of demonstrations, clashes and even assassination attempts' might begin within the next few days. Many soldiers were angry that Habyarimana had yielded to foreign pressure when the army had not been decisively defeated. Discontent was most discernable among senior officers, who expected to be among the first demobilized because of their age. Tensions spread to local government administrators. Like the soldiers, some burgomestres and prefects feared losing their positions – within three months of the installation of the Broad-Based Transitional Government, those found to be incompetent or involved in prior human rights abuses were to be removed. Having seen a similar review process remove about one quarter of the burgomestres in February 1993, many administrators had no desire to expose themselves to the same fate (HRW, 1999a: 125–6).

The RPF also began to subvert the Accords and prepared for a final military assault. Human Rights Watch state that:

> In late July or early August 1993, the RPF brought increasing numbers of young people to their zone to train them as political agents to broaden this network within the country. RPF supporters organized several hundred cells during 1993, each including between six and twelve members.
>
> (1999a: 129–30)

Matters were made considerably worse on 21 October when the elected Burundian president Melchior Ndadaye was assassinated. According to Lemarchand, 20,000 Tutsi men women and children were hacked to pieces, and an equal number of Hutus were killed in all-Tutsi army reprisals. This caused 300,000 Hutus to seek refuge in Rwanda (1998: 6). Southern Rwanda became as charged with violent tensions as the rest of the country. On 23 October 1993, a 'Hutu power' rally was held in Kigali. It included all the major internal parties. Addressing the rally, the Second Vice President of the MDR, Frodauld Karamira, reportedly accused the RPF, and specifically Paul Kagame, of being among the plotters who killed Ndadaye (HRW, 1999a: 138).

In these circumstances, few were surprised that the provisions of the Accords were not duly implemented. Again, Western powers turned on the pressure. France withdrew its forces in December 1993, signalling the Rwandan government's complete isolation. Belgium underlined its transfer of loyalties by using its contingent in the United Nations force (UNAMIR, mandated to Rwanda in terms of the Accords) to provide a military escort for an RPF battalion to Kigali, ostensibly for the protection of

RPF parliamentarians. By this time there was no pretence of neutrality by any Western power. At the end of 1993 the crucially important donors' roundtable on Rwanda took place, not in Kigali, but in Mulindi – the base of RPF operations against the government. Early in 1994 the World Bank announced that all credits to Rwanda were suspended on the grounds that the government was illegal (EIU, 1994).

On 14 January 1994, Belgian and US ambassadors and the French Chargé d'Affairs visited Habyarimana to urge implementation of the Arusha Accords (HRW, 1999a: 154). At a meeting in Dar es Salaam on 3 April 1994, Western powers again exerted pressure upon Habyarimana to comply with all the terms of the Accords. Habyarimana met with the ambassadors of France, Belgium and Germany. He was threatened with a UNAMIR pull-out and another RPF offensive. The German ambassador expressed satisfaction with the result: 'We can no longer talk of stumbling blocks. I think everything is on the right path. I personally expect the establishment of institutions in the course of this week' (cited in Omaar, 1994: 87). Two days later the UN Security Council voted to extend the UNAMIR mandate. On returning to Rwanda on 6 April, Habyarimana's plane was shot down in a missile attack.

Mass slaughter

Among the dead were Habyarimana, Burundi's new President Cyprien Ntaryamira, Rwandan military chief of staff General Deogratias Nsabimana, also Hutu 'militants' Major Thaddée Bagaragaza, the chief of the Presidential Guard, and Colonel Elie Sagatwa, Habyarimana's private secretary and brother-in-law (Madsen, 1999: 108). While no one appeared to have the facts about the circumstances and perpetrators of the missile attack at that time, most NGOs and analysts speculated that Hutu extremists were responsible. No less a figure than Herman Cohen lent his weight to this explanation. He told the investigation led by Senator Quilès into the French role in Rwanda that only the militant Hutus could have been responsible (Madsen, 1999: 124). This fitted the thesis that the eruption of violence on 6 April was triggered by the plane crash as a planned signal for the commencement of a programme of genocide against Tutsis (African Rights, 1995: 22). The *Akazu*, an extremist clique centred upon Habyarimana's wife Agathe, is said to have masterminded the operation as a desperate 'all or nothing' strategy (Prunier, 1995: 213–26). However, what could have motivated Agathe Habyarimana to conspire to murder her husband, her brother and Bagaragaza is not clear.

An alternative explanation is gaining credibility. In a public statement in April 2000, former RPF officer Jean-Pierre Mugabe alleges that after signing the Arusha Accords, RPF general Paul Kagame:

> ... started visiting our unit commands and the areas controlled by the RPF. He told army soldiers not to believe at all in the accords: 'Be ready with your military equipment, we are going to fight for the final war against the Kigali government.'
>
> (ISSA, 2000)

Mugabe gives a detailed account of the military training and preparation for this 'final war', naming individual officers in charge of secret operations to infiltrate men and arms into the capital. His statement is supported by the accounts of two further RPF defectors who, along with Mugabe, in February 1997 submitted evidence to James Lyons, the local head of UN investigations for the International Criminal Tribunal for Rwanda (ICTR). Lyons, a former FBI agent seconded to the ICTR by the US State Department, led a 20-member team investigating, among other issues, who was responsible for shooting down Habyarimana's plane on 6 April 1994. According to Lyons, the RPF defectors gave credible and highly detailed testimony regarding the planning and execution of the rocket attack. They claimed that Kagame formed a commando type group known as the 'network', and that he and his senior advisors put into effect a plan to shoot down the presidential aircraft as it approached Kigali airport. Michael Hourigan, Lyons's team leader, briefed the ICTR Chief Prosecutor, Louise Arbour, on the matter, and was invited to The Hague in order to discuss it further. At the meeting, however, Arbour unexpectedly ordered the investigation to be shut down, claiming the attack on the President's plane was outside the Tribunal's jurisdiction (Lyons, 2001). Former French Minister of Cooperation Bernard Debri gives additional circumstantial evidence of the RPF's responsibility for the assassination, claiming that records of RPF communications prove its soldiers were ordered to begin advancing toward Kigali on the morning of 6 April (cited in HRW, 1999a: 182). If these claims prove to be true, accounts that relate the plane crash to the planning of genocide will be discredited.

The response of sections of the Rwandan army and the Interahamwe and Impuzamugambi militias to the news of the President's assassination is now well known. Mass slaughter followed. Initially, individuals in Kigali known or assumed to be supportive of the RPF were targeted. The killings then spread into rural areas. Prime targets were Tutsi civilians, though many southern Hutu, assumed to be MDR supporters, were also massacred. By the time the RPF emerged the victor in late July, 500,000 to 800,000 people had been slaughtered. The scale of the killing was unprecedented in Rwanda's history.

Yet the atrocities were not quite as one-sided as most analysts have perceived them to be. While the role of the Interahamwe militia and Rwandan military and civilian officials in the killings has been intensively researched and publicized, the RPF's responsibility for civilian massacres during their final offensive has been treated differently. It appears that the diplomatic support given to the RPF by the US included suppression of information on RPF atrocities. This suppression extended to the highest levels of the United Nations, which covered up evidence of RPF atrocities revealed by its own investigators.

Robert Gersony was leading a UNHCR team trying to speed up refugee repatriations when he was confronted with evidence of widespread atrocities. The Gersony team investigated these atrocities from 1 August to 5 September 1994, visiting 91 sites in 41 of the 145 communes in Rwanda, gathering detailed information from ten others, and visiting nine refugee camps in neighbouring countries. They found that men, women and children had been killed indiscriminately, and that 'the great majority of these killings had apparently not been motivated by any suspicion whatsoever of personal participation by victims in the massacres of Tutsi in April 1994' (cited in HRW, 1999a: 727). Gersony estimated that between April and August 1994 the RPF had killed 25,000 to 45,000 civilians (HRW, 1999a: 728). While even the upper 45,000 estimate is a small percentage of the total death toll during this period, what is telling is the way in which these allegations were dealt with internationally. According to Human Rights Watch, on receiving these findings, UN Secretary-General Boutros Boutros-Ghali dispatched Kofi Annan to brief the Rwandan prime minister. Annan reportedly offered assurances that that the UN would do its best to minimize the attention given to Gersony's findings because the international community understood the difficult context in which the new government was operating. In the meantime, the information would be kept confidential. When the representative of the UN's Special Rapporteur tried, in April 1996, to obtain more information about Gersony's findings from the UNHCR, he was told: 'the Gersony report does not exist'. Leading authorities at the UN and several leading governments were reluctant to make criticisms that would weaken the new Rwandan regime (HRW, 1999a: 728–31). US officials were reportedly aware of the UN decision not to make the report public and agreed with it. As one US policy-maker explained:

> We have three choices. Support the former genocidal government. That is impossible. Support the RPF. That is possible. Support neither. That is unacceptable because it might result in those responsible for the genocide coming back to win.
>
> (cited in HRW, 1999a: 732–3)

The US Assistant Secretary of State rejected Gersony's finding that the RPF's killings were 'systematic', and added that America, like Belgium and Germany, was supporting the RPF 'with its eyes open' (cited in HRW, 1999a: 732). Although the story of the Gersony report was leaked to the press, its suppression effectively preserved the one-sided account that had by then become a widely held consensus. In the revised edition of his influential work, *Rwanda: History of a Genocide*, Gérard Prunier admits his earlier dismissal of the report was wrong and says he has been persuaded to accept it as authentic and reliable.

Learning the lessons?

For human rights advocates, the term 'genocide' captures all that took place in Rwanda between April and August 1994, and has also been applied retrospectively to the preceding years. The period between the end of the Cold War and April 1994 is often described in terms of preparations or 'dress rehearsals' for genocide (for example, Melvern, 2000). An account of the role of ordinary Rwandan Hutus in the genocide is forcefully made by Ugandan analyst Mahmood Mamdani: 'The design from above involved a tiny minority and is easier to understand. The response and initiative from below involved multitudes and presents the true moral dilemma of the Rwandan genocide' (2001: 7). The claim that ordinary people were lead actors in genocide does indeed pose a 'moral dilemma' by suggesting that ordinary Rwandan citizens are prone to genocidal actions and incapable of acting morally. The tendency of the 'New Wars' approach to understand the conflict as a product of extremist manipulation of the mindset or culture of the majority of the citizens of Rwanda, ethnic Hutus, is prevalent in much of the literature. It is at best a gross caricature, and at worst a racist one. While Rwandan society did polarize over Hutu and Tutsi political identities, and huge numbers of Tutsi civilians were targeted simply as Tutsis, this development was far from inevitable and cannot simply be reduced to the determination of Hutu 'extremism'. Yet this is what the 'New Wars' perspective claims to be the case.

To the same extent as the 'New Wars' discourse demonizes Rwandan people, it downplays the importance of Western backing for the RPF and accommodation to each step of the RPF's military offensive. Investigation into the dynamics of the peace process reveals that what was achieved with the signing of the Arusha Accords in August 1993 was the basis, not for a peaceful and democratic resolution of Rwanda's conflict, but for an arms race between the warring parties and for heightened insecurity and fear across the whole population. The Arusha Accords created an untenable situation that would lead only to more and greater violence. The absence of critical investigation of the Arusha peace process and the obsession with the psychology of Hutu extremism is testimony to the pervasiveness of the human rights discourse of 'New Wars'. This discourse understands war and conflict in the non-Western world as an extreme form of human rights abuse. A moral analysis of the conduct of war effectively supersedes a political analysis of the dynamics of war. The result is that complex and dynamic processes tend to be reduced to black and white moral narratives, dehumanizing populations caught up in conflict as either irrational abusers or as helpless victims requiring international assistance.

Ironically, the humanitarian 'New Wars' discourse has done no favours at all to those whose plight it was specifically intended to help: the ordinary citizens of Rwanda. The understanding of the communal violence as a genocide in which the masses killed under the direction and control of a small number of state officials removes the context of a war that a rebel army, almost exclusively Tutsi, was winning. It has also established in Rwanda a double standard where atrocities are concerned. This war, and the involvement of ordinary civilians in massacres, should be explained by way of examining the complex dynamics between domestic and international forces that were unleashed after the Cold War. Instead, this discourse has reduced the Rwandan tragedy into a simplistic good versus evil parable of Tutsi victims, Hutu extremists and a civilian population transformed suddenly into mass murderers by means of incitement by extremists. A genocide understood in these terms has provided a moral certainty whose force is used to silence debate. This moral certainty is the sole source of legitimacy of a repressive, militaristic and expansionist regime. It has also created a politically acceptable means of criminalizing Rwandan Hutus. Mamdani captures this well in his quote from a political commissar in the RPF: 'When we captured Kigali, we thought we would face criminals in the state; instead, we faced a criminal population' (2001: 7).

The majority of the Rwandan people have been judged guilty of the most serious of all crimes: genocide. It would therefore seem to follow that such people ought to forfeit, or at least have suspended, their democratic rights. If the RPF ended a genocide in which the majority of the population were guilty participants, then a relationship of moral superiority between the RPF and the rest of society is established in which the denial of democratic rights appears reasonable. A war that began after the formulation of a democratic constitution ended with the dictatorship of a morally constituted elite. The 'New Wars' discourse has played an essential role in problematizing the Rwandan population, legitimizing this contemporary form of benevolent dictatorship.

The moral certainties that are generated by this discourse explain why those who responded to earlier attacks upon Rwandan Tutsis by demanding Western intervention against the government of the day have not responded with anything like the same degree of zeal to massacres subsequently committed by the present government. The treatment of the Gersony report, the response to the massacre of thousands of internally displaced Rwandans at Kibeho in April 1995, and the muted response toward allegations of Rwandan atrocities in the ongoing war in neighbouring Congo (where the death toll has far surpassed Rwanda's) are all illustrative of the double standard established by this process. Western double standards are not new. The use of human rights-based arguments in the denial of democratic rights is a more serious and dangerous development.

9
Moral Combat: Advocacy Journalists and the New Humanitarianism

Philip Hammond

Introduction

A striking feature of media coverage of post-Cold War conflicts has been the emergence of a 'journalism of attachment', or 'advocacy journalism', which explicitly rejects neutral and dispassionate reporting in favour of moral engagement and seeks to influence Western public opinion and policy. This chapter first outlines the claims of advocacy journalists, examining how they view their work as an improvement on past practice. It then considers the examples of Bosnia and Rwanda – both key conflicts for the development of this style of journalism – which suggest that it can have disastrous consequences. Our understanding of these conflicts has been distorted by simplistic narratives of good versus evil, and the sympathies developed by some reporters have led them to welcome attacks on those designated as unworthy victims. It is argued that the journalism of attachment should be viewed in the context of broader political changes during the post-Cold War era. Although often presented as a critical and oppositional stance, its real significance lies in the promotion of a morally loaded, human rights-based discourse which has echoed and encouraged the development of similar themes by powerful Western governments. Journalism which advocates tough military intervention by Western powers has often left the consequences of actual Western involvement largely unexamined.

'Attachment' and 'objectivity' in war reporting

In Britain the best-known proponent of the journalism of attachment is Martin Bell, the former BBC correspondent who coined the phrase.

He describes it as journalism which 'cares as well as knows', and which 'will not stand neutrally between good and evil, right and wrong, the victim and the oppressor'. Bell rejects the 'dispassionate practices of the past', and confesses he is 'no longer sure what "objective" means' (Bell, 1998: 16–18). In the United States a similar argument, in favour of 'advocacy journalism', is perhaps most prominently associated with CNN reporter Christiane Amanpour, who maintains that: 'In certain situations, the classic definition of objectivity can mean neutrality, and neutrality can mean you are an accomplice to all sorts of evil' (quoted in Ricchiardi, 1996).

Notwithstanding Amanpour's and Bell's comments, contrasting attachment with objectivity is imprecise, since 'objectivity' refers to at least three distinct, though interrelated, concepts. First, it primarily entails a commitment to truthfulness: reporting factually accurate information. Second, objectivity is often thought to imply neutrality and balance: seeking to be impartial and unbiased in the process of selection which reporting inevitably involves and, where there are conflicting interpretations of an event, presenting different viewpoints even-handedly. Third, objectivity is also often understood to imply emotional detachment: a dispassionate approach which separates fact from comment and allows news audiences to make up their minds about events rather than being offered a journalist's own response. These are interrelated in that journalists are supposedly dispassionate and neutral so as not to let their own emotional responses and political allegiances get in the way of reporting truthfully.

Yet the core meaning of objectivity in journalism – factual accuracy and truthful reporting – is not discarded by advocacy journalists, who still claim to be reporting truthfully. 'My neutrality has gone out of the window long ago', says the *Guardian*'s Ed Vulliamy (1999a), referring to his decision to appear as an expert witness for the prosecution at the UN's International Criminal Tribunal for former Yugoslavia, and reflecting more generally on his experience of covering the Bosnian war. Yet Vulliamy maintains that objectivity and accuracy are 'sacred' (ibid.). What is rejected is an aspect of objectivity: 'neutral' reporting, and, at least in some cases, emotional disengagement.

The key reason for repudiating neutrality appears to be a moral one: that faced with a clear division between good and evil reporters must not be neutral and detached. As Amanpour elaborates:

Once you treat all sides the same in a case such as Bosnia, you are drawing a moral equivalence between victim and aggressor. And from here it is a short step to being neutral. And from there it's an even shorter step to becoming an accessory to all manners of evil.

(Quoted in Hume, 1997: 6)

This morality exists not within a religious framework, but within the framework of human rights: reporters have a moral obligation to expose human rights abuses and reveal the plight of victims. In pursuing this claimed human rights agenda, today's advocacy journalists consider they are making a stand against the moral failings of Western governments. Amanpour, for example, famously berated President Bill Clinton on live television in May 1994 for not articulating a tough policy on Bosnia (Ricchiardi, 1996).

The apparent divergence between Western policy-makers and morally attached reporters suggests a contrast, not so much with the principle of objectivity, as with the tradition of 'objective journalism'. As many critics of war reporting have observed, in practice 'objective journalism' has generally been subservient to dominant political perspectives. Daniel Hallin (1986), Mark Pedelty (1995) and Robert Jensen (1992), for example, respectively discussing US coverage of Vietnam, El Salvador and the Persian Gulf War, all conclude that much of the reporting of these conflicts broadly conformed to professional standards of 'objective journalism' but was nevertheless deeply flawed, in each case tending to reflect the views of official sources in the US government and military. As Pedelty puts it: 'objective journalism is a political perspective ... a perspective most closely associated with political centrism' (1995: 171). In contrast, advocacy journalists present themselves as being at odds with those in authority. Roy Gutman, for instance, complains of Western governments trying to 'throw sand in everybody's eyes' when he tried to publicize atrocities in Bosnia (1999), and Bell recounts how the British government dismissed him and his colleagues as 'the something-must-be-done club' (1996: 138). Where 'objective journalism' has been criticized for its tacit support of powerful Western political interests, the journalism of attachment claims to be independent and critical, challenging Western governments to do the right thing.

Indeed, advocacy journalists have been highly critical of their fellow reporters for following the allegedly neutral agenda of Western politicians. Vulliamy contends that the 'neutrality' of the 'international community' has been 'nowhere more evident than in the media' (1999b). The BBC's Allan Little describes how in the early 1990s he was 'bewildered' by what seemed a general consensus over Bosnia:

> That the Balkan tribes had been killing each other for centuries and that there was nothing that could be done. It was nobody's fault. It was just, somehow, the nature of the region. It was a lie that Western governments at that time liked. It got the Western world off the hook. When I and others argued that you could not blame all sides equally, the moral implications were that the world should – as it later did – take sides. We were denounced – derided even – by government ministers as laptop bombardiers.
>
> (Little, 2001)

Reporters have described a similar consensus about Rwanda. According to BBC correspondent Fergal Keane:

> The mass of early reporting of the Rwandan killings conveyed the sense that the genocide was the result of some innate inter-ethnic loathing that had erupted into irrational violence ... [S]everal of the world's leading newspapers ... bought the line, in the initial stages, that the killings were a straightforward 'tribal war'.
>
> (1995: 6–8)

The Joint Evaluation of Emergency Assistance to Rwanda, an international study commissioned by the UN, also concluded that 'inadequate and inaccurate reporting by international media' had 'contributed to international indifference and inaction' (JEEAR, 1996: Study II, section 4.3).

In addition to governments and the media, attached journalists have also heavily criticized the neutral stance of humanitarian agencies. In common with some aid workers, journalists have argued that the traditional neutrality of peacekeeping and humanitarianism results at best in helplessness, and at worst in complicity with evil. Keane argues that the UN troops in Rwanda 'had a mandate that turned them into little more than spectators to the slaughter', and endorses the view of Médecins sans Frontières that the refugee camps which developed on Rwanda's borders in the wake of the mass killings of 1994 were a '"humanitarian haven" for the killers' (1995: 124, 186). Similarly, Bell sympathizes with UN troops in Bosnia, forced into the role of 'bystanders', and sarcastically describes humanitarian aid as ensuring that victims 'should not be starving when they were shot' (1996: 135, 190). Condemning what they saw as half-hearted humanitarianism, the goals of advocacy journalists covering both Bosnia and Rwanda were to identify clear human rights villains and victims, explaining conflicts in unambiguous moral terms, and to encourage Western military intervention by bringing public pressure to bear through media reports.

This study argues that on every count the journalism of attachment is the opposite of what it claims to be. Instead of truthful reporting, the agenda of advocacy journalism has sometimes made reporters highly selective, leading them to ignore inconvenient information. Rather than exercising critical independence, advocacy journalism has frequently coincided with the perspectives and policies of powerful Western governments. And despite claims to be pursuing a moral, human rights agenda, the journalism of attachment has led to the celebration of violence against those perceived as undeserving victims.

Bosnia

By their own admission, advocacy journalists presented the Bosnian war as a simple tale of good versus evil. According to *Washington Post* journalist Mary Battiata: 'There was only one story – a war of aggression against a largely defenseless, multi-ethnic population. It was very simple' (quoted in Ricchiardi, 1996). For Amanpour: 'sometimes in life, there are clear examples of black and white ... I think during the three-and-a-half-year war in Bosnia, there was a clear aggressor and clear victim' (ibid.). Committed to a 'simple', 'black and white' outlook, reporters placed events into this framework even when the available evidence strongly suggested they did not fit.

A well-documented example is the 5 February 1994 marketplace massacre in Sarajevo, in which a mortar explosion killed 68 people and injured 197. Amanpour maintains that she 'put [the shelling] in context':

> What I said was that over the years, our [UN] briefers had explained to us and shown us, numerically and by their own measure and statistics, that the overwhelming number of mortar shells and sniper fire and fire into the city was from the Serb side. Therefore, statistically, the likelihood is that it came from the Serb side. And furthermore, there's never been any forensic evidence to suggest that the Bosnians were shooting at themselves.
>
> (ibid.)

After extensive investigations, the UN declared it was unable to determine whether the mortar had been fired by Serb or Muslim forces, but a number of UN sources suggested the Bosnian Muslims were the most likely perpetrators (Binder, 1994–5). As Nik Gowing concludes: 'on a clear balance of probabilities, all evidence pointed to the fatal mortar being fired by Bosnian [Muslim] forces' (1997: 31). Yet, for Amanpour supplying 'context' meant disregarding the possibility that responsibility for the massacre lay with the Bosnian Muslims, and explaining to her viewers the lack of 'any forensic evidence' meant discounting the crater analyses carried out by UN ballistics experts.

A similar line was taken by the *Guardian's* Ian Traynor, who wrote that 'UN and diplomatic sources in Zagreb, Geneva and New York ... unanimously maintain that they know of no instance where the Muslims have committed atrocities against their own side' (8 February 1994). The 1994 marketplace massacre was not the first time that Bosnian Muslim forces had been suspected by UN officials of staging atrocities, and Traynor sought to challenge earlier reporting – by Leonard Doyle in the *Independent* (22 August 1992) – of several similar incidents in Sarajevo, including the 27 May 1992 bread queue massacre which occurred on the eve of a scheduled UN vote on sanctions against Serbia, and a 'choreographed' mortar attack on 17 July 1992 which coincided with a visit to the city by British Foreign Secretary Douglas Hurd. Ignoring the evidence presented by Doyle as well as the more recent revelations, Traynor quoted UN sources dismissing all such allegations as 'completely fabricated and trumped up'.

Yet although Amanpour and Traynor both cited UN sources to disallow the possibility that the Bosnian Muslims staged atrocities in order to win international sympathy, it is clear that these suspicions originated from within the UN. Vulliamy says that Doyle's 1992 article was essentially 'Serbian propaganda', based on a Bosnian Serb press release 'leaked to gullible newspapers' (1999b), but this is simply not the case. Doyle cited UN officials, not Bosnian Serbs. While reporters portrayed the Bosnian Muslims as defenceless victims, many senior Western officials and military officers involved in Bosnia did not share journalists' black-and-white explanation of the conflict. UN General Francis Briquemont, for example, accused the Bosnian Muslims in Sarajevo of provoking the Bosnian Serbs 'on a daily basis' (quoted in Binder, 1994–5: 73). European Community mediator David Owen and UN General Phillipe Morillon voiced the same complaint, accusing Bosnian Muslim forces of trying to draw fire against Sarajevo's Kosevo hospital by using it as a mortar position (Bogdanich and Lettmayer, 2000), and General Charles Boyd, Deputy Commander in Chief of US European Command during the Bosnian war, suggested that contrary to the claims of journalists and

Western governments, 'no seasoned observer in Sarajevo doubts for a moment that Muslim forces have found it in their interest to shell friendly targets' (Boyd, 1995).

The memoirs of Phillip Corwin, who served as the UN's Chief Political Officer in Sarajevo, reveal that there were many among the UN staff who were willing to misrepresent the nature of the conflict for political reasons (Corwin, 1999). But when at least some UN personnel took their mandate as impartial 'peacekeepers' seriously and aired facts and views which shed doubt on media reporting of the war, some journalists, having abandoned neutrality themselves, attempted to discredit the UN. Little, for example, portrays the UN's public refusal to attribute blame definitively for the 1994 marketplace massacre as absurd neutrality – 'spokesmen would condemn nobody until they could condemn everyone in equal measure' – and suggests that, off the record, the UN mounted 'a sustained and systematic whispering campaign to try to blame the victims' (2001). Little thus appears to suggest it was wrong in principle for the UN even to investigate and try to establish the facts through examining the evidence, depicting this effort as nothing more than a covert smear campaign. This is one of the most troubling aspects of the journalism of attachment: not just that advocacy journalists may report inaccurately, but that they often apparently refuse even to examine the evidence or to countenance the possibility that things may not have been as black and white as they wished.[1] It is difficult to have much confidence in reporting conducted on this basis.

Vulliamy accuses the entire 'international community' of 'meddling with the truths of the war to stifle intervention and foster appeasement' and of 'spreading ... lies and distortions that would equate aggressor and victim' (1999b). Western 'neutrality', he charges, amounted to de facto support for the Serbs. Yet despite claiming to be critics of Western policy, and despite clashes with particular UN personnel, the simplistic perspective adopted by advocacy journalists was fully in tune with Western – particularly US – policy. Little acknowledges that Madeleine Albright, America's Ambassador to the UN and later Secretary of State, 'built a new consensus': 'Suddenly it was OK to describe Mr. Milošević as the driving force of the war. Suddenly it did not sound "unbalanced" or "partisan" to lay the blame squarely on the shoulders of one regime' (2001).

It may not have appeared as such, given that it reflected a consensus forged by the US State Department, but blaming the Serbs for the break-up of Yugoslavia undoubtedly was unbalanced and partisan. Indeed, sustaining the notion that one individual, regime or nation was to blame for the war required extraordinary selectivity on the part of both journalists and Western policy-makers. While the Serbian President Slobodan Milošević was routinely condemned as an ultra-nationalist, comparatively little attention was given to the political doctrines of Croatian President Franjo Tudjman and Bosnian leader Alija Izetbegovic, both of whom had espoused an exclusivist nationalism prior to the conflict.

Contrary to the claims of Little and others, Western policy-makers had blamed the Serbs for the war from the start. Presumably he and his colleagues simply think it is a massive coincidence that – before Albright established a consensus for military action against the Serbs – Yugoslavia was already subject to international sanctions and diplomatic censure, while the Croatian and Bosnian governments enjoyed the support of powerful Western states. As David Binder argues, US policy throughout the 1990s was ruled by 'a simplistic dogma that blames one nation, the Serbs, as the origin of evil in the Balkans' (2000). This 'unwritten doctrine', he suggests, was 'endorsed and spread by the mainstream media'. Similarly, Gowing notes that 'by and large the media took their cue from the regular declarations by Western ministers. The Serbs were the main guilty party' (1994: 55). Corwin describes a 'juggernaut of pro-Bosnian, anti-Serb sentiment in the international community' for which the Western media constituted 'a powerful public relations arm' (1999: 38). Boyd suggests that 'the linchpin of the US approach has been the under-informed notion that this is a war of good versus evil, of aggressor against aggrieved' (1995). An illustration of this is provided by former UN commander General Sir Michael Rose, who describes an aerial tour of Bosnia on which he and an American officer were accompanied by a woman from the US Embassy. Flying toward Tuzla by helicopter, the woman 'exclaimed excitedly': 'Look at what the criminal Serbs have done.' Rose pointed out that the scene below was of Croat villages razed by Bosnian Muslim forces. Arriving later at Mostar, she cried out: 'Well, at least this was done by the criminal Serbs', and nearly burst into tears when Rose pointed out that the Croats had been to blame (*Times*, 10 November 1998).

It was not ignorance but Western policy which established the framework within which the Serbs, reluctant to dismember the Yugoslav Federation and live under new states in which they could be persecuted and treated as second-class citizens (as happened in Croatia prior to the war), were perceived as 'aggressors'. German-led support for the secession of Slovenia and Croatia from the federation in 1991, and American pressure for international recognition of Bosnia in 1992, inevitably cast the Serbs as the villains. Even when confronted with evidence of Serb suffering, the black-and-white framework adopted by advocacy journalists often made them reluctant to report it. BBC World Affairs editor John Simpson, for example, recalled:

> Once, when I was in Sarajevo, the UN discovered that Muslim troops were holding a couple of dozen Serbs in a section of drainage pipe three feet high. They opened the front of the pipe once a day to throw food into the darkness inside. The journalists, many of them committed to the principle of not standing neutrally between victim and oppressor, showed no interest at all in this story. It was inconvenient and, as far as I know, was not reported.
>
> (*Sunday Telegraph*, 14 September 1997)

It is disturbing that an approach to journalism supposedly driven by moral concern for victims should deliberately make certain victims invisible. Canadian film-maker Garth Pritchard witnessed Croat atrocities committed against Serbs in the Krajina region in 1993 and 1995, but having documented horrors 'beyond most atrocities that I've tried to record, including the killing fields in Kosovo', he found that the National Film Board and 'other so-called Canadian national "news" agencies' were completely uninterested in the story. Despite the fact that his film had been commissioned, and despite the presence of Canadian UN troops at the incidents he had recorded, he could not get his work broadcast (*Toronto Sun*, 12 August 2001).

Journalists were not responsible for creating Western policy, but by faithfully reflecting it their reporting may be said to share some responsibility for its appalling consequences. First, like US policy, media reporting is accused of having helped to prolong the war. General Rose describes the international media as part of the Bosnian government's 'propaganda machine', accusing them of a 'mischievous distortion of reality' which hindered peacekeeping efforts (quoted in Owen, 1995: 187). Similarly, Corwin notes that reporters' 'oversimplified view of the Bosnian civil war', and the decision of many to side with the Bosnian government, 'undermined the peace process' (1999: 8–9). 'When,' he asks, 'was it ever a news story that the Bosnian government opposed peace [or] that the US government was urging them to continue fighting?' (ibid.: 113). Since journalists were preoccupied with attempting to encourage greater Western involvement, the military support given to Croatian and Bosnian Muslim forces by Germany, the US and other foreign powers was depicted as a lack of support. Indeed, more than five years after the end of the conflict the BBC persisted in presenting documentary evidence of covert Western arms drops to Croatia as confirmation of a lack of US involvement (*Correspondent*, BBC2, 24 June 2001). Second, some of the worst atrocities of the war, carried out with the diplomatic and military support of the United States, were actually welcomed by journalists. Thus, when the Croats forcibly expelled around 200,000 Serbs from Krajina in August 1995, killing an estimated 2,500 in the process, the *Guardian*'s Martin Woollacott wrote that the attack was 'to be welcomed', describing the slaughter of civilians as 'a hold on Serbian aggression' (5 August 1995), while the *Independent*'s editorialist said it was 'tempting to feel euphoric' (7 August 1995).

Third, NATO airstrikes were also encouraged and celebrated by journalists, with few questions asked about the pretext for such action. NATO's first attack against the Bosnian Serbs, in April 1994, was ostensibly a response to the Serbian assault on Gorazde, in which thousands were said to have been killed or wounded. It later transpired that the attack – deliberately provoked by Bosnian Muslim forces from within the nominally demilitarized Gorazde safe area – caused 'closer to 200 than 2,000 casualties', mostly soldiers, and that the extent of the fighting had been exaggerated by UN officials. General Rose, who had argued against the airstrikes, later revealed that the destruction of the town had largely resulted not from the Serbian shelling but from previous Bosnian Muslim attacks which had driven 12,500 Serbs from the area (Bogdanich and Lettmayer, 2000). In 1995 NATO bombed again, following a second marketplace massacre in Sarajevo on 28 August which had killed 37 and wounded 90. Again there is evidence that the atrocity was staged by the Bosnian Muslims in order to encourage outside intervention, but this time the information was effectively suppressed by the United States. Having threatened airstrikes the day before the August 1995 marketplace attack, the US announced that the Serbs were to blame without even waiting for the UN report on the incident. In any case, the UN report did blame the Serbs unequivocally, and it only emerged much later that the British and French UN officers who had investigated the scene had found no evidence that the Serbs had been to blame and suspected the Bosnian Muslims (*Times*, 1 October 1995).[2] At the time, their findings were summarily overruled by a senior US officer. NATO bombing commenced less than 48 hours after the 1995 marketplace massacre, to the evident satisfaction of journalists who had long campaigned for such action. Bell describes the reaction of reporters in Sarajevo to the NATO bombardment: 'through the jaded press corps in the battered hotel there spread a feeling new to all of us – a sense of awe and wonderment' (1996: 281).

Advocacy journalists covering Bosnia helped to create a climate in which NATO bombing and a US-sponsored Croatian offensive against

Serb civilians were seen as a welcome change from neutral humanitarianism and a helpful step toward a resolution of the conflict. Their colleagues did something very similar in Rwanda.

Rwanda

Media coverage of Rwanda has been subjected to much criticism. Initial reporting of the mass killings in April–June 1994 has been criticized for being insufficient, and, as noted above, for its confused and misleading emphasis on 'ancient tribal hatreds'. When Western media paid far greater attention to Rwanda, during the huge refugee exodus in July 1994 and the ensuing cholera epidemic in the refugee camps in Zaire, a further criticism was that journalists simply called for humanitarian aid and did not explain why the refugees were fleeing (McNulty, 1999: 279–80; Philo et al., 1999: 223–4). In fact most criticism of both stages of the coverage centred on the same issues: that reporters had been too neutral in not apportioning blame for the massacres, not explaining the killings as genocide, and not identifying the refugees as 'genocidaires'. Morally attached reporting certainly cannot be criticized on these grounds, and journalists themselves, such as Fergal Keane (1995: 6–8) and Philip Gourevitch (2000: 333–4), are among those who have voiced these criticisms. Yet in reporting both the causes and aftermath of the 1994 massacres advocacy journalism gave rise to its own problems.

A less remarked but highly significant aspect of coverage of Rwanda is the way that the moral certitudes which quickly became established in much reporting inhibited investigation of the causes of the massacres, and of the context of civil war in which they took place, just as effectively as tribalist explanations had done. Like Bosnia, Rwanda became a morality play, presented in simple, black-and-white terms. And as in Bosnia, this is justified by many commentators in terms of refusing to equate victims and abusers or to mitigate the crimes committed. It has therefore become axiomatic to isolate the slaughter of Tutsis and supporters of Hutu opposition parties as a discrete event – the genocide – which exists separately from the preceding years of civil war between the government of Juvénal Habyarimana and the Rwandan Patriotic Front. Alain Destexhe, for example, argues that 'genocide has nothing to do with war' (1995: 68), and Gourevitch writes that 'although the genocide coincided with the war, its organization and implementation were quite distinct from the war effort' (2000: 98). Failure to make this separation is seen as a failure to put the killings in a proper moral context. Interviewing former Rwandan Minister of Justice Stanislas Mbonampeka,

Gourevitch suggests that:

> By regarding the genocide ... as an extension of the war between the RPF [Rwandan Patriotic Front] and the Habyarimana regime, Mbonampeka seemed to be arguing that the systematic state-sponsored extermination of an entire people is a provokable crime – the fault of the victims as well as the perpetrators.
>
> (ibid.)

Yet the consequences of the black-and-white moral perspective adopted by writers such as Gourevitch are, firstly, that the role of Western powers in polarizing Rwandan society is rewritten as a helpful attempt toward encouraging democratization; and secondly, that instances when the RPF have also been perpetrators tend to be downplayed or ignored, while all Hutus (the vast majority of the Rwandan population) are viewed as, at best, unworthy victims, all more or less implicated in the crime of genocide.

Gourevitch goes on to argue that the massacres were provoked, not by war, but by the 'threat of peace' posed by the Arusha Accords (ibid.: 99), an agreement brokered by Western 'donors' in August 1993. Yet, as Barrie Collins' chapter in this volume makes clear, the Arusha 'democratization' process sharpened divisions in Rwandan society. From the perspective of the Habyarimana regime, the power-sharing arrangements envisaged by the Accords promised to reward the aggressive strategy of the RPF, which had repeatedly invaded from 1990 onwards, with vastly disproportionate influence under a proposed new government. The RPF, meanwhile, must have been acutely aware that democratization would eventually leave it as a minority party with no hope of overall electoral success. Though both signed the Accords, both sides were preparing for conflict.[3] Yet while there has been severe criticism of France for its support of the Rwandan government, there has been almost no acknowledgement that the arguably far more significant US-led intervention through the Arusha negotiations had catastrophic results for Rwanda. Nor has much attention been paid to the US role in supporting the RPF. According to Wayne Madsen the US officially began providing military training in January 1994 (1999: 125), and indirect training and support is known to have begun much earlier, when the RPF was exiled in Uganda prior to the 1990 invasion. RPF leader Paul Kagame, along with other senior officers, benefited from American training in the US as well as in US- and British-run facilities in Uganda. Kagame himself came to assume command of the 1990 invasion direct from Fort Leavenworth.

As Mahmood Mamdani notes, the civil war had a devastating effect on Rwandan society. Each RPF offensive produced greater and greater waves of internally displaced refugees as people fled en masse from the invading force: around 80,000 in 1990, 350,000 in 1992 and 950,000 following the February 1993 offensive (Mamdani, 2001: 187). By 1994, the displaced included one in every seven Rwandans. In addition, 300,000 refugees fled to Rwanda from Burundi following the October 1993 assassination of the elected Hutu president and the collapse of the democratization process in a civil war which killed over 50,000 people. Compounding Rwanda's already severe economic problems, the successive refugee crises created 'widespread hunger and starvation' (ibid.: 203). Abuses by the RPF had been documented following earlier invasions, but after the final 1994 offensive evidence of massacres by the RPF was suppressed. Following the RPF's victory in July 1994, a UNHCR team headed by Robert Gersony uncovered evidence of 'clearly systematic murders and persecution of the Hutu population in certain parts of the country' carried out by the RPF. According to Human Rights Watch Gersony's team estimated that 25,000 to 45,000 people had been killed by the RPF between April and August 1994, including the indiscriminate killing of women, children, the elderly and the handicapped (1999a). Reluctant to undermine the new RPF government, the UN suppressed the report, claiming it did not exist and forbidding Gersony himself to speak about it.

If this context of civil war is not properly taken into account, other factors have to be invoked to explain the speed, ferocity and widespread participation in the killings of April–June 1994. Perhaps the most common explanation offered is that Rwandan culture made people exceptionally deferential to authority and they therefore unquestioningly obeyed orders to kill. As some critics have pointed out, however, this explanation is not only implausible, since it overlooks evidence of 'a growing defiance of authority' in early 1990s Rwanda (Mamdani, 2001: 200), it also offers a 'cultural' version of the very tribalist framework it seeks to avoid (Collins, 1998). With the context of ongoing civil war bracketed out, and the evidence of RPF massacres effectively suppressed, the RPF has been widely depicted as a benign force, to be praised for 'ending the genocide', despite the fact that, as Human Rights Watch notes, RPF strategy was designed to secure overall military victory rather than to rescue the maximum number of Tutsi civilians, and despite the fact that the RPF strongly opposed UN proposals at the end of April 1994 to send 'a larger peacekeeping force ... with a broader mandate to protect civilians' (HRW, 1999a). Meanwhile, if the context of war and RPF aggression is ignored or minimized, Hutu fear of the RPF can be dismissed as having no real basis, and as simply the result of propaganda blindly believed because of Rwanda's alleged culture of conformity and the gullibility of Hutu peasants (see, for example: Keane, 1995: 9; Destexhe, 1995: 33).

As the good Tutsi/evil Hutu framework became entrenched in the months and years following RPF victory, journalists grew increasingly critical of the provision of relief to Hutu refugees and regretted the initial media sympathy for the tens of thousands of cholera victims who died in the camps. As Gourevitch puts it, humanitarian aid workers were 'openly exploited as caterers to what was probably the single largest society of fugitive criminals against humanity ever assembled' (2000: 267). With the evidence of RPF massacres exposed by Gersony covered up, it was argued that the one million refugees in Zaire had nothing to fear if they returned to Rwanda and that something else must be keeping them in the camps: either they were guilty, or were being held through 'propaganda and brute force' as a 'human shield' for those who were (ibid.: 266–7). In April 1995, according to UN and NGO workers, around 8,000 internally displaced Hutus were killed when RPF troops opened fire with machine guns and rocket-propelled grenades on the Kibeho camp inside Rwanda. The initial response, however, of both the British government and some journalists was to blame the refugees. Echoing the claim of UK Development Minister Baroness Linda Chalker that 'These camps are full of Hutu extremists with weaponry', the *Times* described Kibeho as 'the last redoubt of the Interahamwe – the Hutu death squads in Rwanda' and suggested, without offering any evidence, that 'the [RPF] soldiers were menaced by the mobs of machete-wielding Hutu extremists present in the camp' (editorial, 25 April 1995). Details of the Kibeho massacre emerged over the following weeks, but did not alter fundamental Western attitudes. By the following year, evidence of continuing violence in Rwanda was again forgotten as journalists continued to present Hutu refugees in eastern Zaire as the problem. The *Guardian*'s Chris McGreal, for example, while conceding that not everyone in the camps was guilty and that conditions in Rwanda were 'not ideal' for returnees, nevertheless wrote of 'armed camps of fanatics' in which Western aid was 'sustaining the genocidal dogma' of Hutu extremists (23 October 1996).

In autumn 1996 the RPF invaded eastern Zaire and attacked the refugee camps. Mugunga camp, which had already absorbed thousands of refugees fleeing attacks on other sites, was shelled for six hours on 15 November with heavy mortar and artillery. Mass killings continued over several months as the refugees were, in the words of Refugees International, 'herded and hunted' across Zaire. By April 1997 it was estimated that 10,000 refugees had been killed since the previous November, and UN official Roberto Garreton reported 'indubitable evidence of mass graves and massacres' (Refugees International, 1997: 82, 58). But we will probably never know precisely what happened: the UN investigation into the killings was abandoned after obstruction by the new Zairian leadership which the RPF intervention had helped to install.

The massacres of refugees in 1996–7 were legitimized by the way Rwanda had come to be viewed as a simple tale of good victims versus genocidal abusers. The *Independent*, for example, hailed the violent break-up of Mugunga camp and the forced repatriation of thousands of refugees as 'some good news from Africa', describing it as 'the outcome everyone wished for' (16 November 1996). Oxfam's Director of Emergencies, Nick Stockton, has described how journalists, wishing to compensate for their failings in 1994, helped condone the attacks on refugees:

> ... some of the best British correspondents who knew the region and its politics rapidly promoted a consensus that here, at last, was the chance to deal with an entirely murderous group [the Hutu] who had been foolishly succoured by aid.
>
> (quoted in Gowing, 1998: 36)[4]

Gowing's interviews with humanitarian workers and journalists reveal how the mass killings of Hutu refugees were justified and legitimized by reporters who viewed events through a 'lens of sympathy'. Many were 'readily pro-Tutsi to the exclusion of what one journalist accepted was "any other more balanced possibility"', while 'all Hutus were often implicitly written off as "killers" or "extremists"' (ibid.: 40–1). Much reporting of the violent assault on the Zairian refugee camps continued to suggest that the Hutu refugees were the threat: *Times* correspondent Sam Kiley described those who did not return to Rwanda as 'heading deeper into the interior of [Zaire] to fulfil a military plan to establish a "safe and sure base" for a future invasion of Rwanda' (19 November 1996).

As one of Gowing's interviewees, an NGO doctor, indicates, this pattern of reporting was entirely in line with Western policy: 'The international community wanted a "moral legitimacy" for Kagame' (1998: 40). At a meeting of regional African leaders in October 1996 US Secretary of State Warren Christopher called for the camps to be closed, effectively encouraging the attacks on what Washington described as 'centres of terrorism' (*Guardian*, 23 October 1996). Furthermore, in the weeks prior to the RPF invasion of Zaire, the US was providing training, supposedly simply to 'professionalize' the RPF military, but in fact including training in psychological warfare and special forces operations.[5] Yet the role of Western governments, particularly the USA, was obscured. Following the forced return of refugees in November 1996, some humanitarian organizations continued to highlight the plight of around 700,000 who had not repatriated, but the US provided overflight data which drastically underestimated the number of refugees who had fled. Some aid workers also believe that information on the location of these 'missing' refugees was passed to the RPF government and their allies in Zaire. In announcing the data at the US Embassy in Kigali, the American military briefer referred to the refugees as 'targets of opportunity', identifying some groups as Interahamwe militia despite having no way of knowing this, and despite the fact that most refugees were women and children (Gowing, 1998: 59–60). As Stockton observes, many journalists failed to question the low US figures, giving the misinformation a 'legitimacy that US official information managers could barely have dreamed of' (quoted in ibid.: 42). Criticism of the West for supposedly excessive 'neutrality' in dealing with the camps amounted to support for the killing of refugees with US approval and training.

New humanitarianism

In understanding the journalism of attachment, it is important to place it in a wider context. Firstly, the explicit rejection of neutrality by some reporters has closely paralleled similar developments among humanitarian organizations. Notwithstanding journalists' criticisms of their 'neutrality', humanitarian agencies have frequently failed to maintain neutrality in practice, and have increasingly rejected it in principle also. Secondly, as I have argued, despite their claim to be critical and independent, advocacy journalists have tended to follow the agenda of powerful Western governments. Their chief complaint – that the West did not intervene early enough or with sufficient strength – was never much of a criticism, and in any case, the intellectual convergence among attached journalists, leading humanitarian agencies and Western policymakers is now clear. Reporters who frame conflicts in terms of a good-versus-evil discourse of abusers and victims and call for ever-greater Western intervention perform a valuable service to governments which, having lost the stable framework of the Cold War, couch their foreign policy in the language of human rights and morality.

When Vulliamy urges that 'the time has come for aid workers to challenge the commandment of neutrality' (quoted in Fox, 2001: 277), he is simply encouraging a development which is already well underway. One of Gowing's interviewees, an aid worker, noted that: 'Most journalists had committed themselves to the idea that the [refugee] camps [in eastern Zaire] were full of genocidal Hutu maniacs, and that they had to be repatriated.' But as Gowing comments: 'Many in the humanitarian community had also made the same commitment' (1998: 24). Predicting an imminent attack on the camps in November 1996, Concern International director Mike McDonagh suggested that 'despite the fact that some innocent people would be killed, the matter will be resolved once and for all' (*Times*, 15 November 1996). Some days later, as it transpired that the attacks were indeed taking place, McDonagh recommended: 'the rebels should be left to get on with clearing out the camps in their own way. They would be doing both us and the refugees a favour' (*Times*, 21 November 1996). Journalists who welcomed the RPF-led offensive against the refugees echoed the sentiments of many aid organizations.

In both Rwanda and the former Yugoslavia, attached journalists were particularly critical of the UN for what they saw as inadequate or weak action, and attacked UN neutrality. Reflecting on a proposed international intervention in Zaire, for example, Kiley lamented the prospect of 'British soldiers [being] asked by the UN to drive food and fresh water into the camps, to give succour to Hutu extremists who will live on to kill' (*Times*, 15 November 1996). Yet in practice UN agencies have not always acted with strict neutrality. UNHCR spokesman Ray Wilkinson took a very similar view to Kiley's, suggesting that the forcible break-up of the camps meant that: 'From a humanitarian point of view a major nut has been cracked. We've got what we wanted' (*Times*, 16 November 1996). Rather than acting neutrally, the UNHCR itself had already attempted to coerce refugees into returning to Rwanda, reducing food rations and refusing to treat new cases of TB or AIDS (Fox, 2000: 24). Similarly, anticipating the 1999 NATO bombing of Yugoslavia the *Independent*'s editorialist recalled how UN troops in Bosnia had been 'forced ... to scuttle around in armoured personnel carriers, dealing out charity', and expressed the hope that: 'Now that humiliation may be over' (25 March 1999). Yet Corwin's memoirs reveal divisions within the UN in Bosnia which meant that: 'The local UNHCR team were clearly part of the politically correct pro-Bosnian government juggernaut', opposing Corwin's suggestion that the UN should protest Bosnian government provocations against the Bosnian Serb Army (1999: 154–5).

As Fiona Fox explains in Chapter 1, humanitarianism has been rede-fined in the post-Cold War era: away from principles of neutrality and impartiality, and towards a human rights-based 'new humanitarianism'. The shift was symbolized by the award of the Nobel Peace Prize to Médecins sans Frontières (MSF) in 1999, in contrast to the award of the prize to the International Committee of the Red Cross at the beginning of the twentieth century (Sellars, 1999). While the ICRC stands for neu-trality, MSF is known for its willingness to condemn human rights abusers and to challenge national sovereignty if governments of coun-tries on the receiving end of Western humanitarianism seek to resist or obstruct intervention. MSF was one of the first NGOs to withdraw from the refugee camps in eastern Zaire, declaring it was 'ethically impossible for MSF to continue aiding and abetting the perpetrators of the Rwandan genocide' (quoted in Halvorsen, 1999: 316). Others followed their lead, so that 'Within a year of the refugees arriving ... the number of relief agencies had dropped from 150 to five' (Fox, 2000: 23).

The new humanitarianism developed by MSF and other NGOs, and the complementary stance adopted by attached journalists, are very close to mainstream Western policy. UK Development Minister Clare Short agreed with MSF that 'humanitarian assistance strengthened the evil forces which had brought about the genocide in Rwanda' (quoted in Fox, 2000: 24), and Secretary of State Albright 'condemned the use of humanitarian aid "to sustain armed camps or to support genocidal killers"' (Gourevitch, 2000: 350). The 'new consensus' developed by Albright on Bosnia, which Allan Little describes as vindicating his sup-port of military intervention, was on full display in the 1999 NATO bombing of Yugoslavia – a war which was justified using precisely the terminology of human rights and new humanitarianism. Appropriately, after NATO's 'liberation' of Kosovo, MSF's founder, Bernard Kouchner, was appointed as governor of the new UN protectorate: NATO's aggres-sive bombing of a sovereign state exemplified the 'right to intervention' which he had long championed.

Advocacy journalists also deserve some credit for legitimizing the NATO bombing. As *Guardian* reporter Maggie O'Kane boasted: 'it was the press reporting of the Bosnian war and the Kosovar refugee crisis that gave [British Prime Minister Tony Blair] the public support and sympathy he needed to fight the good fight against Milošević' (quoted in Glass, 1999). In the buildup to the conflict many journalists not only urged NATO bombing, but deliberately distorted events in order to encourage it. At the negotiations brokered by NATO powers ostensibly to resolve the Kosovo crisis, for example, 'rafts of journalists' were told by a senior State Department official that NATO had 'deliberately set the bar higher than the Serbs could accept' because Yugoslavia 'needed a little bombing' (Kenney, 1999), but all of them failed to report this. During the air war, reporters frequently did their best to excuse NATO 'accidents' and 'collateral damage': although NATO's bombings of ethnic Albanian refugees attracted some negative publicity, there was only minimal and muted media criticism of strikes against passenger trains, buses, bridges, domestic heating plants, electricity stations, factories, television buildings and marketplaces. At the same time, reporters repeated and embellished NATO claims of Serb mass killing, failing to question the figures of 100,000 and more dead given by State Department spokesmen at the time, which have since proven false (Hammond and Herman, 2000).

Although not all reporters explicitly endorse the strongly held views of advocacy journalists, the devaluation of neutrality and dispassionate reporting, coupled with the espousal of a 'moral' line, both complements and encourages the new humanitarianism promoted by Western governments and NGOs. In this respect the journalism of attachment may seem little different from the flawed tradition of 'objective journalism': claiming independence but actually closely following the agenda of powerful interests. By abandoning even the pretence of neutrality, however, today's advocacy journalism also recalls that of an earlier era: the American 'yellow press' of the 1890s. This too was a journalism which, in the words of one of its leading exponents, James Creelman, was 'thrilled by the consciousness of its moral responsibility', and which aimed to encourage US military intervention abroad through what Frederic Moritz charitably characterizes as 'human rights reporting' but which is more generally viewed as 'irresponsible, jingoistic sensationalism' (Moritz, 1997a and 1997b). Apparently thrilled with its sense of moral responsibility, contemporary 'human rights journalism' involves suppressing inconvenient information, distorting public understanding of conflicts, applauding the deaths of designated Western hate-figures (including the civilians associated with them), and ignoring evidence of the destructive effects of Western involvement in countries such as Rwanda and the former Yugoslavia.

The actual irresponsibility of the journalism of attachment derives from its being a part of the broader 'new humanitarian' discourse. The logic of the moralized approach to conflicts is to seek to escalate violence in order to deal with 'evil' human rights abusers. Hence, for example, many commentators complained that the Kosovo bombing was insufficiently violent. Vulliamy disparaged it as merely 'half a war, a war that doesn't have soldiers in it' (1999a). Michael Ignatieff criticized the contemporary view of war as a 'surgical scalpel', instead advising that we should see it as a 'bloodstained sword', and should resolve that 'when the sword is raised, it must be used to strike decisively' (2000a: 215, 213). David Rieff bemoaned the 'limited' and 'hesitant' character of the bombing, and advocated the 'recolonization of part of the world' under a system of 'liberal imperialism' (1999b: 10). As Ignatieff (2000a: 213) acknowledges, there is a 'potential for self-righteous irrationality which lies hidden in abstractions like human rights':

> For high-flown abstractions carry an inherent justification of every-thing done in their name. What is to prevent moral abstractions like human rights from inducing an absolutist frame of mind which, in defining all human rights violators as barbarians, legitimizes bar-barism? ... In theory, [the language of human rights] will not lend itself to dividing human beings into higher and lower, superior and inferior, civilized and barbarian. Yet something very like a distinction between superior and inferior has been at work in the demonization of human rights violators.

In today's circumstances, advocacy journalism and the broader human rights discourse of which it is a part do indeed legitimize barbarism.

Notes

1. The UN made a report on the 1994 massacre available to journalists, yet only one – *New York Times* correspondent David Binder – followed it up. Even then, Binder was obliged to publish his investigative article about the incident else-where since his newspaper declined to carry it (Gowing, 1997: 31; Hume, 1997: 9).
2. Binder (1995) also recorded similar suspicions on the part of two further UN officers (a Canadian and a Russian), an American military officer and a US government official.
3. This is confirmed by the public statement of former RPF intelligence officer Jean-Pierre Mugabe, now an adviser to the US International Strategic Studies Association, issued on 21 April 2000.
4. Page numbers refer to the version of Gowing's paper available at <http://www.usip.org/oc/vd/mic/micwebcast.html> (quoted with the author's permission).
5. See the reports by Lynne Duke in the *Washington Post*, 16 August 1997 and 14 July 1998.

10
Morality's Avenging Angels: the New Humanitarian Crusaders

Edward S. Herman and David Peterson

Introduction

Operation Allied Force was not a moral venture. It was, however, carried out in the name of a humanitarian action on behalf of the Kosovo Albanians, and it won support in the NATO-bloc countries by a widespread belief in the authenticity of its moral goals. But such goals are contradicted by the nature of states and the kinds of forces that determine state policy, by the compelling evidence of other, non-humanitarian ends shaping NATO policy, by the character of the leadership of the dominant NATO powers and by the actual results of the war.

States are not moral institutions and their foreign policies are shaped by economic and political interests and strategic considerations, not by humane values. When humanitarian crises abroad receive attention within a society, and the government responds to them, as the US and several other NATO-power governments did in 1998–9, it is necessary to explain the source of that attention, which regularly turns out to be serviceable to larger material and political interests and not unwelcome to the policy-making authorities. Conversely, the same point can be made as regards the lack of attention to humanitarian crises where focused attention would be objectionable to those powerful interests shaping policy. Neither a random process nor the scale of human rights abuses can explain the Great Power officials', media's and parallel New Humanitarians' virtual neglect of mass killings and ethnic cleansings of the Kurdish population in Turkey during the 1990s or of the East Timorese in 1998–9, and their intense focus on human rights in the Balkans, 1991–2001.[1]

NATO's 'humanitarian war' against Yugoslavia was damaging to human rights, human welfare and most of the objectives claimed by the war-makers. The 78-day bombing campaign greatly intensified an already ugly civil war that had produced between 1800 and 2000 dead on all sides – most of them ethnic Albanians – in the year prior to the start of the bombing (Dientsbier, 2000: para. 42; Chomsky, 2000: 104). This war had been largely brought under control by an agreement signed by the six member Contact Group and Belgrade in October 1998, thus allowing many of the 300,000 refugees from the first round of fighting to return home (OSCE, 1999a). This relatively stable situation held throughout the fall and winter months through the end of the Rambouillet process (18 March 1999), the OSCE's withdrawal of its Kosovo Verification Mission and the onset of NATO's war.

From 1 January 1998 through to the 10 June end of the war, perhaps as many as 7000 people were killed in Kosovo on all sides,[2] and the war itself produced a refugee crisis five times *worse* than that of 1998, causing some 863,000 ethnic Albanians to flee the province, along with 100,000 ethnic Serbs and other minorities, and with another 590,000 people displaced internally (OSCE, 1999a). In the words of Canadian OSCE observer Rollie Keith, NATO's war 'turned an internal humanitarian problem into a disaster' (Keith, 1999), and according to UN Special Rapporteur for Human Rights in Yugoslavia, Jiri Dienstbier, 'has not solved any human problem, but only multiplied the existing problems' (cited in *Czech News Agency*, 2000). Furthermore, war-related destruction and environmental damage throughout Serbia (Kosovo included) was massive, with serious long-term ramifications for its citizens and other countries in the region as well.

It has also been documented that the NATO powers, the United States especially, had underwritten the insurgency of the Kosovo Liberation Army (KLA) (Walker and Laverty, 2000; Beaumont et al., 2001). This support for 'terrorists' (US Special Envoy Robert Gelbard's assessment of the KLA in February 1998) and failure to curb ongoing KLA provocations call into question NATO's concern over human rights violations in Kosovo. On the contrary, their literal encouragement, and NATO's 'raising the bar' to preclude a negotiated settlement at Rambouillet, suggests NATO's determination to go to war for other reasons.[3]

President Clinton said at the time that the aims of the war were to bring 'stability' to the region, to end the 'ethnic cleansing' of the Kosovo Albanians thus allowing the refugees to return to their homes and the people to live together based on 'the principle of multi-ethnic, tolerant, inclusive democracy' (Clinton, 1999). But the much greater second wave of refugees was produced *during* the bombing, and the war both inflamed and entrenched ethnic hatreds. These unnecessary catastrophes were followed by a postwar ethnic cleansing by KLA cadres, killing large numbers (well over a thousand) and causing the flight of an estimated 330,000 ethnic non-Albanians (Dienstbier, 2000: para. 43). All of this was contrary to both Clinton's and NATO's stated goals as well as the commitment undertaken by the UN at the end of the bombing, under Security Council Resolution 1244, to demilitarize the KLA and protect minorities. This NATO-protected ethnic cleansing was more ecumenical than anything done by the Serbs in Kosovo that supposedly justified the resort to war; Jan Oberg has called it 'the largest ethnic cleansing in the Balkans [in percentage terms]' (Oberg, 2000).

Today, the province of Kosovo has become a peculiar non-state in transition to an unknown but unpromising destiny: fear-ridden, lawless, with a high level of inter-ethnic conflict, and – on the model of Bosnia-Hercegovina – a de facto colony run by foreign powers (NATO, the European Union and dozens of NGOs) in the name of 'democracy'. It is an 'artificially multi-ethnic' state with its multi-ethnicity shrinking steadily by voluntary exit and ethnic cleansing, and with 'sham elections' covering over the absence of either local authority or democratic institutions (Hayden, 1998; Chandler, 2001). Finally, by supporting and providing a home base for the KLA, NATO has made Kosovo a haven for organized crime and the drug trade, and allowed other incarnations of the KLA to launch serious insurgencies within Macedonia and southern Serbia. In short, the consequences of NATO's war provide overwhelming evidence that, from a humanitarian perspective, the war was a disaster, taking a heavy human toll and exacerbating ethnic hatred, and wreaking havoc throughout the region.

Despite this sorry record, and despite the traditional aversion of human rights advocates and the Left to war as a policy option, one of the most striking features of NATO's war against Yugoslavia was the support given to it by intellectuals, human rights officials, lawyers and jurists, and 'advocacy journalists' (see Hammond, this volume, Chapter 9), a number presenting themselves as 'on the Left', who accepted the official claim that NATO's main objective was humanitarian. This of course gave them ready access to the mainstream media, where they complemented official sources and the media's own war-supportive biases, and helped put the war in a good light.

The defining characteristics of the New Humanitarians are that (1) they take sides, and have done so in parallel with NATO policy; (2) they reject traditional humanitarianism's principles of neutrality, impartiality, independence, non-violence and the provision of care; and (3) they advocate a 'humanitarian' right to intervene by state violence to terminate human rights abuses. In the following section we will discuss briefly who they are, their commitments, and their sources of influence. In the final section we will deal in more detail with their views and analyses of events in the Balkans.

The New Humanitarians to the barricades

Among the New Humanitarians, and the set that we will study most intensively, are Timothy Garton Ash, Václav Havel, Christopher Hitchens, Michael Ignatieff, Tim Judah, Mary Kaldor, Bernard Kouchner, Aryeh Neier, David Rieff, Geoffrey Robertson, Kenneth Roth and Susan Sontag. But there are many others worthy of mention, including M. Cherif Bassiouni, Antonio Cassese, Ivo Daalder, Bogdan Denitch, Richard Falk, Michael Glennon, Richard Goldstone, Philip Gourevitch, Roy Gutman, Jürgen Habermas, David Held, Louis Henkin, Paul Hockenos, Stanley Hoffman, Bernard-Henri Levy, Andrew Linklater, James Mayall, Martha Minow, Michael O'Hanlon, Diane Orentlicher, Steven Ratner, David Rohde, William Shawcross, Brian Urquhart, Ruth Wedgwood, Marc Weller, Nicholas J. Wheeler and Ian Williams. The 40 individuals listed here fall into a number of sometimes overlapping categories: Havel is an intellectual and political leader, at least eight have worked for governments or NATO-related organizations involved in Balkan policy (Cassese, Goldstone, Daalder, Havel, Hockenos, Kouchner, O'Hanlon, Urquhart), four are or have been affiliated with human rights organizations (Kouchner, Neier, Orentlicher and Roth), 10 are journalists, 20 are academics, six of the academics are professors of law (Bassiouni, Falk, Orentlicher, Ratner, Wedgwood, Weller), one is a lawyer (Robertson), and Sontag is a free-floating artist and writer.

The New Humanitarians very openly and quickly 'chose sides', many of them entering the lists during the struggle within Bosnia in the early 1990s and immediately attaching themselves to the Bosnian Muslims, then engaged in civil wars with Bosnian Croat and Bosnian Serb forces. David Rieff, for one, forthrightly espoused 'the Bosnian cause', and with reference to Kosovo was not only 'in favor of more bombing' but asserted that: 'I would be in the lead vehicle in a ground war' (cited in Henwood, 1999). Rieff refers to his comrade Ignatieff as having 'campaigned' for NATO's 1995 bombing of the Bosnian Serbs, and lauds him as 'an advocate' of a policy of greater force (Rieff, 2000b).

The New Humanitarians have been members of a network of like-minded people who are often friends who work in coordination with government officials and government-linked thinktanks, bonding and hobnobbing among themselves in Sarajevo or at international confer- ences and being fed information by US and Bosnian Muslim officials.[4] They review one another's books and cite and laud one another as authorities profusely.[5] Sometimes, they work together in establishment operations such as the Independent International Commission on Kosovo (Richard Falk, Richard Goldstone, Michael Ignatieff, Mary Kaldor, Martha Minow), the International Crisis Group (William Shawcross), the American Academy in Berlin (Paul Hockenos), George Soros' Open Society Institute (Aryeh Neier), and offshoots of these and similar institutions. The first three groups are heavily funded by NATO governments, and have on their boards numerous NATO government officials, past and present. Indeed, the important human rights group Human Rights Watch, which was vocally supportive of NATO's war against the Bosnian Serbs and later Serbia itself, takes money from the US government and has on its board a number of US government offi- cials, past and present.[6]

Rieff lauds Ignatieff's 'close relations with such important figures in the West's political and military leadership as Richard Holbrooke and Gen. Wesley Clark' (Rieff, 2000b) and, in his book *Virtual War*, Ignatieff acknowledges his debt to Holbrooke, Clark and former Hague chief pros- ecutor Louise Arbour, among others (Ignatieff, 2000a: 6). It is clear that the New Humanitarians are members of an establishment that includes NATO, the Hague Tribunal and human rights group officials, as well as the mainstream media, which treats them as authentic and objective experts. Their privileged access to the media, which they share with their comradely friends in the State Department and Pentagon, helps produce a media echo chamber in which few opposing views or even corrections of error can be heard.

Having chosen sides, and made a simple-minded identification of the people doing evil and those who are innocent victims of the evildoers, the New Humanitarians take an extremely narrow view of humanitarian and human rights issues. This was true in the Bosnian wars, and it continued in Kosovo, where the welfare of the Kosovo Albanians, as seen by the Albanians themselves, has been the New Humanitarians' main if not exclusive standard of appraisal. The obverse has been a dehumanization of the Serbs in a process that approaches racism, evidenced by the fact that their writings show them to be minimally troubled by the wartime and postwar hardships and ethnic cleansings suffered by the Krajina Serbs or by the Serbs, Roma, Turks, Jews and other ethnic minorities of Kosovo.

Bernard Kouchner, the New Humanitarian proconsul in post-bomb- ing Kosovo, stated in public to the Kosovo Albanians: 'I love all peoples, but some more than others, and that is the case with you.' He also said that: 'You have fought for a better Kosovo, a Kosovo where people can lead a peaceful and happy life.' But in reply to a Kosovo Serb who asked why the West couldn't stop the violence by the 'liberated' Albanians, and allow people to live together, Kouchner stated that 'I know the history of the Serbian people ... We know well that because of the evils to which the Albanian people were subjected, a common life is not possible at this time' (cited in Radomirovic, 1999). This staggering expression of bias, with the Serbs (and other non-Albanians) apparently not entitled to 'a common life', and his de facto alliance with the KLA – under Kouchner the KLA was incorporated into the Kosovo Protection Corps, its war criminal leaders Hashim Thaci and Agim Ceku given honoured status[7] – helps explain Kouchner's complaisance at the massive ethnic cleansing under his New Humanitarian rule in Kosovo.

Kouchner is not alone. Almost uniformly the New Humanitarians use the word 'Kosovar' to mean an ethnic *Albanian* inhabitant of Kosovo only, and their concern for the mistreatment of non-Albanians has been minimal. Thus Ian Williams can write at the war's end about the urgency of resettling the 'Kosovar refugees', while at the same time suggesting that the 'Serbian population of Kosovo, like that of Krajina, will probably and wisely take the road back to Serbia. And in five years, there will be an independent Kosova' (Williams, 1999a). Some ethnic cleansings are outrageous; others are entirely acceptable.

What has driven the New Humanitarians into supporting a series of cruel and devastating Great Power wars over the past decade? We have no doubt that most of them have done this with the best of motives, even if they have been, as we firmly believe (and attempt to show below), badly misguided, self-deceived and atrocious analysts and historians. Some have been overwhelmed by the portrayals of one side's suffering and victimization as filtered through an effective propaganda system, including many working 'on the scene' in Sarajevo. Also important, with the old Soviet threat no longer available, it is useful to find an area where villains abuse innocent victims allegedly seeking to maintain a multi-ethnic democracy (Bosnia) or struggling for self-determination (Kosovo).

There is also an economic factor: money is available from NATO governments and establishment institutions like George Soros' network of foundations to human rights groups, scholars and journalists who follow the NATO party line. Furthermore, the selling of articles, books and news reports is conditioned on feeding into accepted perspectives. Those that meet the quickly established consensus will sell; those that contest it will not and may even be vilified as 'apologetics for Milošević'.

The New Humanitarians as propaganda agents of NATO

Channelled benevolence

As we have noted, the New Humanitarians have focused on Yugoslavia, and their alignment there with those opposing the Serbs was in complete accord with US and NATO policy.[8] It is interesting to observe, also, that massive human rights abuses in countries supported by the NATO powers, such as Turkey, Indonesia in East Timor, Colombia and Israel in its Occupied Territories, received slight or zero attention from the New Humanitarians. Thus a large sample of the recent mainstream media publications of 12 leading New Humanitarians that dealt with human rights issues shows that while they concerned themselves with the Yugoslav conflicts in 101 articles, human rights issues relating to East Timor, Israel, Colombia and Turkey were mentioned, briefly, in only three.[9]

The selectivity of US and NATO human rights policy flies in the face of the New Humanitarians' claim that human rights 'has taken hold not just as a rhetorical but as an operating principle in all the major Western capitals on issues that concern political crisis in poor countries and failing states' (Rieff, 1999b), and that 'the military campaign in Kosovo depends for its legitimacy on what fifty years of human rights have done to our moral instincts ... strengthening the presumption of intervention when massacre and deportation become state policy' (Ignatieff, quoted in ibid.). Why do these 'instincts' shrivel and why does the 'operating principle' cease to work for massacre and deportation in East Timor, Colombia and elsewhere? Rieff cites Aryeh Neier's 'eloquent' reply, that 'a human rights double standard where powerful countries like China are concerned does not mean nothing has changed' (ibid.). But Indonesia, Colombia, Israel and Turkey are not powerful countries, and their exemption suggests that the moral instinct is easily overridden, that there is no 'operating principle' at all, and that we must look for factors other than a new morality to explain the Kosovo intervention.

What is even more interesting is the adaptation of the New Humanitarians to the human rights double standard. Even if commercial and other power-related interests weaken the new morality for political leaders, why must the New Humanitarians replicate this double standard? Shouldn't they be struggling to offset the corrupting forces and make human rights the *real* operating principle? Shouldn't they be campaigning on behalf of East Timorese and other long-standing victims of Western collusion with human rights violators? That they don't do this, but instead join the bandwagon geared to Western interests and convenience, raises serious questions about their own clearly politicized human rights concerns and whether these really serve to advance human rights.

When confronted with the fact that they seem to give little attention to US- and NATO-protected human rights abuses, the New Humanitarians have given a variety of responses. One is that Yugoslavia was in 'Europe's backyard', and being so close, attracted attention. David Rieff quotes approvingly Clinton's statement that NATO acted to prevent 'the slaughter of innocents on its doorstep' (Rieff, 1999b). But Turkey is not only on Europe's doorstep, it is a member of NATO itself, and the interests of the United States and its willingness to intervene with force has been global (for example, the Korean and Vietnam wars, the US interventions in Afghanistan and Iraq, etc.).

A second New Humanitarian response has been that 'you can't do everything', and we may therefore have to be satisfied with what is 'politically possible' (Rieff, 2000a). It does not bother them that their efforts are so well coordinated with those of the imperial powers, and it seems not to occur to them that governments perfectly happy to work with major ethnic cleansers such as Suharto and the Turkish generals may have non-humane agendas in the 'politically possible' places, or that the governments' real agendas might contaminate the outcomes (and a number of them acknowledge that the effects of the Kosovo war were disappointing and may threaten similar humanitarian ventures elsewhere) (Garton Ash, 2000a). The New Humanitarians also neglect the fact that their own intense and indignant focus on unapproved villainy (i.e. the Serbs in Bosnia, Croatia and Kosovo) may deflect attention from sometimes large-scale approved or acceptable villainy (i.e. Turkey's treatment of its Kurds), thereby making it easier to do nothing or even support ethnic cleansing in the latter cases. In the latter cases, also, it might be possible to control abuses without resort to war, by simply terminating or threatening to terminate support.

Advocating war as a humanitarian instrument

As noted, traditional humanitarianism demanded strict neutrality and impartiality, with a mission of assisting victims of conflict. The New Humanitarians not only cast aside these principles, they supported NATO's resort to war against Yugoslavia, often with great enthusiasm. As Michael Ignatieff has written, in certain circumstances 'the international community has to take sides and do so with crushing force' (Ignatieff, 2000c).

The idea that war can serve a humanitarian end, and the very concepts of 'humanitarian war' and 'humanitarian bombing' (Held, 1995: 219–86;

Falk, 1998: 49–107; Linklater, 1998: 179–212), would seem outlandish not only in terms of traditional notions of humanitarianism, but also in the light of historical experience with war. Wars produce a cycle of violence and counter-violence that is hard to contain, and a great deal of cruelty, misery and destruction. That war can be a useful means to humanitarian ends assumes a degree of control, knowledge, restraint and nobility of Great Power objectives that we may call Military Utopianism (as is implicit in Kaldor, 1999a). The New Humanitarians have scanted discussion of postwar Kosovo, perhaps because it illustrates so well the coarsening and brutalizing effects of war, which as Dienstbier says has 'only multiplied the existing problems'.

The New Humanitarians have argued that moral imperatives override the problematic means, ignoring not only the historic record of warfare but also the moral significance of employing dubious means in serving alleged higher ends. They also ignore the possibility that moral imperatives may be manipulated and misperceived, with the result that the means serve immoral or amoral ends (for example, NATO's desire to punish the Serbs and to achieve certain political and geopolitical goals).

Advocating the abrogation of the rule of law

The New Humanitarians have had to deal with the awkward fact that NATO's war against Yugoslavia violated international law at many levels – most importantly, the UN Charter's prohibition of war as an instrument of policy except in self-defence, the barring of intervention in the internal affairs of sovereign states, and NATO's violations of the rules of war in its attacks on civilian facilities and use of illegal weaponry (Brownlie, 2000; see also Laughland and Holbrook, this volume, Chapters 2 and 7).

They have dealt with this mainly by either ignoring the matter entirely or accepting that 'human rights' and 'morality' must sometimes be allowed to override the law. The memorable phrase of the International Commission was that the NATO war was 'illegal but legitimate' (IICK, 2000, 2001), with NATO presumably righting wrongs outside the law as a kind of global Robin Hood. Havel claims that NATO's war took place 'out of respect for the law, for a law that ranks higher than the law that protects the sovereignty of states' (Havel, 1999). In this same speech Havel also claims, falsely, that this was the first war ever waged 'in the name of principles and values'. Kouchner takes it for granted that morality overrides the law, and he even proposes 'preemptive' intervention by the NATO powers *prior* to anticipated immoral actions (Kouchner, 1999a).

Apparently overwhelmed by their eagerness to support NATO's intervention on behalf of the Bosnian Muslims and Kosovo Albanians, the

New Humanitarians have been oblivious to the dangers of abandoning the rule of law. Along with their blasé treatment of the selectivity of human rights attention by the Great Powers, and of those Powers' actual support of serious human rights abuses in 'friendly' states, this opening of the gates for the Great Powers to ignore the rule of law represents a major human rights regression that bodes ill for the future.

Acceptance of the NATO powers as humanitarian instruments

Along with their acceptance of the abandonment of the rule of law, the New Humanitarians have all affirmed their faith in the United States and other NATO powers as the instruments of humanitarian service, some reluctantly, others without any seeming scepticism. Ignatieff bases it on the argument that 'only the United States can muster the military might necessary to deter potential attackers and rescue victims' (Ignatieff, 2000a). He has no doubts that this military might will be appropriately used; his only problem is that while 'principle commits us to intervene ... [it] forbids the imperial ruthlessness necessary to make intervention succeed' (Ignatieff, 1998b).

Many of the New Humanitarians are aware that these powers have a dubious record in supporting regimes of murder, and they occasionally acknowledge that such cases can be found today (Turkey, East Timor), but this has not curbed their willingness to rely on the NATO powers to do good by military intervention. Kenneth Roth, Executive Director of Human Rights Watch, never questions the NATO powers as instruments of human rights, but only urges them to more aggressive action (Roth, 1997). Christopher Hitchens even suggests that their past crimes further justify their new humanitarian role: if we did wrong earlier, 'does this not double or triple our responsibility to remove them [bad men] from power. Do "our" past crimes and sins make it impossible to expiate the offense by determined action?' (Hitchens, 2001).

Acceptance of the tribunal as legitimate and judicial

All of the New Humanitarians accept the International Criminal Tribunal for the former Yugoslavia (ICTY) as a legitimate judicial body dispensing justice – for Neier, establishing the Tribunal was 'the most important step by the United Nations to protect human rights since it adopted the Universal Declaration' and the claim that the Tribunal is a 'tool of the US' he dismisses as unworthy of refutation (Neier, 1998). The New Humanitarians do not discuss the Tribunal's NATO-power origination, purpose, funding and staffing, its less than stellar adherence to Western legal standards or its record of service to NATO in pursuing war criminals selectively and coming to NATO's rescue in times of public relations need (Hayden, 1999b; Skoco and Woodger, 2000; Johnstone 2002). Ignatieff says that: 'The great virtue of legal proceedings is that their evidentiary rules confer legitimacy on otherwise contestable facts' (Ignatieff, 1997). He never examines the evidentiary rules of the Tribunal or evaluates the criticisms made of them – he takes their merits as unchallengable; he knows a priori that the Tribunal does not dispense 'victor's justice' (Ignatieff, 2000d).

Apart from expressing approval, neither Ignatieff nor his comrades discuss the Tribunal's indictment of Milošević on 24 May 1999, which gave NATO a public relations boost by a diversion of attention from NATO's escalating bombing of Serbian civilian infrastructures. This remarkable politicization of a supposed judicial body did not bother the New Humanitarians at all, nor did the Tribunal's refusal even to investigate the numerous claims of NATO's violations of law (with its refusal based on NATO press releases for information) (Mandel, 2001). Having taken sides, legal abuses by the forces of morality were of no interest to them. The moral ends justified the means.

In fact, the very politicization of the Tribunal has served the New Humanitarians well. They regularly cite its findings as definitive confirmation of what they want to prove in their campaigning. Thus David Rieff cites Tribunal indictments of Karadzic and Mladic 'FOR GENOCIDE' as showing what a determined West could have done at any time to bring justice to the Balkans (Rieff, 1995: 260–1). Ian Williams cites numbers produced by Carla Del Ponte on deaths in Kosovo as the final authority that 'should have put questions concerning the death toll to rest' (Williams, 1999b). Rieff points out that national sovereignty no longer protects human rights abusers, 'as Slobodan Milošević learned when at the height of the Kosovo conflict, he was indicted for war crimes by an international tribunal at the Hague' (Rieff, 1999b). Rieff just takes it for granted that this was an act carried out by a wholly independent dispenser of justice – its public relations service to NATO during the bombing of Serbia is unmentioned, perhaps never even strikes this war enthusiast and propagandist.

New Humanitarians' abuse of historical evidence

Acceptance of the demon theory of Balkan history

Almost uniformly, the New Humanitarians explain developments in the Balkans in terms of a demon theory of history, or what Lenard Cohen calls the 'paradise lost/loathsome leaders perspective' that has characterized much of the literature on the breakup of Yugoslavia since 1989–91 (Cohen, 2001: 380ff.). Milošević, virtually single-handedly, pursuing his dream of a Greater Serbia, was responsible for the disintegration of Yugoslavia, was the originator and predominant employer of ethnic cleansing in the region, and refused any peaceful avenues in favour of violence. Garton Ash speaks of his 'poisoned, but calculating mind' (Garton Ash, 2000), and Rieff says that Milošević 'had quite correctly been described by US officials … as the architect of the catastrophe' (Rieff, 1999b). The New Humanitarians repeatedly refer to Milošević's speeches, of 24–25 April 1987 and 28 June 1989, as allegedly announcing his ethnic cleansing programme. Tim Judah refers to Milošević's responsibility for wars in 'Slovenia, Croatia, Bosnia, Kosovo: four wars since 1991 and the result of these terrible conflicts, which began with the slogan "All Serbs in One State" is the cruelest irony' (Judah, 2000b).

This is not history but convenient mythology. The breakup of Yugoslavia was driven mainly by German and elite Croatian and Slovenian incentives to separation, and from 1991 and earlier the Serbs were designated the enemy and were on the defensive. There was no 'war' in Slovenia – the Yugoslav army, which had a legal right to fight against a Slovenian secession, did not do so, but withdrew from the Republic after ten days of skirmishes. Much of the fighting and killing resulted from the insistence of the West on preserving Bosnia-Hercegovina as a single entity under Muslim minority control, and the failure there and in Croatia to allow large ethnic minorities to shift from being parts of artificial republics to less threatening associations (Woodward, 1995a; Hayden, 1999a; Chandler, 2000b; Johnstone, 2002).

Milošević supported many initiatives for resolving these problems, coming into regular conflict with the Bosnian Serb leadership as a result. His 1987 and 1989 speeches did not call for a Greater Serbia; instead, they promised to protect Serbians (i.e. inhabitants of Serbia, not merely ethnic Serbs) and called for ethnic toleration (Milošević, 1987, 1989). Opportunistic, demagogic, ruthless he was, but he failed to meet the demon role fixed by NATO, its media and the New Humanitarians. Judah's statement that it all began with the slogan 'All Serbs in One State' is not 'cruel irony', it is a gross misrepresentation of both the dynamics of those cruel conflicts and the literal language used by Milošević.

The New Humanitarians regularly trace history back to a Serb action – frequently misrepresented – and stop there. Michael Ignatieff writes that: 'We were driven from our homes in the Croatian Krajina, Serbs will tell you. True enough, but only after the Slobodan Milošević regime had tried to strangle Croatian independence at birth' (Ignatieff, 1999b).

Note the straightforward apologetics for massive ethnic cleansing, based on a prior set of events long since terminated; the Croatian ethnic cleansing was carefully planned and extremely brutal, and was not against Milošević but Serb citizens of Croatia. The Serbs 'will also tell you' that there was a mass killing of Serbs by Croats at Gospic in September 1991, and that there is a history of Croat genocidal behaviour against Serbs during the Second World War that caused them to fear an independent Croatia, but that is history inadmissible for Ignatieff.

'Genocide' in Bosnia

The views of many of the New Humanitarians were shaped in the wars over Bosnia, where they gathered in Sarajevo to fight for the 'multi-ethnic Bosnia' and against 'nothing less than genocide' (Sontag, 1995). Their distortions of history and ongoing fact in this conflict are legendary:

1. Repeated allegations of Serb genocide and repetition of the number 200,000 or 250,000 dead, provided by the Bosnian Muslim government and contradicted by all independent authorities and the CIA itself (Kenney, 1998; Johnstone, 2002).
2. Rape inflation based again on contaminated sources, with the added unsupported claim that Bosnia Serb rapes were 'by army order' (Sontag, 1995; Johnstone, 2002).
3. Repeated naming of towns in which Muslims or Croats were killed by Serbs – Vukovar, Dubrovnik, Banja Luka, Sarejevo, Mostar, Tulza, Srebrenica – with a systematic failure to mention the prior large-scale Muslim and Croat slaughters of in-town or nearby Serb civilians (Rooper, 1997; Pumphrey, 1998; Bogdanich and Lettmayer, 2000).
4. A mythical representation of the Alija Izetbegovic government as 'actually committed to the rule of law' and multi-ethic tolerance – 'it was in defense of the ideal of a multinational, multiconfessional Bosnia that the Bosnians shed their blood' (Rieff, 1995: 248–9, 260–1). This ignores not only their acceptance of thousands of radical Muslims from the Middle East and elsewhere, but also Izetbegovic's own explicit commitment to Muslim political domination; in his words:

> There is neither peace nor coexistence between the 'Islamic religion' and non-Islamic social and political institutions ... Having the right to govern its own world, Islam clearly excludes the right and possibility of putting a foreign ideology into practice on its territory.
> (quoted, from his 1970 *Islamic Declaration*, in Johnstone, 2002)

These sentiments, never repudiated, are never cited by the New Humanitarians.

5. Rationalizing the refusal to negotiate a settlement along the lines of the Vance-Owen and later Owen-Stoltenberg peace plans, which Milošević and the Bosnian Serbs accepted, on the ground that 'the United States could not support a plan that "rewarded" ethnic cleansing to such an extent' (Rieff, citing Madeleine Albright, 1995: 255).

6. That the mutual ethnic cleansing was a result of the NATO powers' encouragement of the disintegration of the 'multi-ethnic' Yugoslav state, and their refusal to allow threatened minorities to withdraw from artificial republics that they distrusted, is outside the realm of New Humanitarian understanding.

It is also interesting to note how benignly the New Humanitarians treat the ethnic cleansing of Serbs from Krajina in 1995, carried out by the Croatian army with active US assistance. While admitting it was the largest ethnic cleansing of the Balkan wars, Garton Ash refers to it neutrally as 'a large ground offensive – by Croatian troops' (Garton Ash, 2000b). None of the New Humanitarians have called the bombing-war response by Yugoslavia 'a large ground offensive'. For none of them was the Krajina ethnic cleansing a 'humanitarian disaster', rather, implicitly, a just reward.

Misrepresentations regarding 'ethnic cleansing' in Kosovo

Some New Humanitarians, such as Denitch and Williams, contend that Serb ethnic cleansing in Kosovo prior to the bombing was massive, whereas others like Garton Ash, Rieff, Hitchens, Judah and Ignatieff make the flight and expulsions during the bombing war the crucial mark of Serb ethnic cleansing and genocide.

Several problems confront those claiming pre-bombing ethnic cleansing. One is that it is not supported by any official document, including those of the State Department, OSCE, British House of Commons Defence Review, or any of the three indictments of Milošević. Indeed, prior to the bombing, the German Foreign Office had even denied that the refugee flows constituted a case of ethnic cleansing, contending that: '[The] actions of the security forces [were] not directed against the Kosovo-Albanians as an ethnically defined group, but against the military opponent and its actual and alleged supporters' (Canepa, 1999). Garton Ash claims that: 'Serb forces started systematic cleansing as the Kosovo Verification Mission pulled out, just before the bombing started' (Garton Ash, 2000b). However, he offers no evidence for this charge, nor does anybody else. Garton Ash fails to mention that the mission was withdrawn only four days before the bombing began, with the Serbs fully aware that a bombing war was about to start. He also fails to note that the OSCE Kosovo Verification Mission reported no serious incidents between 15 January and 20 March, the day of their withdrawal.

Another problem for the New Humanitarians is the post-bombing acknowledgement that the United States had given support to the KLA prior to the bombing, which aided and encouraged the KLA to provoke the Serbs in order to justify forceful NATO intervention. The New Humanitarians have ignored such considerations. Michael Ignatieff did, however, refer to the KLA murder of six Serb teenagers, saying:

> Doubtless a KLA provocation, intended to goad the Serbs into overre-action and then to trigger international intervention. The Serbs responded by killing 45 civilians in Racak in mid-January. The international community duly intervened. Yet it is worth asking why the KLA strategists could be absolutely certain the Serbs would react as they did. The reason is simple ... only in Serbia is racial contempt an official ideology.
>
> (Ignatieff, 1999b)

We may note first that for Ignatieff the KLA killing was only a 'provoca-tion', not a murderous act to be severely condemned. Note also that although there is serious evidence that the Racak incident was arranged into a 'massacre' following a furious battle, and is therefore of question-able authenticity, Ignatieff takes it as unquestionably valid. On the cer-tainty of the Serb reaction, provocations such as those carried out by the KLA produce similar responses in civil conflicts everywhere, so that Ignatieff's blaming it on Serb racism is nonsensical for that reason alone. But it also flies in the face of Belgrade's tolerance of Albanians in Serbia, along with Roma – in contrast with Kosovo Albanian intolerance of minorities in NATO-occupied Kosovo.

Yet another problem for the New Humanitarians like Garton Ash, Rieff, Ignatieff, Judah and Hitchens, who focus on the flight and expulsions during the bombing war, is that the bombing itself precipitated the forcible response. These authors reply that an 'Operation Horseshoe' was already in the works designed to do the same anyway, and was only accelerated by the bombing. But Operation Horseshoe was never men-tioned prior to the bombing, and has been exploded as a propaganda fraud (Loquai, 2000). The rapid Serb response showed that they were expecting a NATO attack and were prepared to counterattack if necessary, while at the same time their negotiating position always included acceptance of a large international observer force, incompatible with the implementation of an Operation Horseshoe. It is an interesting fact that the New Humanitarians have never pointed to the rapid NATO bombing response following the failure at Rambouillet as demonstrating a NATO intention to carry out a bombing war. This reflects deep bias.

Still another problem for New Humanitarian apologetics is that there is evidence that the KLA and NATO were fighting the war in coordination, and that Serb attacks and expulsions were concentrated in strong KLA areas and were therefore based on military demands and strategy (Erlanger, 1999; Pearl and Block, 1999). There is also evidence that a higher percentage of Kosovo Serbs than Albanians fled during the bombing period, which calls into question a simple Serb expulsion theory of flight and refugees. The New Humanitarians deal with these awkward considerations by ignoring them. Ignatieff states that: 'Milošević decided to solve an "internal problem" by exporting an entire nation to his impoverished neighbors.' He also describes it as a 'most meticulous deportation of a civilian population' and 'a final solution of the Kosovo problem', statements that would be hard to surpass for misrepresentation (Ignatieff, 2000a: 86–7, 78–9, 84).

A final problem is that the postwar evidence on killings has not supported the inflated claims of NATO officials, which ran up to 500,000. The New Humanitarians are never critical of NATO officials for having made those wildly exaggerated claims, which did help make the moral case for devastating Serbia, and their sole preoccupation has been to protect the wartime image that Serb crimes were immense and constituted 'ethnic cleansing' and even 'genocide'. Ignatieff calls 'revisionists' those who challenged the NATO claims, and accepts that 11,334 bodies should be found, based on Tribunal estimates, which rested on 'Western intelligence sources, eyewitness statements and evidence taken from surviving family members' (Ignatieff, 1999c). He says that whether those bodies will be found 'depends on whether the Serb military and police removed them'. Possible inflation from the Tribunal and its sources he ignores by rule of deep bias. He also never mentions the possibility that many of the bodies might have been of soldiers killed in fighting; he never mentions that the KLA was fighting a war in collaboration with NATO; and he never discusses how 11,334 (as yet unrecovered) bodies are to be reconciled with his own and official claims of 'genocide'.

Misrepresenting Rambouillet

At Rambouillet the NATO powers presented Yugoslavia with an ultimatum: Surrender or be bombed. Eventually, they assured the failure of the negotiations by inserting a proviso in the proposed agreement that would have required Yugoslavia to allow NATO to occupy not just Kosovo but all of Yugoslavia (Kenney, 1999).

This is awkward for the New Humanitarians as it puts them into the position of approving bombing and war as punishment and sanctioning a resort to war by a refusal to compromise or negotiate. The New Humanitarians have handled this by either ignoring the matter altogether or accepting a NATO-friendly and false version of history. David Rieff asks: 'How eager is he [Milošević] to allow NATO troops into a portion of his country's sovereign territory, as called for by the Rambouillet agreement?' (Rieff, 1999a). But Appendix B called for NATO troops to occupy *all* of Yugoslavia. Rieff's misrepresentation was never corrected by him or by the *New York Times*. Michael Ignatieff interpreted the failure as based on the fact that Milošević 'thought that he could call NATO's bluff, could risk a bombing' because he could 'withstand' maybe a week's bombing (Ignatieff, 2000d). Again, no mention of the 'bar' being raised because Serbia 'needed a little bombing' but putting it all on the demon, and getting away with this on PBS's *NewsHour with Jim Lehrer*. Tim Judah acknowledged Appendix B, but he made it into a 'sort of military wish list', even if 'more expansive than the norm' (Judah, 2000a: 210). He did not mention the State Department official's explanation that suggests NATO's intent to bomb, nor does he consider that this might point to the reason for insertion of the controversial clause.

New Humanitarian apologetics for NATO's war crimes

The New Humanitarians have dealt with NATO war crimes mainly by evasion. Many of them like Rieff, Kouchner, Havel and Hitchens simply never discuss them, either considering them insignificant or justified by virtue of NATO's humanitarian enterprise. Shawcross praises NATO profusely for its unprecedented willingness to assist Albanian refugees: 'It is, to say the least, unexpected for one of the parties to a combat to undertake vast humanitarian aid of this sort' (Shawcross, 1999). Nowhere does he recognize that NATO's decision to bomb is what produced the refugees.

Hitchens stated that: 'The NATO intervention repatriated all or most of the refugees and killed at least some of the cleansers. I find I have absolutely no problem with that' (Hitchens, 1999). He thereby ignores the fact that NATO's intervention helped *expatriate* the refugees in the first place. As more than 'cleansers' were killed by NATO, Hitchens' failure to mention them, and his complete disinterest in the ethnic cleansing of Serbs from Krajina or any need to repatriate them, displays a bias that can accommodate any NATO illegalities, if directed against the proper evildoers.

Garton Ash describes a number of NATO killings of civilians as 'errors', based on highly disputable claims by NATO itself. But he also acknowledges the 'deliberate acceptance of civilian casualties' in the bombing of Serbian broadcasting facilities, bridges and trains and other civilian infrastructures, and that the intentional destruction of Belgrade's electrical power grid not only damaged 'the morale' of the population but also 'meant that patients on life-support systems and babies in hospital incubators had their power cut off' (Garton Ash, 2000b). He displays no indignation here and uses no condemnatory language: this was only an 'acceptance' of civilian casualties, not deliberate killing by any poisoned minds. And he never gives figures on casualties or destruction, nor does he ever point out that these NATO actions violate international legal prohibitions against targeting civilian facilities and therefore constitute war crimes.

New Humanitarian neglect and misrepresentation of inhumanitarian developments in NATO-occupied Kosovo

As with NATO's war crimes, the New Humanitarians have largely evaded addressing the inhumanitarian developments in NATO-occupied Kosovo. Like the mainstream media, they have failed to report and reflect on the massive ethnic cleansing of Serbs, Roma and others, which violates UN obligations under Security Council Resolution 1244, and also contradicts the alleged humanitarian aim of the war. They were exceedingly indignant about the alleged ethnic cleansing in Kosovo before and during the bombing, but the real, ecumenical ethnic cleansing under NATO occupation doesn't upset them at all. Rieff says that 'for the first time in the post-cold-war period ethnic cleansing was reversed' (Rieff, 1999c). He apologizes for this as 'the law of revenge', and says that 'the Serbs are leaving, and there is very little the United Nations or KFOR can do to stem the exodus' (Rieff, 1999d). Note the benign language for this 'reversed' ethnic cleansing – the Serbs 'are leaving' in an 'exodus', with no mention of a thousand of more killed or disappeared as an exit inducement, whereas the wartime flight of the Kosovo Albanians was a monstrous and evil thing.

Rieff says that war permitted the return of the 'Kosovars' (i.e. Kosovo *Albanians*), 'a tremendous accomplishment'. But the war was by his own admission the thing that drove them out. Also, that wartime flight created much hatred and a spirit of revenge, but Rieff and his fellow New Humanitarians never point out that the war made reconciliation impossible and brought 'the law of revenge' into play. Rieff mentions the hatred of Serbs by the Albanians, but he never suggests that this was seriously increased by the war he supported. Rieff even misleads with his 'law of revenge' because, as Jiri Dienstbier points out: 'What is happening in Kosovo is not some sort of revenge of ordinary ethnic Albanians' against the remaining Serbs (cited in *Agence France Presse*, 2000). It is a highly organized, systematic policy of expulsion carried out by 'Albanian extremists' (ibid.) protected by NATO and implementing that minority's long drive for an ethnically pure Kosovo and Greater Albania.

Why 40,000 UN troops couldn't do anything about this latest round of ethnic cleansing Rieff fails to explain. Garton Ash also notes the reverse ethnic cleansing of Serbs 'under the very noses of NATO troops', although he fails to mention the ethnic cleansing of Roma, Turks and others (Garton Ash, 2000a). But while Serbia's alleged ethnic cleansing justified NATO's bombing for Garton Ash, he does not suggest that this severe case of 'reverse' ethnic cleansing should be curbed perhaps by a bit of NATO bombing!

Garton Ash, following the NATO party line claiming that the intervention was based not only on humanitarian concerns but 'a long-standing fear for the "stability" of the region', mentions that while Kosovo was 'liberated' it remained 'an almighty mess'. But he fails to acknowledge that NATO's interventions from 1991 on destabilized Yugoslavia and the region, and that the 'almighty mess' in Kosovo is not only unstable, it has provided the KLA with a base to destabilize Macedonia in the interest of a 'Greater Albania' – a real aim that the New Humanitarians have never recognized, in contrast with their preoccupation with the mythical aim of a 'Greater Serbia'.

Garton Ash, at least, honestly recognizes that Kosovo under NATO is 'an almighty mess' and that not only Serbs but 'Albanian women are afraid to go out at night in Pristina, for fear of being kidnapped into forced prostitution by the Albanian mafia, which has moved into the province with a vengeance' (Garton Ash, 2000a). Rieff, on the other hand, like Hitchens, Ignatieff and Williams, a more committed and unrestrained propagandist, says: 'There is something magical and heartening about walking through the streets of Pristina ... and seeing young people who grew up fearful in a Serb police state finally getting to behave like normal teenagers' (Rieff, 2000b).

Conclusion

The New Humanitarians have been openly committed activists, serving what they perceived to be moral causes in the Balkans, and portraying events there through the prism of these commitments and political aims. We believe that we have shown that their reporting and commentaries on developments during and leading up to the Kosovo war, and after its conclusion, have been so biased as to constitute war propaganda rather than objective news and minimally balanced commentaries.

The New Humanitarians did not lead NATO on and press them to do things NATO did not want to do; on the contrary, they followed and put a moral gloss on NATO choices that were evident from the beginning of the 1990s if not earlier, and that were clearly rooted in geopolitical and internal political interests and forces. The New Humanitarians provided a moral cover and helped produce an echo chamber and bandwagon support for intervention, and in fact biased that intervention away from negotiations and toward the use of force.

In the New World Order, with an unchallenged superpower pursuing global interests, there has been a strong tendency for the United States and its allies to use force to achieve their geopolitical ends. There is not the slightest reason to believe that this use of force will be directed toward advancing human rights, although that will surely be part of the cover as it has been in the past. This is new order imperialism, even if not characterized by direct imperial rule. By helping sustain that moral cover, and sanctioning the abandonment of the rule of law in the purported interest of human rights, the New Humanitarians have served as a political and propaganda arm of the new imperialism.

Notes

1. On NATO's real objectives, see Chomsky (1999), Simma (1999), Johnstone (2000), MccGwire (2000), and Johnstone (2002).
2. We caution that estimates of deaths both during and after the war vary, and no definitive accounting has yet to be produced. Our own very tentative estimate of the approximate *maximum* total number of deaths derives from the combined total of known deaths based on bodies recovered within Kosovo during and after the war as of 2000 (3658) and the International Committee of the Red Cross's total of people missing and unaccounted for (3525, of which 2746 were ethnic Albanians and 779 from other ethnic groups) (see, further, Del Ponte, 2000; ICRC, 2001a, 2001b, 2001c). It would seem highly improbable for the actual total to exceed the sum of these numbers and, with the likelihood of duplication of names across both lists of the dead and the missing, may very well turn out to be considerably less.

3. According to former State Department Yugoslav Desk officer George Kenney, after Rambouillet, a US government official told him 'the United States "deliberately set the bar higher than the Serbs could accept". The Serbs needed, according to the official, a little bombing to see reason' (Kenney, 1999).

4. As Timothy Garton Ash writes: 'When I arrive in the late evening ... [at Hotel Tuzla] ... I step into the lift, press the button for the second floor, and at once subside, powerless, into the cellar. The reception committee in the bar consists of Christopher Hitchens, Susan Sontag and David Rieff. When I join them, Sontag is just saying to Michael Ignatieff, "I can't believe that this is your first time here"' (Garton Ash, 1999: 147).

5. 'Garton Ash right again', Tim Judah writes (Judah, 1999); 'Superb', Michael Ignatieff says of David Rieff's work (Ignatieff, 1995); 'an immensely wide-ranging intellect', Rieff in turn says of Ignatieff (Rieff, 2000b).

6. Among the Human Rights Watch board members with ties to the US government, board member Morton Abramowitz was a high-ranking State Department official, a former US Ambassador to Turkey; Paul Goble is the director of the US propaganda news network otherwise known as Radio Free Europe/Radio Liberty; Kati Marton is the president of the Committee to Protect Journalists and the wife of Richard Holbrooke; and Warren Zimmermann was the last US Ambassador to Yugoslavia during its break-up.

7. The KPC, inaugurated in September 1999 and modelled on the US National Guard, was recruited from the KLA. Kouchner stated that it had an 'emergency response' function 'with a mandate to provide humanitarian assistance'. KLA commander Agim Ceku was put in charge, with Kouchner stating at the KFC inauguration: 'I look to him to lead the new members of the Corps in the footsteps of Cincinnatus, the model citizen-soldier of ancient Rome' (Kouchner, 1999a). Ceku had 'masterminded the successful [Croatian] offensive at Medak [in 1993] and in 1995 was one of the key planners of the successful Operation Storm' (*Jane's Defence Weekly*, 10 May 1999). Kouchner must have known this. A few weeks after the inauguration, the ICTY announced it was 'investigating Ceku for alleged war crimes committed against ethnic Serbs in Croatia between 1993 and 1995' (*Agence France Presse*, 1999), though, as in the case of the NATO powers, we doubt the ICTY was serious.

8. The New Humanitarians have often criticized NATO, but almost always for its failure to move against the enemy with sufficient speed and force (for example, Ignatieff, 2000b). This practice of limiting their dissent to a narrow range of themes advocating greater state violence gives their work a false aura of independence and high moral stature, but the sides they chose coincided precisely with those fixed by their political leaders.

9. Data based on a byline search using the Nexis database of 18 print media from the US, the UK and Canada (i.e. the *New York Times, Washington Post, Los Angeles Times, Time* Magazine, *Newsweek, The Nation* and the *New Republic; The Times, The Daily Telegraph, The Financial Times, Guardian, Independent* and the *New Statesman;* and the *Toronto Star, Ottawa Citizen, Gazette* (Montreal), *Vancouver Sun* and *Calgary Herald*) for articles published by our sample of 12 New Humanitarians (i.e. Timothy Garton Ash, Václav Havel, Christopher Hitchens, Michael Ignatieff, Tim Judah, Mary Kaldor, Bernard Kouchner, Aryeh Neier, David Rieff, Geoffrey Robertson, Kenneth Roth and Susan Sontag) during the period 1 January 1998 through to 30 June 2001.

References

Africa Confidential (1991) 'Rwanda: Multi-Hutu', *Africa Confidential*, vol. 32, no. 9.

Africa Confidential (1993a) 'Rwanda', *Africa Confidential*, vol. 34, no. 3.

Africa Confidential (1993b) 'Rwanda: Threats to Arusha', *Africa Confidential*, vol. 34, no. 19.

African Rights (1995) *Rwanda, Not so Innocent: When Women Become Killers* (London: African Rights).

Agence France Presse (1999) 'Kosovo Commander Denies War Crimes in Croatia', 12 October.

Agence France Presse (2000) 'One Ethnic Cleansing in Kosovo has Replaced Another: UN Envoy', 21 June.

Agence France Presse (2001) 'ICTY Spokeswoman Criticizes Croatia's Catholic Church', 26 July.

Allott, Philip (1999) 'The Concept of International Law', *European Journal of International Law*, vol. 10, pp. 31–50.

Amnesty International (1978) *Report of the Inquiry into Allegations of Ill-treatment in Northern Ireland* (London: Amnesty International).

Anderson, Mary (1996) *Do No Harm: Supporting Local Capacities for Peace Through Aid* (Cambridge, MA: Collaborative for Development Action).

Annan, Kofi (1997) 'Advocating for an International Criminal Court', *Fordham International Law Journal*, vol. 21, no. 2, pp. 363–6.

Annan, Kofi (1998) 'Peacekeeping, Military Intervention and National Sovereignty in Internal Armed Conflict', in Jonathan Moore (ed.), *Hard Choices: Moral Dilemmas in Humanitarian Interventions* (Lanham, MD: Rowman & Littlefield).

Annan, Kofi (1999a) 'Secretary-General Calls for Renewed Commitment in New Century to Protect Rights of Man, Woman, Child – Regardless of Ethnic, National Belonging'. *UN Press Release* (SG/SM/6949), 7 April. Available from: <http://www.un.org/News/Press/docs/1999/19990407.sgsm6949.html>.

Annan, Kofi (1999b) 'War Foe of Development, Development Best Form of Conflict-Prevention Secretary-General Tells World Bank'. *UN Staff Press Release* (SG/SM/7187), 19 October. Available from: <http://www.un.org/News/Press/docs/1999/19991019.sgsm7187.doc.html>.

Archard, David (1993) *Children's Rights and Childhood* (London and New York: Routledge).

Archibugi, Daniele (1998) 'Principles of Cosmopolitan Democracy', in Daniele Archibugi, David Held and Martin Köhler (eds), *Re-imagining Political Community: Studies in Cosmopolitan Democracy* (Cambridge: Polity), pp. 198–228.

Archibugi, Daniele (2000) 'Cosmopolitical Democracy', *New Left Review*, no. 4, pp. 137–50.

Archibugi, Daniele (2002) 'Demos and Cosmopolis', *New Left Review*, no. 13, pp. 24–38.

Arendt, Hannah (1959) *The Human Condition* (New York: Doubleday Anchor).

Arendt, Hannah (1972) *Crises of the Republic* (Harmondsworth: Penguin).

Arendt, Hannah (1979) *The Origins of Totalitarianism*, new edn (New York: Harvest).

Aries, Phillipe (1962) *Centuries of Childhood: A Social History of Family Life* (New York: Vintage).

Basu, Kaushik (2001) 'On the Goals of Development', in Gerald M. Meier and Joseph E. Stiglitz (eds), *Frontiers of Development Economics: The Future in Perspective* (New York: Oxford University Press), pp. 61–86.

Bean, Nicola (1999) 'Policing Play'. Paper presented to the Political Studies Association Annual Conference, University of Nottingham, 22–25 March.

Beaumont, Peter, Ed Vulliamy and Paul Beaver (2001) 'CIA's Bastard Army Ran Riot in Balkans', *Observer*, 11 March.

Beck, Ulrich (1994) *Risk Society: Towards a New Modernity* (Cambridge: Polity).

Beetham, David (1991) *The Legitimation of Power* (Basingstoke: Macmillan – now Palgrave Macmillan).

Beetham, David (1999) *Democracy and Human Rights* (Cambridge: Polity).

Bell, Martin (1996) *In Harm's Way*, revised edn (Harmondsworth: Penguin).

Bell, Martin (1998) 'The Journalism of Attachment', in Matthew Kieran (ed.), *Media Ethics* (London: Routledge), pp. 15–22.

Bennhold, Martin (1999) 'Thesen zum Völkerrecht'. Unpublished paper, presented at 'Der Terror des Krieges' international conference, Bonn, 27 May.

Betts, Richard K. (2001) 'The Lesser Evil: The Best Way Out of the Balkans', *National Interest*, Summer, pp. 53–65.

BHHRG (British Helsinki Human Rights Group) (2001) 'Slovakia, 2001: Is It a Law-Governed State?' Available from: <http://www.bhhrg.org>.

Bianchi, Andrea (1999) 'Immunity versus Human Rights: The Pinochet Case', *European Journal of International Law*, vol. 10, pp. 237–77.

Binder, David (1994–5) 'Anatomy of a Massacre', *Foreign Policy*, no. 97, Winter, pp. 70–8.

Binder, David (1995) 'Bosnia's Bombers', *The Nation*, vol. 261, no. 10, 2 October.

Binder, David (2000) 'The Ironic Justice of Kosovo', *MSNBC News*, 17 March. Available from: <http://www.msnbc.com/news/382058.asp#BODY>.

Blair, Tony (1999a) 'A New Generation Draws the Line', *Newsweek*, 19 April.

Blair, Tony (1999b) 'Doctrine of the International Community', speech at the Hilton Hotel, Chicago, Illinois, 22 April. Available from: <http://www.globalpolicy.org/globaliz/politics/blair.htm>.

Blair, Tony (2001) 'Full Text of Tony Blair's Speech to the Labour Party Conference, 2 October 2001', *Guardian*, 3 October.

Bogdanich, George and Martin Lettmayer (2000) *Yugoslavia: The Avoidable War* (documentary film) (USA: Frontier Theater and Film).

Boot, Max (1999) 'Paving the Road to Hell: the Failure of UN Peacekeeping', *Foreign Affairs*, vol. 79, no. 2, pp. 143–8.

Booth, Ken (1995) 'Human Wrongs and International Relations', *International Affairs*, vol. 71, no. 1, pp. 103–26.

Booth, Ken (1999) 'Three Tyrannies', in Tim Dunne and Nicholas J. Wheeler (eds), *Human Rights in Global Politics* (Cambridge: Cambridge University Press), pp. 31–70.

Booth, Ken, Tim Dunne and Michael Cox (eds) (2000) 'How Might We Live? Global Ethics in a New Century', Special Issue, *Review of International Studies*, vol. 26.

Bosco, David (2000) 'Dictators in the Dock', *American Prospect*, 14 August.

Boyd, Charles G. (1995) 'Making Peace with the Guilty', *Foreign Affairs*, vol. 74, no. 50, September–October, pp. 22–38. Available from: <http://www.diaspora-net.org/food4thought/Gen.%20Boyd.htm>.

Boyden, Jo (1990) 'Childhood and the Policy Makers: A Comparative Perspective on the Globalization of Childhood', in Allison James and Alan Prout (eds), *Constructing and Reconstructing Childhood: Contemporary Issues in the Sociological Study of Childhood* (London: Falmer Press), pp. 184–215.

Boyle, Kevin (1995) 'Stock-taking on Human Rights: The World Conference on Human Rights, Vienna 1993', *Political Studies*, vol. 43, Special Issue, pp. 79–95.

Boyle, Kevin and Tom Hadden (1994) *Northern Ireland: the Choice* (Harmondsworth: Penguin).

Boyle, Kevin, Tom Hadden and Paddy Hillyard (1975) *Law and State: the Case of Northern Ireland* (London: Martin Robertson).

Bradlow, Daniel and Claudio Grossman (1995) 'Limited Mandates and Intertwined Problems: A New Challenge for the World Bank and the IMF', *Human Rights Quarterly*, vol. 17, pp. 411–42.

Bratton, Michael and Donald Rothchild (1992) 'The Institutional Bases of Governance in Africa', in Michael Bratton and Goran Hyden (eds), *Governance and Politics in Africa* (Boulder, CO: Lynne Rienner).

Bratton, Michael and Nicholas Van de Walle (1992) 'Toward Governance in Africa', in Michael Bratton and Goran Hyden (eds), *Governance and Politics in Africa* (Boulder, CO: Lynne Rienner).

Brauer, Dieter (2000) 'The Paternalistic Attitude of the World Bank Must Change', Interview with Joseph Stiglitz, *Development and Cooperation*, no. 2, March/April, pp. 26–7.

Brown, Ed (2000) 'Tinkering With the System: Adjusting Adjustment', in Giles Mohan, Ed Brown and Alfred B. Zack-Williams (eds), *Structural Adjustment: Theory, Practice, Impacts* (London: Routledge), pp. 119–44.

Brownlie, Ian (1963) *International Law and the Use of Force by States* (Oxford: Clarendon Press).

Brownlie, Ian (1974) 'Humanitarian Intervention', in J. Norton Moore (ed.), *Law and Civil War in the Modern World* (London: Johns Hopkins University Press).

Brownlie, Ian (2000) 'Memorandum Submitted by Professor Ian Brownlie', House of Commons, Foreign Affairs – Appendices to the Minutes of Evidence, 23 May. Available from: <http://www.parliament.the-stationery-office.co.uk/pa/cm199900/cmselect/cmfaff/28/28ap03.htm>.

Bryan, Dominic (2000) *Orange Parades: the Politics of Ritual, Tradition and Control* (London: Pluto).

Burnham, Rick (2001) 'Jumper Confirmed as Next Air Force Chief', *Air Force Link News*, 3 August. Available from: <http://www.af.mil/news>.

Burton, Frank (1978) *The Politics of Legitimacy: Struggles in a Belfast Community* (London: Routledge & Kegan Paul).

Bush, George W. (2001) 'Full Text of George Bush's Speech to the US Congress, 21 September 2001', *Guardian Unlimited*, 21 September. Available from: <http://www.guardian.co.uk/Archive/Article/0,4273,4261868,00.html>.

Camilleri, Joseph A. and Jim Falk (1992) *The End of Sovereignty? The Politics of a Shrinking and Fragmenting World* (Brookfield, VT: Ashgate).

Canepa, Eric (1999) 'Important Internal Documents from Germany's Foreign Office Regarding Pre-Bombardment Genocide in Kosovo' (trans.). Available from: <http://www.suc.org/kosovo_crisis/documents/ger_gov.html>.

Cantwell, Nigel (1992) 'The Origins, Development and Significance of the United Nations Convention on the Rights of the Child', in Sharon Detrick (ed.), *The United Nations Convention on the Rights of the Child: A Guide to the 'Travaux Preparatoires'* (Dordrecht: Martinus Nijhoff), pp. 19–30.

Carothers, Thomas (2001) 'Promoting Democracy Abroad Makes Good Sense', *Washington Post*, 30 January.

Carvel, John (2000) 'NSPCC Hits Back Over Cash', *Guardian*, 9 December.

Cassese, Antonio (1998) 'Reflections on International Criminal Justice', *Modern Law Review*, vol. 61, no. 1, pp. 1–10.

Cassese, Antonio (1999) '*Ex iniuria ius oritur*: Are We Moving Towards International Legitimation of Forcible Humanitarian Countermeasures in the World Community?', *European Journal of International Law*, vol. 10, pp. 23–30. Available at: <http://www.ejil.org/journal/Vol10/No1/com.html>.

Cassidy, Clare and Karen Trew (1998) 'Identities in Northern Ireland: A Multidimensional Approach', *Journal of Social Issues*, vol. 54, no. 4, pp. 725–40.

CGG (Commission on Global Governance) (1995) *Our Global Neighbourhood* (Oxford: Oxford University Press).

Chandler, David (1999) *Bosnia: Faking Democracy After Dayton* (London: Pluto Press).

Chandler, David (2000a) *Bosnia: Faking Democracy After Dayton*, 2nd edn (London: Pluto Press).

Chandler, David (2000b) 'Western Intervention and the Disintegration of Yugoslavia 1989–1999', in Philip Hammond and Edward S. Herman (eds), *Degraded Capability – The Media and the Kosovo Crisis* (London: Pluto Press), pp. 19–30.

Chandler, David (2000c) 'International Justice', *New Left Review*, vol. 2, no. 6, pp. 55–66.

Chandler, David (2001) 'Faking Democracy and Progress in Kosovo – BHHRG Report on the Provincial Elections, 17 November 2001', British Helsinki Human Rights Group. Available from: <http://www.bhhrg.org/faking_democracy_and_progress_in1.htm>.

Chandler, David (2002) *From Kosovo to Kabul: Human Rights and International Intervention* (London: Pluto).

Charney, Jonathan I. (1999) 'Anticipatory Humanitarian Intervention in Kosovo', *American Journal of International Law*, vol. 93, pp. 834–41.

Charnovitz, Steve (1997) 'Two Centuries of Participation: NGOs and International Governance', *Michigan Journal of International Law*, vol. 18, pp. 183–286.

Chomsky, Noam (1999) *The New Military Humanism: Lessons from Kosovo* (Monroe, ME: Common Courage Press).

Chomsky, Noam (2000) *A New Generation Draws the Line: Kosovo, East Timor, and the Standards of the West* (New York: Verso).

Clinton, Bill (1999) 'Remarks by President Bill Clinton to the American Society of Newspaper Editors Regarding the Situation in Kosovo, The Fairmont Hotel, San Francisco, California', *Federal News Service*, 15 April.

Cohen, Lenard J. (2001) *Serpent in the Bosom: The Rise and Fall of Slobodan Milosevic* (Boulder, CO: Westview Press).

Collier, Paul (2000) 'Conditionality, Dependence and Coordination: Three Current Debates in Aid Policy', in Christopher L. Gilbert and David Vines (eds), *The World Bank: Structure and Policies* (Cambridge: Cambridge University Press), pp. 299–324.

Collins, Barrie (1998) *Obedience in Rwanda: A Critical Question* (Sheffield: Sheffield Hallam University Press).

Cooper, Robert (2000) *The Post-Modern State and the World Order* (London: Demos).

Cooper, Robert (2001) 'Dawn Chorus for the New Age of Empire', *Sunday Times*, 28 October.

Corwin, Phillip (1999) *Dubious Mandate* (Durham, NC: Duke University Press).

Coupland, Douglas (2001) *All Families are Psychotic* (London: Flamingo).

Cowan, Rosie (2001) 'Stormont Assembly put on Ice', *Guardian*, 11 August.

Cowell, David and Kimberley Cowell (1999) 'Human Rights as Conflict Management: the Unionist use of Human Rights Language in Northern Ireland', *Nationalism and Ethnic Politics*, vol. 5, no. 1, pp. 1–28.

Cox, Michael (2000) 'Northern Ireland After the Cold War', in Michael Cox, Adrian Guelke and Fiona Stephen (eds), *A Farewell to Arms? From 'Long War' to Long Peace in Northern Ireland* (Manchester: Manchester University Press), pp. 249–62.

CRS (Catholic Relief Services) (1999) 'Beyond the Protection of Human Rights'. Paper delivered at an internal workshop, 20 May.

Cusk, Rachel (2001) *A Life's Work: On Becoming a Mother* (London: Fourth Estate).

Czech News Agency (2000) 'Dienstbier Criticising NATO Raids, Missions in Kosovo Again', 29 March.

Daley, Suzanne (1999) 'Doctors Without Borders Awarded Nobel Peace Prize', *New York Times*, 20 October.

Deacon, Bob with Michelle Hulse and Paul Stubbs (1997) *Global Social Policy: International Organisations and the Future of Welfare* (London: Sage).

DEC (1998) 'Introductory Remarks', 'The Emperor's New Clothes: The Collapse of Humanitarian Principles', Disasters and Emergency Committee Conference, London, 4 February.

Del Ponte, Carla (2000) 'Statement to the Press by Carla Del Ponte', 20 December. Available from: <http://www.un.org/icty/latest/latestdev-e.htm>.

Des Forges, Alison (1997) 'Genocide in Rwanda and the International Response', in Kenneth W. Thompson and Harry G. West (eds), *Conflict and Its Resolution in Contemporary Africa* (New York: University Press of America).

Destexhe, Alain (1995) *Rwanda and Genocide in the Twentieth Century* (London: Pluto).

Detrick, Sharon (ed.) (1992) *The United Nations Convention on the Rights of the Child: A Guide to the 'Travaux Preparatoires'* (Dordrecht: Martinus Nijhoff).

DFID (1999) 'Principles for a New Humanitarianism', in *Conflict Reduction and Humanitarian Assistance*, UK Government, Department for International Development, Policy Statement. Available from: <http://www.dfid.gov.uk/policieandpriorities/files/conflict_reduction.htm>.

Dickson, Brice (1995) 'Criminal Justice and Emergency Laws', in Seamus Dunn (ed.), *Facets of the Conflict in Northern Ireland* (Basingstoke: Macmillan – now Palgrave Macmillan), pp. 61–79.

Dienstbier, Jiri (2000) 'Unofficial Update Distributed During the 56th Session of the Commission to the Report (E/CN.4/2000/39) of Mr. Jiri Dienstbier, Special

Rapporteur on the Situation of Human Rights in Bosnia and Herzegovina, Republic of Croatia, and the Federal Republic of Yugoslavia, 20 March. United Nations Economic and Social Council. Available from: <http://hri.ca/fortherecord2000/documentation/commission/e-cn4-2000-39.htm>.

Dodge, Toby (2001) 'Who's Winning Now?', *World Today*, vol. 57, no. 3, March, pp. 4–6.

Donnelly, Jack (1998) *International Human Rights*, 2nd edn (Boulder, CO: Westview Press).

Donnelly, Jack (2000) *Realism in International Relations* (Cambridge: Cambridge University Press).

Drury, Shadia B. (1994) *Alexandre Kojève: The Roots of Postmodern Politics* (New York: St. Martin's Press).

Duffield, Mark (1998) *Aid Policy and Post Modern Conflict: A Critical Review.* Occasional paper, University of Birmingham, Department for International Development, School of Public Policy, July.

Duffield, Mark (2001) 'Governing the Borderlands: Decoding the Power of Aid'. Paper presented at a seminar on Politics and Humanitarian Aid, Commonwealth Institute, London, 1 February.

DUPI (Danish Institute of International Affairs) (1999) *Humanitarian Intervention: Legal and Political Aspects* (Copenhagen: Denmark: Danish Institute of International Affairs).

Eagleton, Terry (1999) 'Preface', in The Belgrade Circle (ed.), *The Politics of Human Rights* (London: Verso), pp. v–vii.

Easterly, William (2001) *The Elusive Quest for Growth: Economists' Adventures and Misadventures in the Tropics* (Cambridge, MA: MIT Press).

ECHO (1999) *Towards a Human Rights Approach to European Commission Humanitarian Aid.* European Community Humanitarian Aid Office discussion paper, May.

EIN (2001a) 'Two Thousand Serbs Protest in Gracanica', *European Internet Network*, 24 July.

EIN (2001b) 'Five Roma Injured in Hand Grenade Attack in Kosovo', *European Internet Network*, 9 August.

EIU (1990a) Country Report: *Uganda, Rwanda, Burundi*, No. 2, Economist Intelligence Unit.

EIU (1990b) Country Report: *Uganda, Rwanda, Burundi*, No. 3, Economist Intelligence Unit.

EIU (1991) Country Report: *Uganda, Rwanda, Burundi*, No. 3, Economist Intelligence Unit.

EIU (1992) Country Report: *Uganda, Rwanda, Burundi*, No. 2, Economist Intelligence Unit.

EIU (1993) Country Report: *Uganda, Rwanda, Burundi*, No. 2, Economist Intelligence Unit.

EIU (1994) Country Report: *Uganda, Rwanda, Burundi*, No. 2, Economist Intelligence Unit.

Ellison, Graham and Jim Smyth (2000) *The Crowned Harp: Policing Northern Ireland* (London: Pluto).

Erlanger, Steven (1999) 'Monitors Provide Chronicle of Kosovo Terror', *New York Times*, 5 December.

European Parliament (2000a) *Report on the Establishment of a Common European Security and Defence Policy After Cologne and Helsinki* (A5-0339/2000). Available from: <http://www.europarl.eu.int/>.

European Parliament (2000b) *European Parliament Resolution on the Establishment of a Common European Security and Defence Policy After Cologne and Helsinki* (2000/2005(INI)), Adopted 30/11/00. Available from: <http://www. europarl.eu.int/>.

Evans, Tony (1997) 'Democratization and Human Rights', in Anthony McGrew (ed.), *The Transformation of Democracy? Globalization and Territorial Democracy* (Cambridge: Polity Press/Open University), pp. 122–48.

Falk, Richard A. (1998) *Law in an Emerging Global Village: A Post-Westphalian Perspective* (Ardsley, NY: Transnational).

Falk, Richard A. (2000) 'Global Civil Society and the Democratic Prospect', in Barry Holden (ed.), *Global Democracy: Key Debates* (London: Routledge), pp. 162–78.

Farrell, Michael (1980) *Northern Ireland: the Orange State*, 2nd edn (London: Pluto).

Farren, Sean and Robert F. Mulvihill (2000) *Paths to a Settlement in Northern Ireland* (Gerards Cross: Colin Smythe).

Federle, Katherine H. (1994) 'Rights Flow Downhill', *International Journal of Children's Rights*, vol. 2, pp. 343–76.

Fekete, Liz (2001) 'The Terrorism Act 2000: an Interview with Gareth Peirce', *Race and Class*, vol. 43, no. 2, pp. 95–103.

Ferguson, Niall (2001) 'Welcome the New Imperialism', *Guardian*, 31 October.

Financial Times (2001) *'Controlling Tanzania'*, Editorial, 13 August.

Foley, Conor (1998) 'The Human Rights Deficit', in James Anderson and James Goodman (eds), *Dis/Agreeing Ireland: Contexts, Obstacles, Hopes* (London: Pluto), pp. 162–75.

Foltz, William J. (1993) 'Officers and Politicians', *Africa Report*, May/June.

Forsythe, David P. (2000) *Human Rights in International Relations* (Cambridge: Cambridge University Press).

Fortin, Jane (1998) *Children's Rights and the Developing Law* (London and Edinburgh: Butterworths).

Fox, Fiona (2000) 'The Politicisation of Humanitarian Aid'. Unpublished discussion paper for Caritas Europa.

Fox, Fiona (2001) 'New Humanitarianism: Does it Provide a Moral Banner for the 21st Century?', *Disasters*, vol. 25, no. 4, pp. 275–89.

Franklin, Bob (1995) 'The Case for Children's Rights: a Progress Report', in Bob Franklin (ed.), *The Handbook of Children's Rights: Comparative Policy and Practice* (London: Routledge), pp. 3–22.

Freeman, Michael (1997) *The Moral Status of Children: Essays on the Rights of the Child* (The Hague: Martinus Nijhoff).

Furedi, Frank (2001) *Paranoid Parenting: Abandon Your Anxieties and be a Good Parent* (London: Allen Lane/Penguin).

Galtung, Johan (2000) 'Alternative Models for Global Democracy', in Barry Holden (ed.), *Global Democracy: Key Debates* (London: Routledge), pp. 143–61.

Garton Ash, Timothy (1999) *History of the Present: Essays, Sketches, and Dispatches from Europe in the 1990s* (New York: Random House).

Garton Ash, Timothy (2000a) 'We are Losing the Peace in Kosovo', *Independent*, 18 January.

Garton Ash, Timothy (2000b) 'The War We Almost Lost: Was Nato's Kosovo Campaign a Legitimate Response to a Humanitarian Catastrophe – or Did It Cause One?', *Guardian*, 4 September.

Gilbert, Christopher L. and David Vines (2000) 'The World Bank: an Overview of Some Major Issues', in Christopher L. Gilbert and David Vines (eds), *The World Bank: Structure and Policies* (Cambridge: Cambridge University Press), pp. 10–38.

Gillespie, Paul (2000) 'From Anglo-Irish to British-Irish Relations', in Michael Cox, Adrian Guelke and Fiona Stephen (eds), *A Farewell to Arms? From 'Long War' to Long Peace in Northern Ireland* (Manchester: Manchester University Press), pp. 180–98.

Gilligan, Chris (1997) 'Peace or Pacification Process? A Brief Critique of the Peace Process', in Chris Gilligan and Jon Tonge (eds), *Peace or War? Understanding the Peace Process in Northern Ireland* (Aldershot: Ashgate), pp. 19–34.

Glass, Charles (1999) 'Hacks Versus Flacks: Tales from the Depths', *Z Magazine*, 1 August.

GOLI (Grand Orange Lodge of Ireland) (n.d.) *Covenant for Human Rights*. Available from: <http://www.grandorange.org.uk/covenant1.htm>.

Gordon, Thomas (1970) *P.E.T., Parental Effectiveness Training: the Tested New Way to Raise Responsible Children* (New York: Peter H. Wyden).

Gourevitch, Philip (2000) *We Wish To Inform You That Tomorrow We Will Be Killed With Our Families* (London: Picador).

Gowing, Nik (1994) *Real-Time Television Coverage of Armed Conflicts and Diplomatic Crises: Does it Pressure or Distort Foreign Policy Decisions?*, Working Paper 94-1 (Cambridge, MA: Shorenstein Barone Center, Harvard University).

Gowing, Nik (1997) *Media Coverage: Help or Hindrance in Conflict Prevention?*, Report to the Carnegie Commission on Preventing Deadly Conflict (Washington, DC: Carnegie Corporation).

Gowing, Nik (1998) 'New Challenges and Problems for Information Management in Complex Emergencies'. Paper presented to the 'Dispatches from Disaster Zones' conference, London, 27–28 May.

Graham, Brian (1997) 'Ireland and Irishness: Place, Culture and Identity', in Brian Graham (ed.), *In Search of Ireland* (London: Routledge), pp. 1–15.

Griffiths, Martin, Iain Levine and Marc Weller (1995) 'Sovereignty and Suffering', in John Harriss (ed.), *The Politics of Humanitarian Intervention* (London: Pinter), pp. 33–83.

GRRC (n.d.) Garvaghy Road Residents Coalition website. Available from: <http://www.garvaghyroad.org/>.

Guardian (1999) 'In a Nobel Cause', Editorial, 16 October.

Guardian (2000a) 'Adverts and Admin: Charities Need to Account for Our Money', Editorial, 9 December.

Guardian (2000b) 'Charities Need to Account for Our Money', Editorial, Society, 9 December.

Guardian (2001a) 'Just What They Need – a £28 m Air Defence System', Editorial, 18 December.

Guardian (2001b) 'Not at This Price – Britain Must Block the Tanzania Deal', Editorial, 19 December.

Guelke, Adrian (1992) 'Policing in Northern Ireland', in Brigid Hadfield (ed.), *Northern Ireland: Politics and the Constitution* (Buckingham: Open University Press), pp. 94–109.

Guelke, Adrian (2001) 'International Dimensions of the Belfast Agreement', in Rick Wilford (ed.), *Aspects of the Belfast Agreement* (Oxford: Oxford University Press), pp. 245–63.

Gutman, Amy (ed.) (1994) *Multiculturalism; Examining the Politics of Recognition* (Princeton, NJ: Princeton University Press).

Gutman, Roy (1999) Presentation at the 'Journalists Covering Conflict: Norms Of Conduct' symposium, Columbia University, 28 April, *Preventing Deadly Conflict: Publications of the Carnegie Commission on Preventing Deadly Conflict* (CD-Rom) (Washington, DC: Carnegie Corporation).

Gutman, Roy (2000) 'Twenty-five Years of the Helsinki Process: 1975–2000', *Freedom of the Media Yearbook 1999–2000*, Organisation for Security and Cooperation in Europe. Available from: <http://www.osce.org/fom/publications/yearbook9900/III/149>.

Gutman, Roy and David Rieff (1999) 'Preface', in Roy Gutman and David Rieff (eds), *Crimes of War: What the Public Should Know* (New York: W. W. Norton), pp. 8–12.

Habermas, Jürgen (1996) *Between Facts and Norms: Contributions to a Discourse Theory of Law and Democracy* (Cambridge, MA: MIT Press).

Hallin, Daniel C. (1986) *The 'Uncensored War': The Media and Vietnam* (Oxford: Oxford University Press).

Halmos, Paul (1965) *The Faith of the Counsellors* (London: Constable).

Halmos, Paul (1970) *The Personal Service Society* (London: Constable).

Halvorsen, Kate (1999) 'Protection and Humanitarian Assistance in the Refugee Camps in Zaire: The Problem of Security', in Howard Adelman and Astri Suhrke (eds), *The Path of a Genocide: The Rwanda Crisis from Uganda to Zaire* (New Brunswick, NJ: Transaction Publishers), pp. 307–20.

Hammarberg, Thomas (1994) 'Justice for Children Through the UN Convention', in Stewart Asquith and Malcolm Hill (eds), *Justice for Children* (Dordrecht: Martinus Nijhoff), pp. 59–72.

Hammond, Philip and Edward S. Herman (eds) (2000) *Degraded Capability: The Media and the Kosovo Crisis* (London: Pluto).

Hansard (1999a) vol. 324, col. 605, 1 February. Available from: <http://www.publications.parliament.uk/>.

Hansard (1999b) vol. 328, col. 616–17, 25 March. Available from: <http://www.publications.parliament.uk/>.

Harvey, Colin (2001) 'Human Rights and Equality', in Robin Wilson (ed.), *Agreeing to Disagree? A Guide to the Northern Ireland Assembly* (Norwich: Stationery Office), pp. 103–11.

Havel, Václav (1999) 'Kosovo and the End of the Nation-State', *New York Review of Books*, 10 June.

Hayden, Robert M. (1998) 'Bosnia: The Contradictions of "Democracy" Without Consent', *East European Constitutional Review*, vol. 7, no. 2, Spring 1998. Available from: <http://www.law.nyu.edu/eecr/vol7num2/special/bosnia.html>.

Hayden, Robert M. (1999a) *Blueprints for a House Divided: The Constitutional Logic of the Yugoslav Conflicts* (Ann Arbor: University of Michigan Press).

Hayden, Robert M. (1999b) 'Biased "Justice": Humanrightsism and the International Criminal Tribunal for the Former Yugoslavia', *Cleveland State Law Review*, no. 47.

Hays, Sharon (1996) *The Cultural Contradictions of Motherhood* (New Haven, CT and London: Yale University Press).

Heartfield, James (1996) 'Rights and the Legal Subject'. Unpublished Freedom and Law discussion paper.

Heater, Derek (1999) *What is Citizenship?* (Cambridge: Polity).

Held, David (1995) *Democracy and the Global Order: From the Modern State to Cosmopolitan Governance* (Stanford, CA/Cambridge: Stanford University Press/Polity).

Held, David (1998) 'Democracy and Globalisation', in Danile Archibugi, David Held and Martin Köhler (eds), *Re-imagining Political Community: Studies in Cosmopolitan Democracy* (Cambridge: Polity), pp. 11–27.

Held, David (2000) 'The Changing Contours of Political Community: Rethinking Democracy in the Context of Globalization', in Barry Holden (ed.), *Global Democracy: Key Debates* (London: Routledge), pp. 17–31.

Henkin, Louis (1990) *The Age of Rights* (New York: Columbia University Press).

Henwood, Doug (1999) 'Miscellany', *Left Business Observer*, no. 90, July.

Hillyard, Paddy (1997) 'Security Strategies in Northern Ireland: Consolidation or Reform', in Chris Gilligan and Jon Tonge (eds), *Peace or War? Understanding the Peace Process in Northern Ireland* (Aldershot: Ashgate), pp. 103–18.

Hitchens, Christopher (1999) 'Genocide and the Body-Baggers', *The Nation*, 29 November.

Hitchens, Christopher (2001) 'Of Sin, the Left, and Islamic Fascism', *The Nation* (webpage only), 24 September. Available from: <http://www.thenation.com/doc.mhtml?i=special&s=hitchens20010924>.

Hoff, Karla and Joseph E. Stiglitz (2001) 'Modern Economic Theory and Development', in Gerald M. Meier, and Joseph E. Stiglitz (eds), *Frontiers of Development Economics: The Future in Perspective* (New York: Oxford University Press), pp. 389–459.

Holbrook, Jon (2001) 'Afghanistan: A Pariah Made in the West', *Spiked*, 25 October. Available from: <http://www.spiked-online.com/Articles/00000002D291.htm>.

Holland, Tony (2000) 'Statement on Portadown District LOL No. 1 March', 9 July. Available from: <http://www.paradescommission.org/decisions/details.cfm?decision_id=68>.

Holsti, Kalevi Jacque (1996) *The State, War, and the State of War* (New York: Cambridge University Press).

HRW (Human Rights Watch) (1998) *Justice for All? An Analysis of the Human Rights Provisions of the 1998 Northern Ireland Peace Agreement*. Available from: <http://www.hrw.org/reports98/nireland/>.

HRW (Human Rights Watch) (1999a) *Leave None to Tell the Story: Genocide in Rwanda* (New York: Human Rights Watch). Available from: <http://www.hrw.org/reports/1999/rwanda/>.

HRW (Human Rights Watch) (1999b) 'Joint NGO Statement for an Independent Inquiry into the Killing of Human Rights Defender, Rosemary Nelson'. Available from: <http://www.hrw.org/press/1999/dec/nire1210b.htm>.

Hume, Mick (1997) *Whose War is it Anyway?* (London: Informinc).

Hunter, James (2000) *The Death of Character: On the Moral Education of America's Children* (New York: Basic Books).

ICRC (1907) 'Declaration (XIV) Prohibiting the Discharge of Projectiles and Explosives from Balloons', The Hague, 18 October. Available from: <http://www.icrc.org>.

ICRC (2001a) *Book of the Missing in Kosovo* (last updated 10 April). Available from: <http://www.familylinks.icrc.org/kosovo>.

ICRC (2001b) 'More than 3,500 still Missing in Kosovo', *Agence France Presse*, 10 April.

ICRC (2001c) 'Red Cross Book on Kosovo Grows to 3,525 names', *AP Worldstream*, 10 April.

ICTY (2000) 'Final Report to the Prosecutor by the Committee Established to Review the NATO Bombing Campaign Against the Federal Republic of Yugoslavia', International Criminal Tribunal for the former Yugoslavia, 13 June.

IDC (1999) *International Development Committee's Sixth Report on Conflict Prevention and Post-Conflict Reconstruction.* Volume II, Minutes of Evidence and Appendices, UK Government House of Commons, July.

Ignatieff, Michael (1995) 'The Hopeless War', *New York Times Book Review*, 25 February.

Ignatieff, Michael (1997) 'The Elusive Goal of War Trials', *Harper's*, March.

Ignatieff, Michael (1998a) *The Warrior's Honor: Ethnic War and the Modern Conscience* (London: Chatto & Windus).

Ignatieff, Michael (1998b) 'When Force is the Only Language for Liberals', *Sunday Times*, 22 February.

Ignatieff, Michael (1999a) 'Only in Truth Can Serbs Find Peace: There Is Racism Everywhere in Europe, but Only in Serbia Is Racial Contempt an Official Ideology', *Calgary Herald*, 26 June.

Ignatieff, Michael (1999b) 'Counting Bodies in Kosovo', *New York Times*, 21 November.

Ignatieff, Michael (2000a) *Virtual War: Kosovo and Beyond* (New York/London: Metropolitan Books/Chatto & Windus).

Ignatieff, Michael (2000b) 'The Next President's Duty to Intervene', *New York Times*, 13 February.

Ignatieff, Michael (2000c) 'A Bungling UN Undermines Itself', *New York Times*, 15 May.

Ignatieff, Michael (2000d) *The NewsHour with Jim Lehrer* (Transcript 6,740), 31 May.

Ignatieff, Michael (2000e) 'The Right Trial for Milošević', *New York Times*, 10 October.

IICK (Independent International Commission on Kosovo) (2000) *The Kosovo Report: Conflict, International Response, Lessons Learned* (Oxford: Oxford University Press). Available from: <http://www.kosovocommission.org>.

IICK (Independent International Commission on Kosovo) (2001) *The Follow Up: Why Conditional Independence?* Available from: <http://www.kosovocommission.org>.

International Monetary Fund and the International Development Association (2001) *Tanzania: Poverty Reduction Strategy Paper-Progress Report: Joint Staff Assessment.* Mimeo, 1 November.

ISSA (International Strategic Studies Association) (2000) 'An Eye Witness Testimony to the Shooting Down of the Rwandan President Plane'. Released 21 April. Available from: <http://www.StrategicStudies.org>.

JEEAR (Joint Evaluation of Emergency Assistance to Rwanda) (1996) *The International Response to Conflict and Genocide; Lessons From the Rwanda Experience.* Available from: <http://www.um.dk/danida/evalueringsrapporter/1997_rwanda/>.

Jennings, Anthony (ed.) (1990) *Justice Under Fire: The Abuse of Civil Liberties in Northern Ireland* (London: Pluto).

Jensen, Robert (1992) 'Fighting Objectivity: The Illusion of Journalistic Neutrality in Coverage of the Persian Gulf War', *Journal of Communication Enquiry*, vol. 16, no. 1, Winter, pp. 20–32.

Jessup, Philip Caryl (1948) *A Modern Law of Nations* (Hamden, CT: Archon Books).

Johnstone, Diana (2000) 'Nato and the New World Order: Ideals and Self-Interest', in Philip Hammond and Edward S. Herman (eds) *Degraded Capability: The Media and the Kosovo Crisis* (London: Pluto Press), pp. 7–18.

Johnstone, Diana (2002) *The Ninth Crusade: NATO's Conquest of Yugoslavia* (London: Pluto Press).

Judah, Tim (1999) 'Garton Ash Right Again', *The Herald*, 15 July.

Judah, Tim (2000a) *Kosovo: War and Revenge* (New Haven, CT: Yale University Press).

Judah, Tim (2000b) 'Is Milošević Planning Another Balkan War?', *Scotland on Sunday*, 19 March.

Kaldor, Mary (1999a) *New and Old Wars: Organized Violence in a Global Era* (Stanford, California/Oxford: Stanford University Press/Polity Press).

Kaldor, Mary (1999b) 'Transnational Civil Society' in Tim Dunne and Nicholas J. Wheeler (eds), *Human Rights in Global Politics* (Cambridge: Cambridge University Press, 1999), pp. 195–213.

Kaldor, Mary (2001) *Analysis*, BBC Radio Four, 29 March.

Kanbur, Ravi and Lyn Squire (1999) *The Evolution of Thinking about Poverty: Exploring the Interactions*, September. Available from: <http://www.worldbank.org/poverty/wdrpoverty.evolut.pdf>.

Kanbur, Ravi and Lyn Squire (2001) 'The Evolution of Thinking about Poverty: Exploring the Interactions', in Gerald M. Meier, and Joseph E. Stiglitz (eds), *Frontiers of Development Economics: The Future in Perspective* (New York: Oxford University Press), pp. 183–226.

Kanbur, Ravi and David Vines (2000) 'The World Bank and Poverty Reduction: Past, Present and Future', in Christopher L. Gilbert and David Vines (eds), *The World Bank: Structure and Policies* (Cambridge: Cambridge University Press), pp. 87–107.

Keane, Fergal (1995) *Season of Blood: A Rwandan Journey* (Harmondsworth: Viking).

Keeble, Richard (2000) 'New Militarism, and the Manufacture of Warfare', in Philip Hammond and Edward S. Herman (eds), *Degraded Capability: The Media and the Kosovo Crisis* (London: Pluto Press), pp. 59–69.

Keegan, John (2001) 'West Claimed Moral High Ground With Air Power', *Daily Telegraph*, 16 January.

Keen, David (1995) 'Short-Term Interventions and Long-Term Problems: the Case of the Kurds in Iraq', in John Harriss (ed.), *The Politics of Humanitarian Intervention* (London: Pinter).

Keith, Rollie (1999) 'Failure of Diplomacy', *The Democrat* (Canada), May.

Kelsen, Hans (1950) *The Law of the United Nations* (London: Stevens).

Kennedy, Helena (2000) 'Foreword', in Francesca Klug, *Values for a Godless Age: The Story of the UK's New Bill of Rights* (London: Penguin), pp. xi–xv.

Kenney, George (1998) 'Kosovo: A Short History', *The Nation*, 6 July.
Kenney, George (1999) 'Rolling Thunder: the Rerun', *The Nation*, 14 June.
King, Michael (1997) *A Better World for Children: Exploration in Morality and Authority* (London and New York: Routledge).
Klaus, Marshall, John Kendell and Phyllis Klaus (1996) *Bonding: Building the Foundations of Secure Attachment and Independence* (London: Cedar).
Klinghoffer, Arthur J. (1998) *The International Dimension of Genocide in Rwanda* (Basingstoke: Macmillan – now Palgrave Macmillan).
Klug, Francesca (2000) *Values for a Godless Age: The Story of the UK's New Bill of Rights* (London: Penguin).
Knightley, Phillip (2000) *The First Casualty: the War Correspondent as Hero and Myth-maker from the Crimea to Kosovo*, revised edn (London: Prion Press).
Köhler, Martin (1998) 'From the National to the Cosmopolitan Public Sphere', in Daniele Archibugi, David Held and Martin Köhler (eds), *Re-imagining Political Community: Studies in Cosmopolitan Democracy* (Cambridge: Polity), pp. 231–51.
Korey, William (1999) 'Human Rights NGOs: The Power of Persuasion', *Ethics and International Affairs*, vol. 13, pp. 151–74.
Kouchner, Bernard (1999a) 'Establish a Right to Intervene Against War, Oppression; It's Time for a Global Moral Code that Can Stop Wars Before They Start and Murderers Before They Kill', *Los Angeles Times*, 18 October.
Kouchner, Bernard (1999b) 'The Right to Intervention: Codified in Kosovo', *New Perspectives Quarterly*, vol. 16, no. 4, Summer.
Krasner, Stephen (1983) *International Regimes* (Ithaca, NY: Cornell University Press).
Kuperman, Alan J. (2001) *The Limits of Humanitarian Intervention: Genocide in Rwanda* (Washington DC: Brookings Institution).
Lasch, Christopher (1977) *Haven in a Heartless World: the Family Besieged* (New York: Basic Books).
Lasch, Christopher (1978) *The Culture of Narcissism: American Life in an Age of Diminishing Expectations* (New York: W. W. Norton).
Lasch, Christopher (1985) *The Minimal Self: Psychic Survival in Troubled Times* (New York: W. W. Norton).
Laughland, John (1997) *The Tainted Source: The Undemocratic Origins of the European Idea* (London: Little, Brown).
Laughland, John (1999a) 'The Anomalies of the International Criminal Tribunal are Legion. This Is not Victors' Justice in the Former Yugoslavia – In Fact, It Is no Justice at All', *The Times*, 17 June.
Laughland, John (1999b) 'The Massacres That Never Were', *Spectator*, 30 October.
Laughland, John (1999c) 'I Was Right About Kosovo', *Spectator*, 20 November.
Lawyers Committee for Human Rights (1993) *Human Rights and Legal Defense in Northern Ireland: The Abuse and Intimidation of Defense Lawyers and the Murder of Patrick Finucane* (New York: Lawyers Committee for Human Rights).
Lemarchand, René (1996) *Burundi, Ethnic Conflict and Genocide* (Cambridge, MA: Woodrow Wilson Center).
Lemarchand, René (1998) 'Genocide in the Great Lakes: Which Genocide? Whose Genocide?', *African Studies Review*, vol. 4, no. 1.
Lenin, Vladimir Ilyich (1965) 'On the Slogan for a United States of Europe', in *Lenin, Marx, Engels, Marxism*, 7th edn (Moscow: Progress Publishers).
Lewis, C. S. (1945) *That Hideous Strength: A Modern Fairy-Tale for Grown-Ups* (New York: Simon & Schuster, 1996).

Lewis, Norman (1998) 'Human Rights, Law and Democracy in an Unfree World', in Tony Evans (ed.), *Human Rights Fifty Years On: A Reappraisal* (Manchester: Manchester University Press).

Lijphart, Arend (1977) *Democracy in Plural Societies: a Comparative Exploration* (New Haven, CT: Yale University Press).

Lijphart, Arend (1996) 'The Framework Document on Northern Ireland and the Theory of Power-Sharing', *Government and Opposition*, vol. 31, no. 3, pp. 267–74.

Lillich, Richard B. (1967) 'Forcible Self-help by States to Protect Human Rights', *Iowa Law Review*, vol. 53, pp. 34–51.

Linklater, Andrew (1998) *The Transformation of Political Community: Ethical Foundations of the Post-Westphalian Era* (Columbia, SC: University of South Carolina Press).

Little, Allan (2001) 'The West Did Not Do Enough', *BBC Online*, 29 June. Available from: <http://news.bbc.co.uk/hi/english/world/from_our_own_correspondent/newsid_1413000/1413764.stm>.

Littman, Mark (1999) *Kosovo: Law and Diplomacy* (London: Centre for Policy Studies).

Loquai, Brigadier General Heinz (2000) *Der Kosovo-Konflikt. Wege in einen vermeidbaren Krieg* ('The Kosovo Conflict: Paths into an Avoidable War') (Baden Baden: Nomos).

Lucy, Gordon (2001) 'Questions of Emphasis', *Fortnight*, October, no. 399.

Lyons, James (2001) 'Covert Action in Africa: a Smoking Gun in Washington DC' Public statement at a conference organized by US Congresswoman Cynthia McKinney, 16 April. Available from: <http://www.house.gov/mckinney/news/pr010416.htm>.

McAllister, Brendan (1999) 'Encountering the Strange: Mediation and Reconciliation in Northern Ireland's Parades Conflict'. Paper presented to conference, 'Promoting Peace Through Reconciliation and Co-existence Alternatives', the American University, Washington, DC. Available from: <http://www.mediation-network.org.uk/html/mediation_paper.html>.

MccGwire, Michael (2000) 'Why Did We Bomb Belgrade?', *International Affairs*, vol. 76, no. 1, January–March.

McGillivray, Anne (1994) 'Why Children Do Have Equal Rights: in Reply to Laura Purdy', *International Journal of Children's Rights*, vol. 2, no. 3, pp. 243–58.

McNulty, Mel (1999) 'Media Ethnicization and the International Response to War and Genocide in Rwanda', in Tim Allen and Jean Seaton (eds), *The Media of Conflict* (London: Zed Books), pp. 268–86.

McVeigh, Tracy (2001) 'Children May Die in Care Crisis', *Guardian*, 16 September.

Madsen, Wayne (1999) *Genocide and Covert Operations in Africa, 1993–1999* (Lewiston, NY: Edwin Mellen Press).

Malanczuk, Peter (1993) *Humanitarian Intervention and the Legitimacy of the Use of Force* (Hingham, MA: Martinus Nijhoff International).

Malinvaud, Edmund (ed.) (1997) *Development Strategy and Management of the Market Economy* (Oxford: Oxford University Press).

Mamdani, Mahmood (2000) 'The Political Diaspora in Uganda and Background to the RPF invasion', in Didier Goyvaerts (ed.), *Conflict and Ethnicity in Central Africa* (Tokyo: Tokyo University of Foreign Studies).

Mamdani, Mahmood (2001) *When Victims Become Killers: Colonialism, Nativism, and the Genocide in Rwanda* (Princeton, NJ: Princeton University Press).

Mandel, Michael (2001) 'Milošević Has a Point', *Toronto Globe and Mail*, 6 July. Available from: <http://www.globalpolicy.org/intljustice/tribunals/2001/0706milo.htm>.

Marwitz, Harald (1994) 'Another Side of Rwanda's Bloodbath', *Washington Times*, 11 August.

Meehan, Elizabeth (2000) 'Europe and the Europeanisation of the Irish Question', in Michael Cox, Adrian Guelke and Fiona Stephen (eds), *A Farewell to Arms? From 'Long War' to Long Peace in Northern Ireland* (Manchester: Manchester University Press), pp. 199–213.

Melton, Gary B. (1994) 'Is There a Place for Children in the New World Order?' in Stewart Asquith and Malcolm Hill (eds), *Justice for Children* (Dordrecht: Martinus Nijhoff), pp. 26–58.

Melvern, Linda (2000) *A People Betrayed: The Role of the West in Rwanda's Genocide* (London: Zed Press).

Midgley, Mary (1999) 'Towards an Ethic of Global Responsibility', in Tim Dunne and Nicholas J. Wheeler (eds) *Human Rights in Global Politics* (Cambridge: Cambridge University Press), pp. 160–74.

Miller, David (1994) *Don't Mention the War: Northern Ireland, Propaganda and the Media* (London: Pluto).

Mills, Kurt (1997) 'Reconstructing Sovereignty: A Human Rights Perspective', *Netherlands Quarterly of Human Rights*, vol. 15, no. 3, pp. 267–90.

Millwood, David (ed.) (1995) *The International Response to Conflict and Genocide: Lessons from the Rwanda Experience* (Copenhagen: Steering Committee of the Joint Evaluation of Emergency Assistance to Rwanda).

Milošević, Slobodan (1987) 'Speech by Slobodan Milošević in Kosovo Polje', *BBC Summary of Worldwide Broadcasts*, 28 April.

Milošević, Slobodan (1989) 'Slobodan Milošević Addresses Rally at Gazimestan', *BBC Summary of Worldwide Broadcasts*, 30 June.

Minnow, Martha (1990) *Making All the Difference: Inclusion, Exclusion, and American Law* (Ithaca, NY: Cornell University Press).

Mkandawire, Thandika and Charles C. Soludo (1999) *Our Continent, Our Future: African Perspectives on Structural Adjustment* (Dakar, Senegal: CODESRIA).

Moghalu, Kingsley Chiedu (1999) 'The Indictment of Milošević: A Revolution in Human Rights', *New Perspectives Quarterly*, vol. 16, no. 4, pp. 13–16.

Morgenthau, Hans (1973) *Politics Among Nations: The Struggle for Power and Peace* (New York: Knopf).

Moritz, Frederic (1997a) 'Human Rights Journalism: Born in Purple Prose'. Available from: <http://www.worldlymind.org/creelover.htm>.

Moritz, Frederic (1997b) 'American Human Rights Reporting: Digging Up Its Deeper Roots'. Available from: <http://www.worldlymind.org/birth1.htm>.

Müllerson, Rein (1997) *Human Rights Diplomacy* (London: Routledge).

Mutua, Makau wa (1996) 'The Ideology of Human Rights', *Virginia Journal of International Law*, vol. 36, pp. 589–657.

Narayan, Deepa (1997) *Voices of the Poor: Poverty and Social Capital in Tanzania* (Washington, DC: World Bank).

Narayan, Deepa with Raj Patel, Kai Schafft, Anne Rademacher and Sarah Koch-Schulte (2000a) *Voices of the Poor: Can Anyone Hear Us?*, Vol. 1 (Oxford: Oxford University Press).

Narayan, Deepa, Robert Chambers, Meera K. Shah and Patti Petesch (2000b) *Voices of the Poor: Crying Out for Change*, Vol. 2 (Oxford: Oxford University Press).

Narayan, Deepa and Michael Walton (eds) (2000c) *Voices of the Poor: From Many Lands*, Vol. 3 (Oxford: Oxford University Press/World Bank).

Neier, Aryeh (1998) 'A Force for World Justice', *Washington Post*, 5 May.

Neier, Aryeh (2001) 'A Quest for Justice', *New York Review of Books*, 8 March.

New York Times (1999) 'Then and Now/Reflections on the Millennium: The Powerful Idea of Human Rights', Editorial, 8 December.

Newbury, Catherine (1995) 'Background to Genocide: Rwanda', *Issue: A Journal of Opinion*, vol. 23, no. 2.

NIHRC (Northern Ireland Human Rights Commission) (n.d.), 'What We Do: Functions of the Commission'. Available from: <http://www.nihrc.org/files/%25whatwe1.htm>.

Nolan, James (1998) *The Therapeutic State: Justifying Government at Century's End* (New York: New York University Press).

Oberg, Jan (2000) 'UN Broke in Kosovo', Transnational Foundation for Peace and Future Research, 7 February. Available from: <http://www.transnational.org/pressinf/2000/pf86.html>.

O'Brien, Brendan (1993) *The Long War: the IRA and Sinn Fein 1985 to Today* (Dublin: O'Brien Press).

O'Clery, Conor (1996) *The Greening of the White House, the Inside Story of How America Tried to Bring Peace to Ireland* (Dublin: Gill & Macmillan).

O'Leary, Brendan (1989) 'The Limits to Coercive Consociationalism in Northern Ireland', *Political Studies*, vol. 37, no. 4, pp. 562–88.

O'Leary, Brendan (1999) 'The Nature of the British-Irish Agreement', *New Left Review*, no. 233, pp. 66–96.

O'Leary, Brendan (2001) 'The Protection of Human Rights under the Belfast Agreement', *Political Quarterly*, vol. 72, no. 3, pp. 353–65.

Omaar, Rakiya (1994) *Rwanda: Death, Despair and Defiance* (London: African Rights).

O'Neill, Brendan (2001) 'The Great Parades Debate', *Spiked*, 14 August. Available from: <http://www.spiked-online.com/Articles/00000002D1E9.htm>.

O'Neill, Brendan (2002) '"Today it's Just Pure Naked Bigotry": an Interview With Peter Shirlow', *Spiked*, 17 January. Available from: <http://www.spiked-online.com/Articles/00000002D3B4.htm>.

O'Neill, Onora (1992) 'Children's Rights and Children's Lives', in Philip Alston, Stephen Parker and John Seymour (eds), *Children's Rights and the Law* (Oxford: Clarendon Press), pp. 24–42.

OSCE (Organization for Security and Cooperation in Europe) (1999a) *Kosovo/Kosova: As Seen, As Told. The Human Rights Findings of the OSCE Kosovo Verification Mission October 1998 to June 1999*. Available from: <http://www.osce.org/kosovo/reports/hr/part1/p0cont.htm>.

OSCE (Organization for Security and Cooperation in Europe) (1999b) *Kosovo/Kosova: As Seen, As Told. June to October 1999*. Available from: <http://www.osce/org/kosovo/reports/hr/part2>.

Österdahl, Inger (1998) *Threat to the Peace* (Uppsala: Iustus Forlag).

Owen, David (1995) *Balkan Odyssey* (CD-Rom Standard Edition, Version 1.1) (London: Electric Company).

Pape, Matthias (1997) *Humanitäre Intervention* (Baden-Baden: Nomos).

Parton, Nigel (1985) *The Politics of Child Abuse* (London: Macmillan).

Pearl, Daniel and Robert Block (1999) 'Body Count: War Was Cruel, Bitter Savage; Genocide It Wasn't', *Wall Street Journal*, 31 December.

Pedelty, Mark (1995) *War Stories: The Culture of Foreign Correspondents* (London: Routledge).

Pelzer, Dave (2001) *A Child Called It* (London: Orion Paperbooks).

Pender, John (2001a) 'From "Structural Adjustment" to "Comprehensive Development Framework": Conditionality Transformed?', *Third World Quarterly*, vol. 22, no. 3, pp. 397–411.

Pender, John (2001b) 'Why Shouldn't Tanzania Have Air Traffic Control?', *Spiked*, 21 December. Available from <http://www.spiked-online.com/Articles/00000002D377.htm>.

Philo, Greg, Lindsey Hilsum, Liza Beattie and Rick Holliman (1999) 'The Media and the Rwanda Crisis: Effects on Audiences and Public Policy', in Greg Philo (ed.), *Message Received* (Harlow: Longman), pp. 213–28.

Pieterse, Nederveen J. (1997) 'Sociology of Humanitarian Intervention: Bosnia, Rwanda and Somalia Compared', *International Political Science Review*, vol. 18, no. 1, pp. 71–93.

Popkewitiz, Thomas S. and Marianne N. Bloch (2001) 'Administering Freedom: A History of the Present, Rescuing the Parent to Rescue the Child for Society', in Kenneth Hultqvist and Gunilla Dahlberg (eds), *Governing the Child in the New Millennium* (New York and London: Routledge/Falmer), pp. 85–118.

Prest, Michael (1996) 'Special Report: Wolfensohn's World Bank', *Prospect*, August/September, pp. 68–71.

Prunier, Gérard (1995) *The Rwanda Crisis, 1959–1994: History of a Genocide* (London: Hurst).

Prunier, Gérard (1997) *The Rwanda Crisis: History of a Genocide*, 2nd edn (London: Hurst).

Pumphrey, George (1998) '"The Srebrenica Massacre": A Legend?', *Dialogue*, vol. 7, no. 7, Autumn/Winter.

Pupavac, Vanessa (1999) *Children's Rights and the Culture of Paternalism* (Sheffield: Sheffield Hallam University Press).

Pupavac, Vanessa (2000) 'Securing the Community? An Examination of International Psychosocial Intervention'. Paper presented at 'Balkan Security: Visions of the Future' Conference, Centre for South-East European Studies, School of Slavonic and East European Studies, University College London, 16–17 June.

Pupavac, Vanessa (2001a) 'Misanthropy Without Borders: The International Children's Rights Regime', *Disasters*, vol. 25, no. 2, pp. 95–112.

Pupavac, Vanessa (2001b) 'Therapeutic Governance: Psycho-social Intervention and Trauma Risk Management', *Disasters*, vol. 25, no. 4, pp. 216–30.

Purdie, Bob (1990) *Politics in the Streets: the Origins of the Civil Rights Movement in Northern Ireland* (Belfast: Blackstaff).

Rabkin, Jeremy (1999) 'Nuremberg Misremembered', *Johns Hopkins SAIS Review*, Summer–Fall, pp. 223–39.

Radomirovic, Vladimir (1999) 'A Man Who Does Not Sleep Well', *The Reporter* (Banja Luka) 22 December. Available from: <http://www.cdsp.neu.edu/info/students/marko/reporter/reporter9.html>.

Rawls, John (1993) 'The Law of Peoples', in Stephen Shute and Susan Hurley (eds), *On Human Rights* (New York: Basic Books), pp. 41–68.

Reed, William Cyrus (1995) 'The Rwandan Patriotic Front: Politics and Development in Rwanda', *Issue: A Journal of Opinion*, vol. 23, no. 2.

Refugees International (1997) *The Lost Refugees: Herded and Hunted in Eastern Zaire* (Washington, DC: Refugees International).

Reisman, Michael W. (1990) 'Sovereignty and Human Rights in Contemporary International Law', *American Journal of International Law*, vol. 84.

Reisman, Michael W. and Myers S. McDougal (1973) 'Humanitarian Intervention to Protect the Ibos', in Richard B. Lillich (ed.), *Humanitarian Intervention and the United Nations* (Charlottesville: University Press of Virginia).

Rhodes, Aaron (1999) 'Human Rights in the "New Europe": Some Problems', in The Belgrade Circle (ed.), *The Politics of Human Rights* (London: Verso), pp. 189–93.

Ricchiardi, Sherry (1996) 'Over the Line?', *American Journalism Review*, September.

Rieff, David (1996) *Slaughterhouse: Bosnia and the Failure of the West* (New York: Simon & Schuster).

Rieff, David (1999a) 'What Bombs Can't Do', *New York Times*, 25 March.

Rieff, David (1999b) 'A New Age of Liberal Imperialism?', *World Policy Journal*, vol. 16, no. 2, Summer, pp. 1–10.

Rieff, David (1999c) 'The Precarious Triumph of Human Rights', *New York Times*, 8 August.

Rieff, David (1999d) 'The Law of Revenge Rules', *Newsweek*, 23 August.

Rieff, David (2000a) 'The Crusaders: Moral Principles, Strategic Interests, and Military Force', *World Policy Journal*, vol. 17, no. 2, Summer.

Rieff, David (2000b) 'Virtual War: Kosovo and Beyond', *Los Angeles Times*, 3 September.

Roberts, Adam (1999) 'Willing the End but Not the Means', *World Today*, vol. 55, no. 5, May, pp. 8–12.

Roberts, Adam (2001) 'Intervention: Suggestions for Moving the Debate Forward', Round Table Consultation, London, 3 February, *Discussion Paper*. International Commission on Intervention and State Sovereignty. Available from: <http://web.gc.cuny.edu/icissresearch/london%20discussion%20paper.htm>.

Robertson, Geoffrey (1998) 'A Question of Sovereignty', *Newsweek*, 7 December.

Robertson, Geoffrey (1999) *Crimes Against Humanity: The Struggle for Global Justice* (London: Allen Lane).

Robertson, Geoffrey (2000) *Crimes against Humanity: the Struggle for Global Justice*, revised edn (London: Penguin Books).

Robinson, Anne (2001) *Memoirs of an Unfit Mother* (London: Little, Brown).

Robinson, Mary (1999) 'We Can End This Agony', Saturday Review, *Guardian*, 23 October.

Rodgers, William D. (1991) 'The Principles of Force, the Force of Principles', in David Scheffer (ed.), *Right v Might: International Law and the Use of Force* (New York: Council on Foreign Relations Press).

Rooney, Kevin (1998) 'Institutionalising Division', *Fortnight*, no. 371.

Rooper, Jonathan (1997) 'Srebrenica'. Unpublished paper.

Rorty, Richard M. (1993) 'Human Rights, Rationality, and Sentimentality', in Stephen Shute and Susan Hurley (eds), *On Human Rights* (New York: Basic Books), pp. 111–34.

Rose, Nikolas (1990) Governing the Soul: the Shaping of the Private Self (London: Routledge).

Rose, Nikolas (1999a) *Governing the Soul: The Shaping of the Private Self,* 2nd edn (London and New York: Free Assocation Books).

Rose, Nikolas (1999b) *Powers of Freedom: Reframing Political Thought* (Cambridge: Cambridge University Press).

Roth, Kenneth (1997) 'Why Justice Needs NATO: As Long as War Criminals Go Free, There is No Peace for Bosnia', *The Nation,* 22 September.

Rothchild, Donald (1997) *Managing Ethnic Conflict in Africa: Pressures and Incentives for Cooperation* (Washington, DC: Brookings Institution).

Ruane, Joseph (1999) 'The End of (Irish) History? Three Readings of the Current Conjuncture', in Joseph Ruane and Jennifer Todd (eds), *After the Good Friday Agreement: Analysing Political Change in Northern Ireland* (Dublin: UCD Press), pp. 145–69.

Rubin, Alfred P. (1997) *Ethics and Authority in International Law* (New York: Cambridge University Press).

Rumsfeld, Donald (2001) 'Text of the Defense Secretary's Briefing on the Military Strikes, the Pentagon, 7 October 2001', Associated Press. Available from: <http://www.nytimes.com>.

Ryan, Mark (1994) *War and Peace in Ireland: Britian and the IRA in the New World Order* (London: Pluto).

Ryan, Mark (1997) 'From the Centre to the Margins: The Slow Death of Irish Republicanism', in Chris Gilligan and Jon Tonge (eds), *Peace or War? Understanding the Peace Process in Northern Ireland* (Aldershot: Ashgate), pp. 72–84.

Sanction, Thomas (1999) 'Distinguished Service: Médecins sans Frontières Receives the Nobel Peace Prize', *Time,* vol. 154, no. 17, 25 October.

Savić, Obrad (1999) 'Introduction', in The Belgrade Circle (ed.), *The Politics of Human Rights* (London: Verso), pp. 3–15.

Sellars, Kirsten (1999) 'The New Imperialists', *Spectator,* 23 October.

Sen, Amartya (1997a) 'Development Thinking at the Beginning of the 21st Century', *Development Economics Research Programme,* Series No. 2, Suntory and Toyota International Centres for Economics and Related Disciplines, London School of Economics, March.

Sen, Amartya (1997b) 'What's the Point of a Development Strategy?', in Edmund Malinvaud (ed.), *Development Strategy and Management of the Market Economy* (Oxford: Oxford University Press), pp. 35–60.

Sen, Amartya (1999) *Development as Freedom* (New York: Anchor Books).

SHAPE (1999) 'SHAPE News Summary and Analysis', 12 May. Available from: <http://www.fas.org/man/dod-101/ops/docs99/sa120599.htm>.

Shaw, Martin (1994) *Global Society and International Relations: Sociological Concepts and Political Perspectives* (Cambridge: Polity).

Shaw, Martin (2000) 'On Slaughter: Mass Killing from War to Genocide'. Paper presented to Sussex University International Relations and Social and Political Thought joint seminar series 'The New World Order Ten Years On: Norms, Values and Morality in Contemporary Politics'. Available from: <http://www.sussex.ac.uk/Users/hafa3/slaughter>.

Shawcross, William (1999) 'Wandering in the Wilderness', *Newsweek,* 19 April.

Shawcross, William (2000) *Deliver Us From Evil: Warlords and Peacekeepers in a World of Endless Conflict* (London: Bloomsbury).

Shea (1999) 'Press Conference given by NATO Spokesman, Jamie Shea and SHAPE Spokesman, Major General Walter Jertz', 17 May. Available from: <http://www.nato.int/kosovo/press/p990517b.htm>.

Shestack, Jerome J. (1997) 'Globalization of Human Rights Law', *Fordham International Law Journal*, vol. 21, no. 2, pp. 558–68.

Short, Clare (1998) 'Principles for a New Humanitarianism'. Speech by the Secretary of State for International Development, 'Principled Aid in an Unprincipled World: Relief, War and Humanitarian Assistance', Conference hosted by ECHO and the Overseas Development Institute, 7 April.

Simma, Bruno (1999) 'NATO, the UN and the Use of Force: Legal Aspects', *European Journal of International Law*, vol. 10, no. 1. Available from: <http://www.ejil.org/journal/Vol10/No1/ab1.html>.

Simpson, Mark (2001) 'Government Preparing for Poll "Flak"', *BBC News*. Available from: <http://news.bbc.co.uk/hi/english/uk/northern_ireland/newsid_1553000/1553161.stm>.

Sisk, Timothy (2001) 'Peacemaking Processes: Forestalling Return to Ethnic Violence', in I. William Zartman (ed.), *Preventive Negotiation: Avoiding Conflict Escalation* (New York: Rowman & Littlefield).

Skoco, Mijana and William Woodger (2000) 'War Crimes', in Philip Hammond and Edward S. Herman (eds), *Degraded Capability: The Media and the Kosovo Crisis* (London: Pluto Press), pp. 31–8.

Slim, Hugo (1997) *Positioning Humanitarianism in War: Principles of Neutrality, Impartiality and Solidarity* (Oxford: Oxford Brookes University, Centre for Development and Emergency Planning).

Slim, Hugo and Isobel McConnan (1998) *A Swiss Prince, A Glass Slipper and the Feet of 15 British Aid Agencies: A Study of DEC Agency Positions on Humanitarian Principles* (Oxford: Disasters Emergency Committee).

Slim, Hugo and Emma Visman (1995) 'Evacuation, Intervention and Retaliation: UN Humanitarian Operations in Somalia 1991–1993', in John Harriss (ed.), *The Politics of Humanitarian Intervention* (London: Pinter).

Solomon, Norman (2001) 'TV News: A Militarized Zone', 8 October. Available from: <http://www.fair.org/media-beat>.

Sommaruga, Cornelio (1999) 'The 50th Anniversary of the Geneva Conventions: The Challenges of Protecting Civilians in Times of Armed Conflict'. Speech delivered by the President of the International Committee of the Red Cross, RSA, London, 13 October.

Sontag, Susan (1995) 'A Lament for Bosnia', *The Nation*, 25 December.

Stammers, Neil (1999) 'Social Movements and the Social Construction of Human Rights', *Human Rights Quarterly*, vol. 21, pp. 980–1008.

Statewatch (1999) 'Documents Confirm Collusion'. Available from: <http://www.poptel.org.uk/cgi-bin/dbs2/statewatch?query=northern+ireland&mode=records&row_id=19639>.

Stern, Nicholas (1997) 'Macroeconomic Policy and the Role of the State in a Changing World', in Edmund Malinvaud (ed.), *Development Strategy and Management of the Market Economy* (Oxford: Oxford University Press), pp. 143–74.

Stern, Nicholas and Joseph E. Stiglitz (1997) 'A Framework for a Development Strategy in a Market Economy', in Edmund Malinvaud (ed.), *Development Strategy and Management of the Market Economy* (Oxford: Oxford University Press), pp. 253–95.

Stiglitz, Joseph E. (1998) 'More Instruments and Broader Goals: Moving Towards the Post-Washington Consensus', *WIDER Annual Lecture*, 2 January.

Stiglitz, Joseph E. (1999) 'The World Bank at the Millennium', *Economic Journal*, no. 109, November, pp. 577–97.

Stiglitz, Joseph E. (2000) 'Introduction', in Christopher L. Gilbert and David Vines (eds), *The World Bank: Structure and Policies* (Cambridge: Cambridge University Press), pp. 87–107.

Stockton, Nicholas (1998) 'In Defence of Humanitarianism'. Speech at 'The Emperor's New Clothes: The Collapse of Humanitarian Principles', Disasters and Emergency Committee Conference, London, 4 February.

Thakur, Ramesh (2001) 'Global Norms and International Humanitarian Law: An Asian Perspective', *International Review of the Red Cross*, no. 841, pp. 19–43.

Thurer, Daniel (1999) 'The "Failed State" and International Law', *International Review of the Red Cross*, no. 836, pp. 731–61.

The Times (2001) 'Government Collapses as Ministers Quit', 30 June.

Tomlinson, Mike (1995) 'Fortress Northern Ireland: a Model for the New Europe?', in Patrick Clancy, Sheelagh Drudy, Kathleen Lynch and Liam O'Dowd (eds), *Irish Society: Sociological Perspectives* (Dublin: Institute of Public Administration), pp. 432–64.

Totton, Nick (2000) *Psychotherapy and Politics* (London: Sage).

Townshend, Charles (1993) *Making the Peace: Public Order and Public Security in Modern Britain* (Oxford: Oxford University Press).

Trew, Karen (1992) 'Social Psychological Research on the Conflict', *The Psychologist: Bulletin of the British Psychological Society*, no. 5, pp. 342–4.

Tuveson, Ernest Lee (1968) *Redeemer Nation: The Idea of America's Millennial Role* (Chicago: University of Chicago Press).

UKFCO (1986) 'Foreign Office Policy Document No. 148', *British Year Book of International Law*, vol. 57, The Royal Institute of International Affairs (London: Oxford University Press).

UKSCD (2000) *Select Committee on Defence Thirteenth Report: Iraqi No-Fly Zones* (HC 453) (London: HMSO). Available from: <http://www.parliament.the-stationery-office.co.uk/pa/cm199900/cmselect/cmdfence/453/45302.htm>.

UN (1996) *States Must be Honest About Human Rights, Accept Constructive Criticism, Third Committee Told in Rights Debate*, United Nations Press Release (GA/SHC/3400), 22 November.

UN (1998) *Assembly President Stresses 'Creative Force' of Universal Declaration*, United Nations Press Release (GA/SM/4398), 10 December.

UN (1999) *Secretary-General says Global Effort Against Armed Conflict Needs Change From 'Culture of Reaction to Culture of Prevention'*, United Nations Press Release (SC/6759), 29 November.

UN (2000a) '"We the Peoples": The Role of the United Nations in the 21st Century', *Millennium Report of the Secretary-General* (A/54/2000) (New York: United Nations). Available from: <http://www.un.org/millennium/sg/report>.

UN (2000b) *Emerging Issues for Children in the Twenty-first Century*, UN General Assembly Economic and Social Council (A/AC.256/3 – E/ICEF/2000/13), 4 April. Available from: <http://www.unicef.org/specialsession/documentation/archive.htm>.

UN (2001) *We the Children: End-decade Review of the Follow-up to the World Summit for Children. Report of the Secretary-General*, UN General Assembly (A/S-27/3). Available from: <http://www.unicef.org/specialsession/documentation/archive.htm>.

UNICEF (1997) *The Progress of Nations 1997*. Available from: <http://www.unicef.org/pon97/>.

UNICEF (2001) 'Early Childhood: Choices to be Made', *The State of the World's Children 2001*. UNICEF. Available from: <http://www.unicef.org/sowc01/1-1.htm>.

United Republic of Tanzania (2000) *Poverty Reduction Strategy Paper*, 1 October.

United Republic of Tanzania (2001) *Poverty Reduction Strategy Paper Progress Report*, 14 August.

Urquhart, Brian (2000) 'In the Name of Humanity', *New York Review of Books*, 27 April.

USC (1994) *Hearing before the United States Congress, House of Representatives: Committee on Foreign Affairs, Subcommittee on Africa*, 103rd Congress, 2nd Session, 4 May (Washington DC: US Government Printing Office).

USDoS (2000) *On the Record Briefing Secretary of State Madeleine K. Albright and Assistant Secretary of State for Democracy, Human Rights and Labour Harold Hongju Koh on the Country Reports on Human Rights Practices for 1999*, Washington, DC, 25 February.

Uvin, Peter (1998) *Aiding Violence: The Development Enterprise in Rwanda* (West Hartford, CT: Kumarian Press).

Uvin, Peter (1999) *The Influence of Aid in Situations of Violent Conflict. Synthesis Report* (Paris: OECD Development Assistance Committee), September.

Vulliamy, Ed (1999a) Presentation, 'Journalists Covering Conflict: Norms Of Conduct' symposium, Columbia University, 28 April, *Preventing Deadly Conflict: Publications of the Carnegie Commission on Preventing Deadly Conflict* (CD-Rom) (Washington, DC: Carnegie Corporation).

Vulliamy, Ed (1999b) ' "Neutrality" and the Absence of Reckoning: A Journalist's Account' (reproduced from the *Journal of International Affairs*, vol. 52, no. 2, Spring 1999), *Preventing Deadly Conflict: Publications of the Carnegie Commission on Preventing Deadly Conflict* (CD-Rom) (Washington, DC: Carnegie Corporation).

Vulliamy, Ed (1999c) 'Crimes of War', Speech in Session V at Journalism, War and Law, Weapons of War, Tools of Peace Symposium IV: 'The Role of the Media and International Humanitarian Law in the Protection of Civilians in Conflict', Cape Town, South Africa, 17–19 November.

Waal, Alex de (1997a) *Famine Crimes: Politics and the Disaster Relief Industry in Africa* (Oxford: James Curry/Indiana University Press).

Waal, Alex de (1997b) 'Becoming Shameless: The Failure of Human-Rights Organizations in Rwanda', *Times Literary Supplement*, 21 February, pp. 3–4.

Wade, Robert (2001) 'Showdown at the World Bank', *New Left Review*, vol. 2, no. 7, January/February, pp. 124–37.

Wagenseil, Steven (1999) 'Human Rights in US Foreign Policy', *Journal of Intergroup Relations*, vol. 26, pp. 3–13.

Walker, Clive (1992) 'The Role and Power of the Army in Northern Ireland', in Brigid Hadfield (ed.), *Northern Ireland: Politics and the Constitution* (Buckingham: Open University Press), pp. 110–29.

Walker, Tom and Aidan Laverty (2000) 'CIA Aided Kosovo Guerrilla Army', *Sunday Times*, 12 March.

Wedgwood, Ruth (1999) 'NATO's Campaign in Yugoslavia', *American Journal of International Law*, vol. 93, pp. 828–34.

Weller, Marc (1999a) 'Armed Samaritans', *Counsel*, August, pp. 20–2.

Weller, Marc (1999b) 'The US, Iraq and the Use of Force in a Unipolar World', *Survival*, vol. 41, no. 4, pp. 81–100.

Westendorp, Carlos (1999) 'Lessons Bosnia Taught Us', *Wall Street Journal*, 19 May.

Wheeler, Nicholas J. (1996) 'Guardian Angel or Global Gangster: A Review of the Ethical Claims of International Society', *Political Studies*, vol. 44, no. 1, pp. 123–35.

Wheeler, Nicholas J. (1997) 'Agency, Humanitarianism and Intervention', *International Political Science Review*, vol. 18, no. 1, pp. 9–26.

Whyte, John (1990) *Interpreting Northern Ireland* (Oxford: Clarendon Press).

Williams, Ian (1999a) 'Waging Diplomatic War', *Salon*, 9 June. Available from: <www.Salon.com>.

Williams, Ian (1999b) 'Counting Bodies in Kosovo', *Knight-Ridder/Tribune*, 23 November.

Williamson, Anne (2000) 'The Rape of Russia', *Laissez Faire City Times*, vol. 4, no. 31, 31 July. Available from: <http://zolatimes.com/V4.31/williamson_russia. html>.

Williamson, Anne (forthcoming) *The Global Money Racket* (New York: Thomas Nelson).

Williamson, John (1990) 'What Washington Means by Policy Reform', in John Williamson (ed.), *Latin American Adjustment: How Much Has Happened?* (Washington, DC: Institute for International Economics), pp. 7–20.

Wolf, Martin (1995) 'Troubled Giant of H Street', *Financial Times*, 6 October.

Wolf, Naomi (2001) *Misconceptions: Truth, Lies and the Unexpected on the Journey to Motherhood* (London: Chatto & Windus).

Wolfensohn, James D. (1998a) 'Rethinking Development – Principles, Approaches, and Projects', in *Annual World Bank Conference on Development Economics 1998* (Washington, DC: IBRD/World Bank), pp. 59–61.

Wolfensohn, James D. (1998b) 'The Other Crisis', Annual Meetings Address, 6 October. Available from: <http://www.worldbank.org/html/extdr/am98/jdw-sp/am98-en.htm>.

Wolfensohn, James D. (2000a) 'Rethinking Development – Challenges and Opportunities', Remarks to Tenth Ministerial Meeting of UNCTAD, Bangkok, Thailand, 16 February. Available from: <http://www.worldbank.org/html/extdr/extme/jdwsp021600.htm>.

Wolfensohn, James D. (2000b) 'Remarks at the Second Annual ABCDE Conference in Europe on Development Thinking at the Millennium', Paris, 26 June.

Woodrow, Alain (1999) 'The Commandos of Compassion', *The Tablet*, 23 October.

Woodward, Susan L. (1995a) *Balkan Tragedy: Chaos and Dissolution After the Cold War* (Washington, DC: Brookings Institution).

Woodward, Susan L. (1995b) *Socialist Unemployment: The Political Economy of Yugoslavia 1945–1990* (Princeton, NJ: Princeton University Press).

Woodward, Susan L. (1997) 'International Aspects of the Wars in Former Yugoslavia', in Jasminka Udovicki and James Ridgeway (eds), *Burn This House: The Making and Unmaking of Yugoslavia* (Durham, NC: Duke University Press).

Woollacott, M. (2001) 'Blair is Right to Revive the Idea of a "New World Order"', *Guardian*, 5 October.

World Bank (1989) *Sub-Saharan Africa: From Crisis to Sustainable Growth* (Washington, DC: World Bank).

World Bank (1998) *Assessing Aid: What Works, What Doesn't and Why* (New York: Oxford University Press).

World Bank (1999) *Entering the 21st Century: World Development Report 1999/2000* (New York: Oxford University Press).

World Bank (2000a) *Attacking Poverty: World Development Report 2000/2001* (Oxford: Oxford University Press).

World Bank (2000b) 'Transcript of World Bank Group Press Conference on Voices of the Poor', Prague, Czech Republic, 21 September.

World Bank (2002) *Building Institutions for Markets: World Development Report 2002* (Oxford: Oxford University Press).

Žižek, Slavoj (1999) *The Ticklish Subject: The Absent Centre of Political Ontology* (London: Verso).

Index